Library of
Davidson College

HEGEL AND THE HISTORY OF PHILOSOPHY

HEGEL AND
THE HISTORY OF PHILOSOPHY

Proceedings of the 1972
HEGEL SOCIETY OF AMERICA
Conference

edited by

JOSEPH J. O'MALLEY
K.W. ALGOZIN
FREDERICK G. WEISS

MARTINUS NIJHOFF - THE HAGUE - 1974

193
H46xhe

75-7902

© *1974 by Martinus Nijhoff, The Hague, Netherlands*
All rights reserved, including the right to translate or
to reproduce this book or parts thereof in any form
ISBN 90 247 1712 4

TABLE OF CONTENTS

I.	"The Pilgrimage of Truth through Time : The Conception of the History of Philosophy in G.W.F. Hegel" A. Robert Caponigri, University of Notre Dame	1
II.	"Hegel as Historian of Philosophy" Quentin Lauer, S.J., Fordham University	21
III.	"The History of Philosophy and the *Phenomenology of Spirit*" Joseph C. Flay, The Pennsylvania State University	47
IV.	"Hegelianism and Platonism" John N. Findlay, Boston University	62
V.	"On Hegel's Platonism" Lucia M. Palmer, University of Delaware	77
VI.	"Cartesian Doubt and Hegelian Negation" Frederick G. Weiss, The Citadel	83
VII.	"Liebniz and Hegel on Language" Daniel J. Cook, Brooklyn College, CUNY	95
VIII.	"Hegel's Critique of Kant" John E. Smith, Yale University	109
IX.	"Kant and Hegel on Practical Reason" Peter Laska, The University of Arizona	129
X.	"Moral Autonomy in Kant and Hegel" Heimo E.M. Hofmeister, The American University	141
XI.	"Hegel and Solovyov" George L. Kline, Bryn Mawr College	159

XII.	"Hegel and Peirce" Max H. Fisch, The University of Illinois	171
	Bibliography Joseph C. Flay	194
	Index	237

FOREWORD

The papers published here were given at the second biennial conference of the Hegel Society of America, held at the University of Notre Dame, November 9-11, 1972. They appear in an order which reflects roughly two headings : (1) Hegel's conception of the history of philosophy in general, and (2) his relation to individual thinkers both before and after him.

Given the importance of the history of philosophy for Hegel, and the far-reaching impact of his thought upon subsequent philosophy, it becomes immediately apparent that we have here only a beginning. At the conference, cries went up "Why not Hegel and Aristotle, Aquinas, Husserl and Hartmann?" Indeed, why not? The answer, of course, might be given by Hegel himself : if we wish to accomplish anything, we have to limit ourselves. We trust that future conferences and scholarship will bring to light these relationships and the many more which testify to Hegel's profound presence in the mainstream of past and present thought. It is furthermore no accident that the renaissance of Hegelian studies has brought with it a rebirth of the history of philosophy as something relevant to our own problems. For Hegel, the object of philosophy is alone the truth, the history of philosophy is philosophy itself, and this truth which it gives us cannot be what has passed away.

The editors wish to thank the Departments of Philosophy at the University of Notre Dame, Marquette University, and The Citadel for their support in conducting the conference and in the preparation of this manuscript.

J.J. O'MALLEY
K.W. ALGOZIN
F.G. WEISS

To the memory of
H.B. Acton
† June 16th 1974
Professor of Moral Philosophy
University of Edinburgh

and

Paul M. Byrne
† May 13th 1974
Chairman of Philosophy
Marquette University

THE PILGRIMAGE OF TRUTH THROUGH TIME : THE CONCEPTION OF THE HISTORY OF PHILOSOPHY IN G.W.F. HEGEL

A. ROBERT CAPONIGRI

University of Notre Dame

An intimation that a very special relationship must obtain between philosophy and its own history has long haunted western thought. Equally persistent has been the premonition that the exploration of this relationship must have a profound effect, not on the historiography of philosophy alone, but on the idea of philosophy itself as well. Hegel makes vocal and brings into focus intimation and premonition alike when he writes : "... the history of philosophy because of the special nature of its subject matter (i.e. philosophy itself), is different from other histories",[*1] In what way is the history of philosophy different, in what way is this difference determined by the nature of philosophy and in what way does this difference, in turn, affect philosophy? This is the essential theme.

Efforts to reach an understanding in principle of this special relation between philosophy and its own history have produced the most divergent views. To bring some order into this diversity a continuum might be constructed. The poles of this continuum would be, at the one extreme, the complete objectification of the history of philosophy relative to the activity of philo-

---

[*] References, unless otherwise noted, are to the following titles :
Hegel, G.W.F. : *Lectures on the History of Philosophy* translated by E. S. Haldane and Frances H. Simson. New York : The Humanities Press/London : Routledge and Kegan Paul, Ltd., 3 vs., 1955 (referred to as *Haldane*).
Hegel, G.W.F. : *Vorlesungen über die Geschichte der Philosophie*, herausgegeben von Hermann Glockner, 3 vs., Fr. Frommans Verlag Gunther Holzboog, Stuttgart 1959 (referred to as *Glockner*).
Lauer, Quentin : *Hegel's Idea of Philosophy*, with a new translation of Hegel's *Introduction to the History of Philosophy*. New York : Fordham University Press, 1971 (referred to as *Lauer*).

[1] Haldane : p. 8; Glockner, I, p. 35 : "... der Geschichte der Philosophie, um der besonderen Natur ihres Gegenstandes willen, eine andere Bewandniss hat als mit den Geschichten anderer Gebiete".

sophy and, at the other, the total identification of philosophy with its own history. In the first instance, the historiography of philosophy would possess no intrinsic philosophical character. Though its "content" or "matter" would be philosophy, the history of philosophy would obey methodological canons which dictate a strict objectification of the relation between history and its subject matter whatever the character of the latter; canons which dictate, for example, that political history cannot and ought not to be a form of political action, nor religious history apologetic or catechetical. In the second instance, by contrast, philosophy and the history of philosophy would form a seamless unity, in the sense that the history of philosophy would prove to be a philosophical transaction, indeed, the supreme philosophical act. Other views of this relationship would find their natural places, so to say, along this continuum as each approximated the one or the other of these extremes.

Hegel, it would seem, leaves us no doubt as to where, on this continuum, his own view would fall. It would fall at, or very close to, the extreme of the identification of philosophy and its own history. Hegel writes, "The history of philosophy is itself scientific and thus essentially becomes the high point of the science of philosophy."[2] And, lest any equivocation find entrance, he presses the point : "...this history represents not merely the external, accidental events contained within it, but it shows how that content, or what appears to belong to mere history, belongs to the science of philosophy."[3] Arresting and unequivocal as these assertions are, the basic reason which leads Hegel to make them and thus to assume the position at the extreme point of identification on that continuum is more arresting still. That reason lies in his fundamental philosophical enterprise, the construction of the system. Unless these assertions are valid, the construction of the system of reason is not valid. The Hegelian system is a system of total mediation. That is to say, it is a system in which the world of experience is grounded without residue in the principles of reason, while these in turn are totally concretized or realized in the range of actual or possible experience. The identity of philosophy and its own history is the very core and axis of this system of mediation. The problem, therefore, of the relationship of philosophy and its own history is not, for Hegel, an exercise in mere erudition; it is a central issue in his own speculative system. The best evidence

---

[2] Haldane : p. 6; Glockner, I, p. 33 : "die Geschichte der Philosophie selbst wissenschaftlich ist und sogar zur Wissenschaft der Philosophie der Hauptsache nach wird."

[3] Haldane : p. 6; Glockner, I, p. 33 : "... dass sie nicht bloss das Aeusser, Geschehene die Begebenheiten des Inhalts darstellt, sondern wie der Inhalt, — diess, was als historisch aufzutreten erscheint, — selbst zur Wissenschaft der Philosophie gehört."

for this assertion is to be found in his most inclusive formulation of the problem, a formulation which will provide the constant framework for all his reflections on the issue.

1. The Problem : Hegel's Formulation

Hegel conceives this problem, in its widest reaches, as embodied in a contradiction which must be resolved before the conditions of the system can be fulfilled. "This subject," he writes, "contains an inner contradiction. Philosophy aims at understanding what is unchangeable, eternal, in and for itself. History tells us what at one time has been, at another has vanished. Truth is eternal, it does not fall within the transient. It has no history. But if it has a history and if this history is only a representation of past forms of knowledge the truth is not to be found in it."[4] This contradiction controls his entire address to this problem.

At the same time, this contradiction dictates the task which confronts him. He must establish the counter-thesis which will resolve this contradiction; he must demonstrate that *truth must have a history*, "veritas filia temporis." He must establish that the changing must generate the unchanging, time the eternal, the shifting thought of man abiding truth. Or the task may be stated with equal justice in the converse but symmetrical terms : the unchanging must generate the changing, the eternal time, the one truth conflicting systems of truth, conflicting philosophies, as the condition of its own self-realization. The alchemy by which this transformation will be accomplished will have two names, philosophy and history, but a single reality, the construction of the system.

2. The Point of Departure

Hegel finds the springboard for the accomplishment of this task in a cultural phenomenon which none can fail to observe : the general scepticism toward philosophy as a viable human enterprise bred precisely by incom-

---

[4] Haldane, pp. 7-8; Glockner, I, p. 35 : "Der Gedanke, der uns bei einer Geschichte der Philosophie zunächst entgegen kommen kann, ist dass sogleich dieser Gegenstand selbst einen inneren Widerstreit enthalte. Denn die Philosophie beabsichtigt das zu erkennen, was unveränderlich, ewig, an und für sich ist. Ihr Ziel ist die Wahrheit. Die Geschichte aber erzählt solches, was zu einer Zeit gewesen, zu einer anderen aber verschwunden und durch Anderes verdrängt worden ist. Gehen wir davon aus, dass die Wahrheit ewig ist : so fällt sie nicht in die Sphäre des Vorübergehenden, und hat keine Geschichte. Wenn sie aber eine Geschichte hat, und indem die Geschichte diess ist, uns nur eine Reihe vergangener Gestalten der Erkenntniss darzustellen : so ist in ihr die Wahrheit nicht zu finden; denn die Wahrheit ist nicht ein Vergangenes."

prehension of the history of philosophy. He attacks this scepticism in the form in which it is, ostensibly, most convincing but, in fact, most vulnerable : the plurality of philosophical systems, and the manifest tensions and contradictions among them, which throngs the course of that history. That this plurality of philosophical systems does exhibit itself in history, Hegel is not prepared to deny; neither is he blind to the many conflicts and contradicitions which prevail among those systems. He *is* prepared to deny, however, that this plurality or these conflicts provide a valid basis for scepticism toward philosophy. Such a conclusion, he holds, is without justification and, he adds with an unwonted note of harshness, is evidence of a lack of education in those who so conclude. In truth, this plurality and diversity of philosophical systems, truly comprehended, supports quite the opposite point of view. They become, in Hegel's view, not only evidence for the *possibility* of philosophy, but its *necessary* and *essential* ground. He writes : "It is important to haves a deeper insight into the bearings of this diversity in the systems of philosophy. Truth and philosophy, known philosophically, make such diversity appear in another light than that of abstract opposition between truth and error. We must make the fact conceivable that the diversity and number of philosophies not only does not prejudice philosophy itself, that is to say, the possibility of a philosophy, but that such diversity is and has been absolutely necessary to the existence of a science of philosophy and that it is essential to it."[5]

Thus Hegel defines his task without ambiguity; he approaches it, however, circumspectly, conscious of the pitfalls it may conceal. He seeks to fortify himself with some general reflections concerning this diversity of philosophies, concerning the history of philosophy in general and as it forms part of the wider history of the human spirit, stressing in these remarks the element of necessity and of rationality which informs them. In the first place, he observes, "no matter how different these systems of philosophy have been, they have a common bond in that they were philosophy. Thus whoever may have studied or become acquainted with a philosophy of whatsoever kind...has thereby become acquainted with philosophy."[6] And further : "In the history of philosophy we have to deal with philosophy itself. The facts within that history are not adventures (*Abentheuer*) and contain no mere romance — just as world history is not something merely romantic. (One is reminded of di Negri's characterization of the *Pheno-*

[5] Haldane, pp. 18-19; Glockner, I, 47 : "Aber es kommt wesentlich darauf an, noch eine tiefere Einsicht darein zu haben, was es mit dieser." u.s.w.

[6] Haldane, p. 18; Glockner, I, 47 : "Wer also irgend eine Philosophie studirte oder inne hätte, (wenn es anders eine Philosophie ist) hätte damit doch Philosophie inne."

menology of Mind as "un romanzo.") They are not a collection of chance events...nor is it chance that one thing has been thought here, another there, as though at will; rather in the movement of thinking spirit there is real connection. There is reason in that movement".[7] From the tone, however, in which these reflections are advanced, it is clear that Hegel is not prepared to rest his case on them. They are mere assertions without demonstrative force. He must, therefore, identify the real, and not the merely polemical, point of departure. This he finds in the notion of truth, more specifically still, in the unity of truth.

3. *Truth and Its Unity*

"Certainly," Hegel writes, "the fact is sufficiently well established that there are and have been different philosophies. The truth, however is one. The instinct of reason has this unshakable feeling or faith (*dieses unüberwindliche Gefühl oder Glauben hat der Instinkt der Vernunft*)."[8] The ultimate concern of philosophy is to know this truth, to know, in the sense of bringing that one truth to be. For this one truth, which philosophy seeks to know, though its unity is warranted by the unshakable faith generated by the instinct of reason, is not itself given in its unity, its totality, its realized form by any immediate intuition. It is rather the product of thought. More precisely still, it is the knowledge which thought has of its own self-generation under the dual aspects of that which is thought and the process by which it is thought, in the light of the necessity which rules that process.

This truth, Hegel continues, cannot, therefore, be a solitary (*einfacher*) nor empty (*leerer*) thought; it must be a thought completely differentiated and determined in itself (*in sich bestimmter*).[9] Philosophy seeks to know this one truth just as determined in itself, that is, under the form of the unity within which all such determinations are effected (so that they are determina-

---

[7] Haldane, p. 19; Glockner I, 48 : "Die Thaten der Geschichte der Philosophie sind keine Abentheuer — so wenig die Weltgeschichte nur romantisch ist — nicht nur eine Sammlung von zufälligen Begebenheiten, Fahrten irrender Ritter, die sich für sich herumschlagen, absichtslos abmühen, und deren Wirksamkeit spurlos verschwunden ist. Eben so wenig hat sich hier Einer etwas ausgeklügelt, dort ein Anderer nach Willkür, sondern in der Bewegung des denkenden Geistes ist wesentlich Zusammenhang. Es geht vernünftig zu."

[8] Haldane, p. 17; Glockner, I, 46 : "Es ist allerdings genug gegründete Thatsache, dass es verschiedene Philosophien giebt und gegeben hat. Die Wahrheit aber ist Eine, - dieses unüberwindliche Gefühl oder Glauben hat der Instinkt der Vernunft."

[9] Haldane, p. 20; Glockner, I, 48 : "Das Wesentlichste ist also vielmehr zu erkennen, dass die Eine Wahrheit nicht ein nur einfacher, leerer, sondern in sich bestimmter Gedanke ist."

tions and not mere othernesses) and under the form of the unity which those determinations constitute, on the basis of the total mediation of their othernesses by thought. Moreover, philosophy seeks to know this one truth, so determined within itself, not as an immediate and inert given, but in its process of generation, of coming to be what it is, as the source whence all those determinations flow in their necessity and to which, by a like necessity, they return. That is to say, philosophy seeks to know this one all-generating and all-embracing truth in the actual process of the self-determination of that truth into the totality of its differentations and of the re-constitution of those differentations into the unity of the one truth. Finally, philosophy seeks to know this one truth, and the dual process which transpires within it, of its going out from and its return to its own unity, not as a spectacle which transpires before its eyes but in which it has no part, but as an activity in which it is directly involved, as an activity which is its very own, the activity by which it, philosophy, is contituted and which is, at the same time, the activity by which the one truth is constituted. In a word, what philosophy seeks to know, and what is known in philosophy, is philosophy precisely as that activity by which the one truth in its differentiation and determination and its immanent re-integration is brought into actuality, is realized. In this sense, as can be foreseen, that one truth will be philosophy itself and philosophy will be its own history. But this is yet to come.

4. *The Idea*

Truth, conceived thus in the unity of its determinations, is an architectonic notion. It presents the most inclusive structural pattern of the real, not in its actuality, but merely in its projected schema. It is, in a word which Hegel seems to favor, abstract. And abstract means for him, precisely as in opposition to its own actualization. Truth, in this sense, is, consequently in a condition of diremption, of otherness to itself. And since truth is thought and thought is presence, the form of diremption in which this architectonic truth finds itself is absence. By contrast, the condition of the actuality of truth is presence, total presence to itself. And this total presence of truth must be, not the presence of a given, which would but confirm the diremption, but the presence which embraces its own coming to be as its own proper self-generative activity : presence not as *factum*, but as *fieri*, and *fieri* not as the consequence of the agency of another, but as the consequence of its own action, indeed as wholly contained in its own action, never transcending that act, but eternally residing in it. Truth, in this mode of absolute presence to itself, Hegel calls the *Idea*.

The salient characteristic of the Idea, consequently, would seem to be this diremption. And Hegel muses over this strange circumstance that truth, the Idea, must be other than it is, must become what it is. He writes, "That the Idea should have to make itself what it is seems like a contradiction," and, he goes on, "it may be said that it is what it is," thus tangentially, almost casually, indicating the relationship of his own view to that of the classical metaphysics of Pure Act and the foundations of classical theism.[10]

If, then, its salient characteristic is this diremption, the innermost reality of the Idea is its dynamism toward the closure of this diremption, toward its own coming to be in its actuality and totality in absolute presence. It is, therefore, the nature of the Idea to come to be, through its own immanent and constitutive activity, what it is, according to its total content and its essential form, total determination and total presence. Thus Hegel writes, "It is essentially (*wesentlich*) the nature of the idea to generate its own being (*sich zu entwickeln*) and only through this generation of its own actuality to make itself, to become, what it is."[11] This self-generation, this coming to be through its own inward and constitutive activity, is the essence and the actuality of the Idea.

5. Idea in Its Coming to Be

Central though it is to the entire train of his thought, Hegel yet permits a certain haze of ambiguity to cling about the character of this self-coming-to-be of the Idea; and this haze will continue to cloud the system in the course of its construction. This ambiguity may be symbolized by the two models which he cites as illustrating this process. The one is the seed, the other, the self.[12]

Both these images are illuminating and both eventually find their places in the system. It is rather a question of the range and order which must prevail between them. Each does, indeed, embody a process of coming-to-be in actuality of a principle in potency, as Hegel notes.[13] Yet the difference between them is profound. For the coming to be of the seed to its maturation

---

[10] Haldane, p. 20. The sentence quoted is not found in the Glockner text.
[11] Haldane, p. 21; Glockner, I, 49 : "Wesentlich ist es nun die Natur der Idee sich zu entwickeln und nur durch die Entwickelung sich zu erfassen, zu werden, was sie ist."
[12] Lauer, pp. 76-77.
[13] Haldane, pp. 20-21; Glockner, I, 49 : "Der eine ist das, was als Anlage, Vermögen das Ansichsein (wie ich es nenne) *potentia*, δύναμις bekannt ist. Die zweite Bestimmung ist das Fürsichsein, die Wirklichkeit (*actus*, ἐνέργεια)."

in the fruit, though in a sense inward, is fixed and determined and enclosed, as Hegel notes,[14] in the eternally repetitive cycle of nature. The self-generation of the self, however, is free. While it, too, has an inward principle of necessity, this necessity is not the necessitating force of nature, but the inwardly perceived and apprehended ideality of thought, a logical necessity, which rules, but does not determine, the course of thought; a necessity whose essence is that it can only abide with freedom. Hence it is that the one, the process of the seed in its coming to be in the fruit, can have no history; but the whole reality of the other, the self, can only be its history, for history is always the history of freedom.[15] It is, consequently, of the greatest moment that the form of the coming to be of the Idea be specified with respect to these two images.

Clearly, it is the image of the self which dominates Hegel's view, and rightly so. For the coming to be of the Idea is a free self-creation and not merely the enactment of a predetermined schema, as the program of the development of the seed and, indeed, the whole movement of nature, must be. Nevertheless, the movement of nature, its mode of coming to be what it is as exemplified in the seed, also has its place in the system, in the very life of the Idea itself. For nature, too, proves to be one of the necessary moments of the free self-creation of the Idea, and a most important one, since it is in nature that one dimension of time is projected. But the stages of nature do not provide the primary model of the stages of the life of the Idea. These are indicated rather by the free self-creative movement of thought.

Hegel provides a dual schema of the free movement of thought through which the Idea takes possession of itself, becomes what it is. He speaks first of the movement of thought through the representation, to the concept and thence to the Idea; to this he adds the movement of the Idea from its being-in-itself through *Dasein* to its being-for-itself. These two series have been explored and elaborated by many commentators. For our present purpose it is sufficient to note but one point. It would seem that they are not to be taken as simple alternatives; rather, they represent two different aspects under which the single process of the self-generation of the Idea, the free movement of thought, may be viewed. Yet it is not to be supposed that a simple or direct correlation between them is possible; the attempt

---

[14] Glockner, I, 61 : "Die Natur ist, wie sie ist, und ihre Veränderungen sind deswegen nur Wiederholungen, ihr Bewegen nur ein Kreislauf".

[15] Hegel, G.W.F. : *Lectures on the Philosophy of History*. Introduction translated as *Reason in History*, translator Robert S. Hartman. Indianapolis : Bobbs-Merrill and Co. (Little Library of Liberal Arts No. 35), 1953, pp. 24-25.

to establish such a correlation meets frustrating difficulties. The most profitable manner of dealing with them is to employ them as points of reference as the various modalities of the development of the Idea are examined. Hegel himself suggests the broader notion of mediation as that in which the relation between them can best be expressed. When the notion of mediation is made central to the interpretation of Hegel's thought, however, as Niel's work [16] shows that it profitably may, a different idiom is developed from that in which Hegel conducts his own reflection on the relation between philosophy and its own history.

6. Philosophy

The process of the self-generation of the Idea provides Hegel with the proper context for the broadest definition of philosophy. "The Idea," Hegel writes, "is thus — concrete in itself and self-generative — an organic system, a totality, which contains a wealth of stages and moments within itself. Philosophy is now for itself the knowledge of this self-generation; indeed is, as conceptualizing thought, this development or self-generation of thought."[17] Here again, it may be suggested, Hegel permits a certain ambiguity or indistinction to becloud his expression, if not his thought. This imprecision seems to reside in that single sentence in which he sets forth the dual relation of philosophy to the process of the self-generation of the Idea. In the first member of this compound statement he asserts that philosophy, as it is present to itself, is knowledge of this process; taken in itself, this might admit of a certain distance between philosophy and that process as its object. This distance is immediately closed by Hegel when, in the second member, he asserts rather the identity of philosophy with that process under the specific form of the concept, as the process of conceptualization (*begreifendes Denken*). It is at this moment, consequently, the concept, that the real relation of philosophy to that process of the self-generation is established; it is identity. Philosophy is the self-presence of that process of thought to itself, under the form of the concept, in the moment of conceptualization. The full force of this assertion is felt when the problem of establishing this identity as a time-historical transaction, and hence as belonging to the history of philosophy, is addressed.

---

[16] Niel, Henri : *De la médiation dans la philosophie de Hegel.* Paris : Aubier, 1945.

[17] Haldane, p. 27; Glockner, I, 56 : "Die Idee ist so — konkret an sich und sich entwickelnd — ein organisches System, eine Totalität, welche Reichtum von Stufen und Momenten in sich enthält. Die Philosophie ist nun für sich das Erkennen dieses Entwickeln und ist als begreifendes Denken selbst diese denkende Entwickelung."

7. *The Two Paths*

Philosophy, then, in its most intimate character is identical with the process of the self-development, more precisely, self-generation of the Idea. It is knowledge of that process; but the knowledge involved is self-knowledge, since philosophy is the generative principle of that process, is the process itself. The path of the self-generation of the Idea is not, however, single but complex, as is apparent from Hegel's exposition.

Hegel calls his first exposition of development abstract and formal. This exposition proceeds at two levels. At the first level he indicates the forms of thought, the most encompassing notions. Thought taken in itself may seem something completely abstract; but since, as he has pointed out elsewhere, thought is not something solitary and empty, it must be essentially concrete, that is, determining, indeed, determined. Concretion is determination. Thought as concrete he calls Concept (*Begriff*). The Idea is the concept as it is realized, that is, as completely self-determined so that all of its determinations are posited, and posited as deriving entirely from itself. The movement of the Idea toward becoming what it is, is thus an entirely immanent, non-transitive movement generative both of its own form and content. At the second level this same process is further specified into its constitutive moments : the moment of *being-in-itself*, the moment of being there (*Dasein*), i.e. being manifested in experience, and finally *being-for-itself*. What is in-itself, is not yet the true, however, it is only the abstract; what is abstract, Hegel says, cannot be true; it is the seed, the tendency of the true.[18] It is something simple, i.e. undetermined, though containing all the multiple distinctions which must eventually be posited. But the simple, the in-itself, is precisely what develops. And it develops by positing itself, by entering into existence as something distinct, by becoming manifest, no longer hidden. This is being-there, existential separateness, manifestation in experience. Being-for-itself is the identity of being-in-itself in the process of its existential positing, its being revealed. This reveals at the same time the meaning of development and the manner in which it is to be distinguished from all other change. For the essence of the change which is development is that it is change which reveals identity, the distinction of the two moments of the same. In the kind of change, which is development, the subject of the change enters into itself by going out of itself, i.e., by entering into existence. In this process, it takes possession of itself, by way of its existential positing. In other kinds of change, what results is simply other than that which under-

---

[18] Haldane, p. 24; Glockner, I, 53 : "Ist das Wahre abstrakte, so ist es unwahr."

goes the change.[19] This process transpires fully only in consciousness, indeed only in the self-conscious subject; it transpires only in spirit, not in nature. The totality of this process in the self-conscious subjectivity of man is philosophy. And in philosophy man comes into the fullness of his being, comes to be *wie sie ist*, through the total mediation of his own being in itself which includes by way of its own self-development, experience, the totality of all that is other to man in that its otherness is restored to integrity in his total self-consciousness, his concrete being in and for himself as reason.[20]

In the second exposition of development, a further step is taken: the bifurcation of this process of development into the logical and the temporal strains: the bifurcation which reveals the essential problem of the history of philosophy for Hegel. The *locus* of this bifurcation in the process of development is existence, the being-for-itself of the Idea, its moment of self-manifestation. This process of manifestation is subject to modes: "...the difference in regard to the possible modes of manifestation must be pointed out."[21] These modes are two, the logical and the temporal. In Hegel's own terms: "...the progression of the various stages in the advance of thought may occur with the consciousness of necessity in which case each in succession deduces itself...." "Or else it may come about as does a natural and apparently accidental process so that while inwardly the Idea brings about its result consistently, this consistency is not made manifest...for the whole of these manifestations merely have the form of a succession in time."[22]

This bifurcation of the moments of the manifestation of being-in-itself becomes the basis of the differentiation of the spheres of logic (or, more precisely, of philosophy as logic) and of the history of philosophy. "The one kind of which represents the deduction of the forms, the necessity, thought

---

[19] Haldane, p. 22; Glockner, I, 50-51 : "In die Existenz Treten ist Veränderung, und in demselben Eins und dasselbe bleiben. Das Ansich regiert den Verlauf. Die Pflanze verliert sich nicht in blosse ungemessene Veränderung. So im Keim der Pflanze. Es ist dem Keime nichts anzusehen. Er hat den Trieb sich zu entwickeln, er kann es nicht aushalten nur an sich zu sein. Der Trieb ist der Widerspruch, das er nur an sich ist und es doch nicht sein soll. Der Trieb fesst in die Existenz heraus." u.s.w.

[20] Lauer, pp. 75-80.

[21] Haldane, p. 29; Glockner, I, 58 : "Um diess zu erläutern muss zuerst der Unterschied in Ansehung der Weise der Erscheinung bemerklich gemacht werden, der Statt finden kann." u.s.w.

[22] Haldane, p. 29; Glockner, I, 58 : "Das Hervorgehen der unterschiedenen Stufen im Fortschreiten des Gedankens kann nämlich mit dem Bewusstsein der Nothwendigkeit, nach der sich jede folgende ableitet, und nach der nur diese Bestimmung und Gestalt hervortreten kann." u.s.w.

out and recognized, of the determinations, is the business of philosophy; and because it is the pure Idea which is in question and not yet its particularized form as Nature and as Mind, that representation is, in the main, the business of logical philosophy. But the other method, which represents the part played by the history of philosophy, shows the different stages and moments in development in time, in their manner of occurence, in particular places, in particular peoples or political circumstances, the complications arising thus, and in short, it shows us the empirical form."[23]

The relation between these two movements, in Hegel's view, is isorhythmic. "I maintain," he writes, "that the sequence in the systems of philosophy in history is similar to the sequence in the logical deduction of the notion-determinations in the Idea. I maintain that if the fundamental conceptions of the systems appearing in the history of philosophy be entirely divested of what regards their outward form...the various stages in the determination of the Idea are found in their logical notion. Conversely, in the logical progression, ... there is, so far as its principle elements are concerned, the progression of historical manifestations....It may be thought that philosophy must have another order as to the stages of the Idea than that in which these notions have come forth in time, but in the main, the order is the same." "But it is necessary to have these pure notions in order to know what the historical form contains."[24] And he concludes : "I would only remark this,

---

[23] Haldane, pp. 29-30; Glockner, I, 58 : "Die Eine Weise dieses Hervorgehens, die Ableitung der Gestaltungen, die gedachte, erkannte Nothwendigkeit der Bestimmungen darzustellen, ist die Aufgabe und das Geschäft der Philosophie selbst; und indem es die reine Idee ist, auf die es hier ankommt, noch nicht die weiter besondere Gestaltung derselben, als Natur und als Geist : so ist jene Darstellung vornehmlich die Aufgabe und das Geschäft der logischen Philosophie. Die andere Weise aber, dass die unterschiedenen Stufen und Entwickelungsmomente, in der Zeit, in der Weise des Geschehens, an diesen besonderen Orten, unter diesem und jenem Volke, unter diesen politischen Umständen und unter diesen Verwickelungen mit deselben hervortreten — kurz unter diesen empirischen Form, — dies ist das Schauspiel, welches uns die Geschichte der Philosophie zeigt. Diese Ansicht ist es welche die einzig würdige für diese Wissenschaft ist; sie ist durch den Begriff der Sache die wahre, und dass sie der Wirklichkeit nach ebenso sich zeigt und bewährt, diess wird sich durch das Studium dieser Geschichte selbst ergeben."

[24] Haldane, p. 30; Glockner, I, 58-59 : "Nach dieser Idee behaupte ich nun, dass die Aufeinanderfolge der Systeme der Philosophie in der Geschichte dieselbe ist, als die Aufeinanderfolge in der logischen Ableitung der Begriffsbestimmungen der Idee. Ich behaupte, dass wenn man die Grundbegriffe der in der Geschichte der Philosophie erschienenen Systeme rein dessen entkleidet, was ihre äusserliche Gestaltung, ihre Anwendung auf das Besondere, und dergleichen betrifft : so erhält man die verschiedenen Stufen der Bestimmung der Idee selbst in ihrem logischen Begriffe. Umgekehrt, den logischen Fort-

that what has been said reveals that the study of the history of philosophy is the study of philosophy itself."[25]

8. *The Ideal Genesis of Time*

Having established, or, more accurately, asserted this parallelism between the two sequences, the logical and the temporal, in the self-generation of the Idea, Hegel would seem to have gained the *pou sto* whence he could move the problem of the relation of philosophy to its own history and, more immediately, that of the pluralism of philosophical systems which appear in that history. The sequence of these systems in time and space would be the correlative of the sequence of the ideal moments of the logical development of the Idea. The task of the history of philosophy would then seem to be the concrete exemplification of this correlation. This does not wholly prove to be the case, however. A number of problems assert themselves which must be confronted. The logical sequence of the stages of the development of the Idea is independent of and antecedent to the establishment of the time-space sequence of the systems of philosophy in time. It is *a-priori*, Hegel writes, and hence does not proceed in time. If this is the case, why then does the Idea generate the time sequence of its development?[26]

Hegel, it must be said, is quite aware of this problem and of the fact that he must eventually confront it from the very outset of his discourse. He seems reluctant to do so, however, and on a number of occasions remands it to another moment, protesting that it involves probing the metaphysics of time or again that the justification of the dual sequence of the development of the Idea would carry him too far from his aim.[27] The moment arrives,

---

gang für sich genommen, so hat man darin nach seinen Hauptmomenten den Fortgang der geschichtlichen Erscheinungen;—aber man muss freilich diese reinen Begriffe in dem zu erkennen wissen, was die geschichtliche Gestalt enthält."

[25] Haldane, p. 30; Glockner, I, 59 : "ich bemerke nur noch diess, dass aus dem Gesagten erhellt, dass das Studium der Geschichte der Philosophie Studium der Philosophie selbst ist, wie es denn nicht anders sein kann."

[26] Haldane, p. 32; Glockner, I, 61 : "Die unmittelbarste Frage, welche über diese Geschichte gemacht werden kann, betrifft jenen Unterschied der Erscheinung der Idee selbst, welcher so eben gemacht worden ist,—die Frage, wie es kommt, das die Philosophie als eine Entwickelung in der Zeit erscheint und eine Geschichte hat. Die Beantwortung dieser Frage greift in die Metaphysik der Zeit ein und es würde eine Abschweifung von dem Zweck der hier unser Gegenstand ist, sein, wenn hier mehr als nur die Momente angegeben würden, auf die es bei der Beantwortung der ausgeworfenen Frage ankommt."

[27] Glockner, I, 59 : "... diess näher zu zeigen würde uns aber von unserem Zwecke zu weit abführen." *Ibid.*, 61 : "Die Beantwortung dieser Frage greift in die Metaphysik der Zeit..." u.s.w.

however, in the progress of his argument, when the issue can be postponed no longer and he addresses it, somewhat grudging, however, and protesting that he will give only the elements on which the total solution rests.

The ideal genesis of time, it would seem, is a special thesis in Hegel's general theory of mind. Mind is activity; its being is its activity.[28] In this it differs from nature, which is as it is, whose changes are mere repetitions, whose movements constitute a circle, the circle of the eternal return.[29] The activity which constitutes mind, however, is precisely self-knowledge. But mind's self-knowledge necessitates a moment of scission, in which mind becomes object to itself, other to itself. In establishing this scission, mind constitutes its existence. It becomes, in Hegel's term, "external" (*äusserlich*), other to itself. This otherness, this externality, in which it thus establishes itself, is precisely the universal and distinctive form (*Weise*) of the existence of nature. Now one form of this otherness, this externality or existence according to the conditions of nature, is time. The Idea, therefore, which is essentially thought or mind, must, in order to be itself, become other to itself; and the form of this otherness, of the Idea as it exists according to the conditions of nature is time.[30]

This passage over into time, the time of mind that is, is not a mere being-cast down; it is a free act of mind itself. Time, therefore, has an ideal genesis, i.e. a genesis in the activity of the Idea itself. Even though, therefore, the Idea passes over into a condition of nature, i.e. time, there would seem to be a difference, to Hegel's mind, in the manner in which mind is in nature's time and the manner in which nature itself is in that time. For nature is fixed eternally in the circle of its time; it is forever externality. It cannot deliver itself from that otherness, it is fixed in being-in-itself. The manner of the being of the Idea in the time which is the form of the existence of nature is a transitory thing, as Hegel insists of the multiple systems of philosophy. Eventually in the total movement of the Idea, it is mind which redeems nature from that static condition of otherness, by reclaiming it for mind, and recognizing it as an essential moment of the movement of mind, of the Idea.

The dispersion of the Idea into the externality of time generates, in the first place, the individual consciousness, consciousness as existentialized in the individual thinking subject, which is, therefore, closest to nature in

---

[28] Haldane, p. 32.

[29] Haldane, p. 32; Glockner, I, 61 : "Die Natur ist, wie sie ist, und ihre Veränderungen sind deswegen nur Wiederholungen, ihre Bewegung nur ein Kreislauf."

[30] Haldane, p. 32; Glockner, I, 62 : "Die Eine der Weisen der Aeusserlichkeit aber ist die Zeit," u.s.w.

its condition, most subject to that otherness, most bound to time. In this condition it tends to generate only opinion. Hegel has shown that as such it is alien to philosophy, for there is no such thing as philosophical opinion.[31] That dispersion is, however, also proper to philosophical reflection, to that transcendental consciousness in which philosophical reflection transpires. For mind is not only to be considered as individual mind, finite consciousness, but also as that mind which is universal and concrete within itself. This concrete universality comprehends all the various sides and modes in which mind becomes object to the Idea. The time of transcendental, universal, concrete mind is not identical with the time of individual consciousness, even though it transpires in and through, that is, is immanent in, individual consciousness and hence to the time of that consciousness. This transcendental time is the time of the Idea itself, and the form of otherness in which it appears is the otherness of its own ideal moments to its own ultimate constitutive unity. The time of the Idea is both immanent to the time of nature, taking on its form, therefore, and transcendent to it. In this transcendence it exhibits itself as the temporally dispersed moments of its own unity, a dispersion which establishes its concreteness. Every such moment appears in time-space as a philosophy.[32]

9. *Temporality and History*

This temporalization of the Idea, its deployment into the time-space of nature, and its deployment into its own discrete ideal moments, i.e. the plurality of philosophies, which appear in the time-space discreteness of nature, is not yet history. There would seem to be a fundamental imprecision in Hegel's handling of this point; that is to say, he seems sometimes to speak as though temporality and historicity were the same. Yet the more basic intention of his thought is in quite the opposite direction; that is to say, in the direction of the counter-distinction of temporality and historicity. This would seem to become clear when we observe the inward movement of the Idea. For the deployment of the Idea into the discrete time-space *loci*, both in its natural and in its transcendental movement, is but the "outward" movement, the dispersion of the Idea, its movement toward concrete-

---

[31] Haldane, p. 12; Glockner, I, 40 : "Die Philosophie aber enthält keine Meinungen— es gibt keine philosophische Meinungen. Die Philosophie ist objektive Wissenschaft der Wahrheit, Wissenschaft ihrer Notwendigkeit, begreifendes Erkennen — kein Meinen und kein Ausspinnen von Meinungen."

[32] Haldane, p. 34; Glockner, I, 64 : "Solche vollständige Gestaltung des Gedenkens ist eine Philosophie."

ness, of which this dispersion is the condition. But this dispersion does not generate the presence of the Idea to itself. On the contrary, it generates the absence of the Idea to itself. Historicity is, in its essence, not temporality, but *contretemps*, that is, the movement of the Idea toward its unity, in and through, but counter to, the movement of its dispersion or self-diremption in time.

This is brought out clearly by Hegel in some passages, while in others it seems to be elided. It is brought out most clearly and precisely, in the context of the history of philosophy, with respect to that dispersal in time-space of the pluralism of philosophical systems. For the function of the history of philosophy, and what makes it ultimately a philosophical transaction in its own right, is not the following out of the pattern of this dispersal, but rather the retracing of the path back to the unity of the Idea in and through the dialectic of this plurality. The direction of history, consequently, is not toward the generation of time, but toward eternity; i.e. for that absolute presence of the Idea to itself in the concrete synthesis of all of its determinations; history moves, not toward movement and time, but toward the Idea at rest, the rest which comes after the movement of its self-diremption in the time-forms had been reversed and its concrete unity generated. The Idea at rest is not in time, Hegel writes.[33] And the Idea at rest, is the product of its own self-movement of synthesis, of *contretemps*, of historicity as distinct from temporality. Yet temporality is not a pure mode of alienation; for it is the ground of the concreteness of the Idea in its mediated self-identity. Time is, therefore, an absolute ingredient of the Idea.

10. *The Priority of the Logical*

It is of this complex movement of time and *contretemps* that Hegel asserts that the logical sequence of the Idea, that is, the sequence by which the moments of its movement are deduced *a priori* each from its *a priori* antecedent, without reference to the time-space deployment in temporality and without reference to the *contretemps* of the historical movement of the Idea, but antecedently to the latter movement, is independent condition.[34] While these statements indeed correspond to what Hegel says, they

[33] Haldane, p. 33; Glockner, I, 62 : "Denn die Idee, in ihrer Ruhe gedacht, ist wohl zeitlos."

[34] Haldane, pp. 30-31 : "But in order to obtain a knowledge of its progress as the development of the Idea in the empirical external form in which philosophy appears in history, a corresponding knowledge of the Idea is absolutely necessary..."
Glockner, I, 60 : "Aber um in der empirischen Gestalt und Erscheinung, in der die Philosophie geschichtlich auftritt, ihren Fortgang als Entwickelung der Idee zu erkennen, muss man freilich die Erkenntnis der Idee schon mitbringen."

arouse questions which lead one to wonder whether they accurately represent the deeper drift of his meaning.

The assertion of the isorhythmic movement of the logical and temporal sequences causes no particular problem, although Hegel does not seem to offer any explicit ground for it. It is to be presumed that this ground lies in the unity of truth, and in the unity of the Idea. This isorhythmic movement is all the more persuasive if it is assumed, though this is not always clearly stated, that Hegel would assert it of both the movement of temporality and that of historicity as these have been distinguished earlier. It is rather at a deeper level that the problem arises. This deeper problem involves both the alleged antecedency of the logical sequence to the temporal-historical sequence and eventually the autonomy and the rationale of the logical sequence.

It would seem apparent that to assert the antecedency of either sequence, the logical or the temporal-historical, would be to reduce the other to the status of a redundancy. This is certainly true of the temporal-historical sequence, if the antecedency and the paradigmatic character of the logical sequence is asserted. Hegel himself makes a weak case for the necessity of the temporal-historical sequence when he speaks of it as "exemplifying" the logical sequence of the stages of the development of the Idea *a priori*; it would be difficult to see how any philosophical function could be assigned to the history of philosophy. Exemplification would hardly be construed as meeting the conditions of a philosophical function. Thus the history of philosophy would be reduced to a mere order of chance and contingency since it would have no principle of necessity immanent to itself. Any necessity which informed it would be derivative from the order which it exemplifies; for one would not look to the example as establishing the necessity of the order exemplified. More cogently still, the question arises, what would be the necessity of that manifestation or exemplification? There would seem to be none; the history of philosophy would be but a pageant.

If, on the other hand, the antecedency of the temporal-historical order is asserted, it would seem that the logical sequence is reduced to redundancy. Indeed, this is the exact position assumed in absolute historicism which is based, in the ultimate analysis, upon a critique and a rectification of Hegel. According to this form of historicism, it is the logical sequence which appears as redundant. For if the historical process is functionally autonomous, there is nothing to be determined *a priori*. The only process necessary must be that of historiography from which the Idea itself would be determined in all its dimensions, logical as well as existential. The logical phases of the self-development of the Idea can be, this position would assert, determined only on historiographic grounds; and in this case, since they have no other reference than the process from which they emerged, that is, historiography, the only status which can be assigned them is a methodological one; that is, they can become canons for historiography itself. The *a priori* construction of the logical sequence is thus redundant. Hegel seems to provide grounds for this view; for after asserting that an antecedent knowledge of the Idea is necessary for understanding the appearance and incidence of the plurality of philosophical systems in time, he says "To make you acquainted with this Idea, is the business of the history of philosophy".[35]

Neither of these alternatives, however, solicit assent without qualification. For the two moments, the logical and the temporal-historical, as Hegel perceived, are in some manner essential to the self-generative process of the Idea, for the rational construction of experience. The problem is that of their relation. The identity of philosophy with its own history would seem to be more complex than even Hegel thought.

11. *Historicism and System*

The resolution of this tension between the logical and the time-historical sequences in the self-generation of the Idea is of the utmost importance in Hegel's thought. On it depends, in the last analysis, the definitive form which his philosophy must take. Hegel envisioned the Idea, reality itself, as present to itself in absolute self-consciousness, as system. The Idea at rest, in the full explication and mediation of all its determinations, is the terminus. But this notion is clearly challenged by the inward movement of the time-historical sequence. For the pattern of this latter movement through time and *contretemps* precludes its termination in the pure circle of eternity, in the Idea at rest. Rather, it would seem to imply a time-historical sequence without term, the Idea forever without rest, forever in the moil and labor of its self-generation. How then is this tension to be relaxed and what then would seem to be the ultimate fate of Hegel's great emprise?

The weight of the decision, it would seem, falls not in favor of the aprioricity and the methodological antecedency of the logical sequence to the time-historical, but rather in the autonomy of the latter. The crux of the matter seems to lie in the notion of concretion, of actuality. The self-generation of the Idea involves its total mediation in actuality. Otherwise it remains a

---

[35] Haldane, p. 31; Glockner, I, 60 : "Diese Idee Ihnen nachzuweisen, die Erscheinungen sonach zu erklären—diess ist das Geschäft dessen, der die Geschichte der Philosophie vorträgt."

dream, the thought, which is thought, as Hegel said of his own logic, of God prior to all creation, which, not going out into creation, is essentially dream. But this concretion, this actualization of the process of determination, is realized only in the time-historical process of philosophy and its own history and not in that of the *a priori* deduction of the stages of the self-generation of the Idea. The autonomy of the time-historical thus would seem paramount.

This autonomy would seem, however, to plunge the entire process of philosophy and its own history back into the flux of chance and unreason from which Hegel had sought to rescue it. Not so in fact, however. What this autonomy really implies, it would seem, is rather the deepening of the task of philosophy in its total identity with and immanence to its own history. This task becomes now, not the otiose function which Hegel tended to assign to it, the exemplification of a transcendent, i.e. *a priori*, logical order, but the far more difficult task of the derivation of a logical structure from the time-historical movement itself.

As the vision of the system, then, recedes, it is replaced by another, that of philosophy moving through its own history, not backward upon itself to form the closed circle of the system and hence migrating from the dynamism of time to the dream-like repose of eternity nor driving forever and forlornly toward a future which ever eludes it, but in a complex, spiraling rhythm, though *corsi* and *ricorsi*, deepening its content and its consciousness with each movement of advancement and return, seeking ever the abiding truth which is its freight.

CONCLUSION

The problem of the history of philosophy and its relation to philosophy is then, for Hegel, no tangential concern, but an issue intimate to his own system. The self-mediation of the Idea through time and through the *contretemps* of history is the essential dynamic principle of the construction of the system. This movement of the Idea outward into time and its return through the process of history, its own history, is the reality of the history of philosophy and is identical with philosophy itself in the fullest sense of the term. The distinction, however, between the temporal-historical sequence of the self-generation of the Idea and the logical movement seems to import a radical distortion into the structure of Hegel's thought. In the last analysis Hegel is confronted by this dilemma : if the logical deduction of the stages of the self-generation is valid, then the role of the history of philosophy is redundant and its identification with philosophy untenable. On the other hand, if the history of philosophy, that is the temporal deployment of the Idea and its reconstitution through the *contretemps* movement of history, truly occupies the position he seeks to assign it, then the logical deduction of the stages of the self-generation of the Idea is not only rendered redundant but becomes mythical in character, lacking all actuality. When these alternatives are weighed, in order to reduce this dilemma, it would seem that the weight of the argument must fall in the direction of the history of philosophy, because only through this process is the mediation of the Idea complete, i.e. through existence and actuality. But when the dilemma is resolved in this manner the projective character of Hegel's thought is radically ordered. Ostensibly ordered toward a closed system, its inner logic impels it rather in the direction of an absolute historicism.

HEGEL AS HISTORIAN OF PHILOSOPHY

QUENTIN LAUER, S.J.

Fordham University

Although Hegel's *Lectures on the History of Philosophy* have long provided a source of trenchant quotations illustrating Hegel's philosophical views, and despite the fact that more than one author has pointed out that the best way to begin studying Hegel is with these *Lectures*, rarely do we find any study of just what he is trying to do in treating the history of philosophy and how he goes about doing it. That Hegel himself attached great importance to the history of philosophy is attested to by the fact that he repeated the course so often, revising the course, particularly the introductory lectures, over and over again.[1] Nevertheless, we should look in vain were we to seek in the three posthumously published volumes of these *Lectures* a scholarly presentation or interpretation of past philosophical positions. Hegel was not the sort of historian who gives a disinterested account of exactly what each philosopher said.[2] His task, as he conceived it, was rather to show that the development of pure thought so elaborately worked out in his *Science of Logic* has its exact counterpart in the empirically verifiable development of philosophy from the first faltering steps of Thales to the elaboration of Hegel's own system. If the *Phenomenology of Spirit*, a "historical" account of the development of consciousness — not of philosophy — can be looked on as Hegel's introduction to his *Logic*, so too can

---

[1] We are in the unfortunate position of possessing a critical edition only of the Introduction to the *Lectures* (*Einleitung in die Geschichte der Philosophie*; 3rd ed. Hoffmeister-Nicolin, Hamburg: Meiner, 1959), which assembles all the extant notes for Hegel's introductory lectures to his course on the History of Philosophy. For a critical edition of the rest we must wait and, in the meantime, rely on Michelet's presentation which is found in Vols. 17-19 of *Hegel : Sämmtliche Schriften* (ed. Glockner). What we have, then, may be quite unreliable, but a comparison of Michelet's edition of the Introductory Lectures with the others indicates a substantial identity of content which might justify concluding that the same is true of the remaining lectures.

[2] Cf. *Einleitung*, pp. 134-35, for Hegel's thoughts on a "disinterested" presentation of the history of philosophy.

the *History of Philosophy* be considered a different sort of introduction to the same *Logic* — not exhibiting the development of consciousness to the point where pure speculative thinking can begin but presenting an historical account of the development of speculative thinking itself.[3]

One of the criticisms frequently leveled against Hegel's treatment of the history of philosophy is that it is arbitrary. Having decided what philosophy is, we are told, Hegel simply makes the "moments" of its development fit into the preconceived scheme of its systematic structure. There may, of course, be a certain amount of truth to the contention that Hegel has antecedently made up his mind that the historical development of philosophical thought will correspond to its logical development. It is not true, however, that his procedure is arbitrary. If philosophy is to have a history at all, in the sense in which Hegel understands history, it must throughout its development be identifiable as one and the same, and if its own logic demands the sort of development Hegel has elaborated in his system, it is quite understandable that he should expect to see the "moments" of that development manifested in the historical process.[4] In any event the standpoint from which Hegel surveys the history of philosophy is that of his own *Logic*. Only if we are aware of this can we follow his interpretation of the many philosophies which have been elaborated down through history. By the same token, however, if we grasp the historical development of philosophy as Hegel presents it we shall be in a better position to understand the same process as presented in his *Logic*.

Here, then, our task is to follow the development of philosophy as Hegel presents its history. For methodological reasons, it would seem, the best way to do this is to look first at his Introduction (its many versions constitute a separate book) in which Hegel tells us what to look for in the history of philosophy. Then we can turn to the conclusion at the end of Vol. III to see what Hegel is convinced he has found. Finally we can follow him as he tells the story from beginning to end, in order to determine how he finds what he does find, realizing, of course, that what he *finds* is to a great extent determined by what he *looks for*.

In carrying out this task we must be aware from the outset that history is, for Hegel, more than the record of a succession of events. Its concern, too, is more than just the events themselves; it is the connection of the events with each other, and here Hegel detects a certain logical necessity, whether the events in question be those of world-history or the opinions of philoso-

---

[3] Thus, the *Phenomenology* and the *Lectures* are not "historical" in the same way.
[4] Cf. *Einleitung*, pp. 132, 274-81.

phers who have contributed to philosophy's growth down through the ages. Where the history in question, then, is that of philosophy, subjective opinions are contingent events and as such are not part of philosophy.[5] They are at best the outward manifestation of an inner development, which is that of the rational idea.[6] To such a unified development conflicting positions are not an obstacle; they are the necessary moments of a concrete dialectical process.[7] Philosophy, then, has a life of its own; it is one and continuous; its manifestations are varied, and no one of them is identifiable with philosophy itself. In the *Phenomenology of Spirit* Hegel had sought to show that, if we begin with the absolutely minimal manifestation of human consciousness which we call sensation and follow out all its successive implications we shall inevitably come to the highest form of consciousness, absolute knowing. This absolute knowing is philosophical knowing, the highest function of the highest form of human consciousness. Then, in the *Logic*, Hegel spells out all that philosophical knowing implies. This is the knowing whose process he traces "empirically" in the *Lectures on the History of Philosophy*. In one sense, of course, we can say that there is thought and the process of thought only because there are individuals who think. In another sense, however, thought transcends any and all individuals who engage in the subjective activity of thinking, and so does the process of thought. Philosophy, then, which is thought thinking thought, transcends all philosophers and all particular philosophies, and this is its profound unity throughout all the vicissitudes of its history.[8] Thus, although Hegel's historical investigations are in one sense empirical—the evidence is in the record as given [9]—in another sense he sees a *logical* necessity that the development should be such as he discovers it to be.[10]

The Unity of Philosophy

One can, of course, speak of the unity of philosophy in an abstract, formal way, the way one speaks of the unity of a class concept—all philosophies are united under the one heading, philosophy. This, however, is not the sense in which Hegel intends the unity of philosophy. He speaks rather of a concrete unity, to which multiplicity and diversity are essential, since

[5] *Ibid.*, p. 27.
[6] *Ibid.*, pp. 100-101.
[7] *Ibid.*, p. 91.
[8] *Ibid.*, p. 120.
[9] Cf. *Einleitung*, pp. 252-53, where Hegel speaks of the *works* of philosophers as the events of philosophy's history.
[10] *Ibid.*, p. 278.

they constitute the kind of unity in question, "the unity of differentiated determinations."[11] The history of philosophy reveals the concrescence of these determinations and is, thus, identical with philosophy itself, since philosophy is a process and not a static unity, a process of unification.[12] It is logically necessary that rational thinking should be developmental,[13] and historical investigation shows that the process has, in fact, been rational.[14] What is more, it shows that the historical development corresponds with the logical.[15]

Quite obviously there is a sense in which thinking — even philosophical thinking—is something that a subject does. For Hegel, however, this in no way means that thinking is a merely subjective activity; no merely subjective activity can claim for itself objective validity, and yet it is true of genuinely rational thinking that it validates itself—nothing else could. This is what Hegel means when he says of thought that is is free, autonomous; it need not go outside itself for its justification, its determination. This autonomy, however, is not automatic; it is to be won in a long process of development, of overcoming the multiple forces to which it is in bondage —a process eloquently described in the *Phenomenology*.

The point of all this is that only in rational thinking can man come to grips with reality as it is, and this he can do only if he makes thought itself the object of investigation. Philosophy is precisely thought occupied with itself.[16] When it is occupied with the inevitable implications of thinking as such, the investigation is logical. When it is occupied with the de facto process it has gone through in time, the investigation is historical.[17] In both types of investigation the task is to find out what reason says : in the logical, to find out what reason *must* say; in the historical, to find out what reason *has* said. "In the history of philosophy, however, there is question only of reason, to the extent that it has been expressed in the form of thought."[18] But, to say that thought is rational is to say that it is free, in the sense of not being in the service of something other than thought, whether it be a reality outside thought or a position established by authority, tradition, or custom.[19]

[11] *Ibid.*, p. 30.
[12] *Ibid.*, p. 120.
[13] *Ibid.*, p. 278.
[14] *Ibid.*, p. 122; cf. p. 35.
[15] *Ibid.*, p. 34.
[16] *Ibid.*, p. 83.
[17] *Ibid.*, p. 82.
[18] *Ibid.*, p. 204.
[19] Cf. *ibid.*, p. 218.

It is not, of course, the function of history to validate the very idea of philosophical thinking; that is a logical task.[20] Still, given the idea, the historian of philosophy can eliminate from his account what he sees to be not philosophically significant, either because it is not truly independent thought or because it constitutes no advance in the process of thought.[21] More than that, the fact that someone called a "philosopher" has expressed this or that thought does not make that thought integral to the history of philosophy. Only to the extent that past thought remains somehow integral to our own thinking is it properly historical.[22] Philosophy's past is significant only to the extent that it continues to be part of its present,[23] nor are the thoughts of others interesting simply as such, but only to the extent that they constitute "moments" in the ongoing process of philosophy.[24] As presented, the "principles" of a philosophy may be one sided and therefore to be abandoned, but they can at the same time be integrated into the more comprehensive unity of Philosophy itself. "Thus it is essential to the history of philosophy that onesided principles are made into moments, concrete elements, and retained in a sort of knot."[25] In one sense, no philosophy properly so called is ever refuted, since it is an essential moment of the one Philosophy; in another sense, all are refuted, because they are lifted to a plane of different significance by being integrated into the whole.[26] It is for this reason that at any given time philosophy is the result of its whole past,[27] and, since the process of development is a process of concretion, an earlier philosophy will be more abstract and a later one more concrete.[28] This does not mean that Philosophy itself changes in the course of time, only that it goes more deeply into itself and becomes more profoundly what it is.[29] The process of philosophy is a necessary one, and each historical step in its development is proper to the time when it appears,[30] and although no particular philosophy can advance beyond its time,[31] Philosophy itself

---

[20] *Ibid.*, p. 93.
[21] *Ibid.*, pp. 24, 124.
[22] *Ibid.*, p. 6; cf. p. 133.
[23] *Ibid.*, pp. 12-13.
[24] *Ibid.*, p. 281.
[25] *Ibid.*, p. 132.
[26] *Ibid.*, p. 128.
[27] *Ibid.*, pp. 70, 118-19, 126-27.
[28] *Ibid.*, p. 66.
[29] *Ibid.*, p. 32.
[30] *Ibid.*, p. 125.
[31] *Ibid.*, p. 144.

is not limited to any time.³² Philosophy is its history, the whole of it; "Thus philosophy is developing system; so, too, is the history of philosophy, and this is the main point, the fundamental concept which this treatment of that history will present."³³

After all this one might ask why Hegel bothers doing the history of philosophy at all, since he knows what he is going to find before he does it. His *Logic*, after all, has traced the process of thought without any appeal to its historical development. Although it is not easy to gainsay the charge of arbitrariness in the way Hegel finds historically verified the steps which the *Logic* has revealed to be necessary, it should be remembered that he looks upon his own system as the result of a long process of historical development. There simply would be no *Logic*, had the process which extends from Thales to Hegel himself not taken place. It was, in fact, his insight into the concreteness of becoming over against the abstractness of mere being which revealed to him the need of a dynamic logic to supplement the abstract formal logic bequeathed to the West by Aristotle. Philosophy's coming-to-be is its history, but philosophy's coming-to-be is philosophy itself, and thus philosophy and the history of philosophy are identical.³⁴ We can understand, then, Hegel's contention that the history of philosophy cannot be written without a system as a point of view from which to look at it.³⁵ What he does, so to speak, is to show historically how the system comes to be what it is. This, incidentally, need not conflict with Hegel's further contention that each philosopher is to be interpreted on the basis of what he has said and not in the light of later developments of thought— although there might be reason to question whether Hegel has always remained faithful to his own rule, so convinced is he that the system reveals what its "moments" have to mean. Aside from his reliance on secondary sources for everything he has to say about oriental philosophy and for most of what he has to say about medieval philosophy—and his failure even to mention Lucretius as a source for a knowledge of Epicureanism—he does manifest a tendency to make the words of philosophers fit into the procrustean bed of *his* system.

Since, however, Hegel's concern is to show the system in the process of coming to be, and since he is convinced that it is not simply *his* system but philosophy itself which is in question, his procedure, arbitrary as it may seem, is at least understandable. For this reason we can, before watching

---

[32] *Ibid.*, p. 149.
[33] *Ibid.*, p. 33.
[34] *Ibid.*, p. 120.
[35] *Ibid.*, p. 261-62.

Hegel trace the process down through the centuries, turn to the conclusions he draws from what he has observed. These conclusions will, it is hoped, throw a sort of retrospective light on the whole process as he sees it.

The Overall View

The task Hegel had set himself at the outset of his course of lectures was that of observing philosophical thought, beginning with its first abstract attempts to find in reason the explanation of reality and proceeding to the systematic realization that concretely reason finds all reality in itself. It has taken this thought a long time to come to know itself as it now does:

> The world-spirit has now come to this point. The latest philosophy is the result of all former ones; nothing has been lost, all principles have been retained. This concrete idea is the result of spirit's efforts over almost 2500 years (Thales was born in 640 B.C.)—the result of its most earnest endeavor, that of becoming objective to itself, of knowing itself : *Tantae molis erat, se ipsam cognoscere mentem.*[36]

What has happened is that the task announced at the beginning of the *Logic*, of presenting God "as he is in his eternal essence before the creation of nature and of a single finite spirit,"[37] has now been accomplished again through the medium of history. To say that philosophy is the process of spirit coming to know itself is to say that it is the process of the human spirit coming to know God as God knows himself, and this is to say of philosophy that it is "necessarily *one philosophy* in the process of developing. The revelation of God as he knows himself."[38]

This "one philosophy" has become what it now is by going through a series of stages, by successively discovering the contradiction in each of its positions, and by rediscovering its own unity in the reconciliation of each contradiction. Five steps on that ladder of development were cleared during the period of Greek philosophy from Thales to the neo-Platonists, a period of approximately a thousand years. No further steps were made until the dawn of modern philosophy, a thousand years later, and for modern philosophy three more steps were needed.[39] All of which permits us to understand, in retrospect, why Hegel devoted two thirds of his course (apart from the Introduction) to Greek philosophy and only one third to medieval and modern philosophy combined. In any event, the overall process is one in

---

[36] *Vorlesungen über die Geschichte der Philosophie*, Vol. III (Glockner, 19), p. 685.
[37] *Wissenschaft der Logik* (3rd ed., Lasson, Hamburg: Meiner, 1963), Vol. 1, p. 31.
[38] *Geschichte* III, p. 686.
[39] *Ibid.*, pp. 686-89.

which philosophy again and again manifests itself as one in the midst of diversity, because spirit comes to know itself as one and the same throughout the whole process of its thinking. "To know opposition in unity and unity in opposition, this is absolute knowing; and science is this, to know this unity in its entire development through itself (by knowing itself)."[40]

What has been learned, then, in this course on the history of philosophy is that there is only one philosophy, that its process reveals the logical necessity of its various stages, that each later stage contains all that is significant in the stages which preceded it, and that thus there can be only forward movement in philosophy, no regression.

> The overall result of the history of philosophy is : 1) that throughout the whole of time there is only one philosophy, and its simultaneous differences constitute the necessary aspects of the one principle; 2) that the sequence of philosophical systems is not a contingent one but manifests necessary progress in the development of this science; 3) that at a given time the most recent philosophy is the result of this development, and truth is then in the highest form that the self-consciousness of spirit has of itself. The most recent philosophy, therefore, contains those which preceded it, embraces all levels, is the product and result of all those that went before. One cannot now be a Platonist; one must raise oneself a) above the trivialities of particular opinions, thoughts, objections, difficulties, b) above one's own vanity, as though one had thought in a specially significant way. For to catch hold of the inner substantial spirit is the position of the individual; within the whole individuals are as though blind; the inner spirit drives them.[41]

Philosophy, of course, could not begin—nor, a fortiori, could its history begin—did we not have the conviction that the truth is attainable and that the human mind has the capacity to attain to it. In Hegel's own words, "The first condition for philosophy is that we have assurance of truth and faith in the power of the spirit,"[42] or, to continue in a more eloquent vein :

> Man, because he is spirit, should and must deem himself worthy of the highest. He cannot think too highly of the greatness and the power of his spirit, and, given this belief nothing will be so difficult and hard as not to reveal itself to him. The being of the universe, at first hidden and concealed, has no power which can offer resistance to the courageous pursuit of knowledge, it has to lay itself open before the seeker—to set before his eyes and give for his enjoyment, its riches and depths.[43]

This faith, however, is a long-continuing one, and only as the power of the mind unfolds itself through the successive efforts of individual philo-

---

[40] *Ibid.*, p. 689.
[41] *Ibid.*, pp. 690-91.
[42] *Einleitung*, pp. 5-6.
[43] *Ibid.*, p. 6.

sophers, is it possible to see what riches it does, in fact, reveal. It is this "unfolding" (*Entwicklung*) that Hegel traces in his *Lectures on the History of Philosophy*, beginning with the first independent application of mind to the mysteries of the universe and only after 2500 years coming to the realization that there is no other way to plumb these mysteries than by plunging into the depths of reason itself, where all has been contained since the beginning. The final goal, perhaps only asymptotically approachable, is to see the totality of reality as God sees it; i.e. as God sees himself—and this Hegel comes to grips with in his *Logic*.

Detailed Elaboration

In attempting to see how Hegel goes about tracing philosophy's development one could, of course, simply paraphrase the three volumes of his *History*—a not unrewarding task, perhaps, but a somewhat problematic addition to Hegel's own words. A more manageable and, in the long run, more instructive approach is to take some of the key developments which Hegel detects in philosophy's history and to show how he traces these developments from their abstract beginnings to their concrete fulfillment. Not to make the list too long we can, perhaps, confine ourselves to those salient developments whereby mind becomes progressively aware of its capacity to come to terms with the totality of reality. 1) The first of these is to be found in the progressively more autonomous character of thought, mind's progressive realization that it need make no appeal outside itself for the justification of its affirmations. 2) Secondly, there is the growing realization that what thought *affirms* to be so is more really so than what the senses *take* to be so. 3) Closely allied to this last is the progressive identification of those seeming opposites, thought and being, which is realized only in the gradual dialectical reconciliation of opposites, accomplished in "speculative" thought. 4) A thought which develops in this way is conditioned by the progressive realization that the primary category of both being and thought is subject, not substance. 5) Finally, the mere subjectivity of individual thinking is as arbitrary as is mere opinion, if it is not fleshed out by identification with the universality of thought itself. Each of these developments, it will be seen, culminates in a systematic completeness which is to be found only in Hegel's *Logic*.

1. *Freedom of Philosophical Thought*

In his Introduction Hegel tells us that philosophy begins where thought begins to be free, and this it can do only where men themselves (the philosophers) are free.[44] He thus links freedom of thought with political freedom, both to justify his refusal to accord any philosophical significance to oriental philosophy and to situate the beginning of philosophy in the Greek city-state. One may well question the accuracy of Hegel's interpretation of oriental philosophy—or of oriental political life, for that matter—but his decision to seek the sources of contemporary Western philosophical thinking only in the West is at least understandable. In any event Hegel is convinced that only free men can philosophize,[45] and that the contribution made by the Greeks to the legacy left by the East was precisely the freedom which makes philosophy possible.[46] The important point here, of course, is that thought itself be free, which it begins to be when with the Eleatics it moves away from its dependence on imaginative representation and becomes "for itself".[47] Herein, says Hegel, we find the dialectical character of thought.[48] Freedom, however, is a meaningless concept if individuals as such are not free, and it is in Athens, with the Sophists that the subjective freedom of individuals begins to emerge, that individuals were first encouraged to think for themselves.[49] The principle here is that the individual is free "to admit validity only to that which he himself clearly sees, to what he finds in his own reason".[50] With the Sophists, however, the subjective freedom of ratiocination (*das räsonnierende Denken*) is minimal, and it is only with Socrates that the individual is called upon to take responsibility for his own thinking, i.e. producing his own thoughts: [51]

With regard to the Socratic principle the first characteristic of thought, an important one, although as yet merely formal, is that consciousness produces from itself what is true, and, therefore, has as its function to produce precisely this. This is the principle of subjective freedom, i.e. that consciousness is directed upon itself.[52]

Although Hegel has much to say about Plato and his contributions to the development of thought, he does not distinguish him from Socrates on the question of subjective freedom. Still, he does make much of the dialectic of the *Parmenides*, in Hegel's mind the greatest of Plato's dialogues. That he should have found so little on this point in Plato may well be due

[44] *Ibid.*, pp. 225-27.
[45] *Geschichte* I (Glockner, 17), pp. 183-84.
[46] *Ibid.*, p. 188.
[47] *Ibid.*, p. 300.
[48] *Ibid.*, p. 296.
[49] *Ibid.*, pp. 400-402.
[50] *Geschichte* II (Glockner, 18), p. 20.
[51] *Ibid.*
[52] *Ibid.*, p. 71.

to the fact that he misses the point of Plato's use of myth,[53] which he considers to be only a pedagogical instrument, on which thought no longer has to depend, once the concept is sufficiently advanced.[54] It is Aristotle who brings the concept forward to this point. With Aristotle, then, thought is free because it does not depend on the presence of its object, neither on its physical presence in sensation nor on its imaginative presence in representation.[55]

To understand what Hegel has to say about freedom of thought in the interval between Aristotle and the emergence of the subjective principle at the beginning of the modern period we should do well to turn to his treatment, in the *Phenomenology*, of Stoicism, Scepticism, and the Unhappy Consciousness. The last, which is a religious rather than a philosophical consciousness, in that it relinquishes freedom in favor of a principle which is *beyond* reason, characterizes, for Hegel, the whole of the Middle Ages and permits him to devote very little time to the Medieval period. It is interesting to note, in this connection, that he sees subjective freedom reintroduced not in the philosophical but in the religious sphere with Luther's insistence on freedom of spirit, according to which reason is responsible to itself alone, not to any external authority.[56] Modern philosophical thinking, with its insistence that thought depends on thought alone, begins, properly speaking, with Descartes. It is Descartes who affirms explicitly that what we recognize as true is the product of our own free thinking, in the sense that the evidence for the truth is to be found in consciousness itself.[57] Although Hegel has a good deal to say about the period between Descartes and Kant, with regard to the freedom of thinking he sees very little advance during this time over the principle enunciated by Descartes. With Kant, however, a significant change takes place; he it is who asserts the autonomy of mind with the utmost vigor. "What is true in Kantian philosophy is its grasp of thinking as concrete in itself, self-determining. Thus freedom is recognized."[58] Kant, however, comes in for more criticism than, perhaps, any other philosopher that Hegel treats.[59] The reason for this may be found in Hegel's very notion of criticism: Kant was "so near and yet so far," and the task

[53] Cf. *Einleitung*, pp. 54-55.
[54] *Geschichte* II, p. 189.
[55] *Ibid.*, p. 377.
[56] *Geschichte* III (Glockner, 19), p. 255.
[57] *Ibid.*, p. 338.
[58] *Ibid.*, p. 552.
[59] Cf. Quentin Lauer, S.J., "Hegel's Critique of Kant's Theology," in *God Knowable and Unknowable*, ed. Robert J. Roth, S.J., (New York: Fordham University Press, 1973), pp. 85-105.

of criticism is not to refute but to show how a philosopher's own principles demand to be developed.[60] For Kant theoretical reason is not genuinely independent, since it produces only the form of thought and is dependent on sensual intuition for its content.[61] Only practical reason is thoroughly self-determining, i.e. free.[62] Fichte, who is more "speculative" than Kant, makes more of a case for freedom in the self-development of the absolute concept, the Ego,[63] but the freedom in question is still rather formal, since it consists in a progressive determination of the object by the subject, not a self-development of the concept itself.[64] With Schelling, on the other hand, all knowing is produced by the interior activity of the subject,[65] but the mode is that of intellectual intuition,[66] not the "logical" development that pure thought demands.[67]

2. *The Objectivity of Thought*

If all Hegel could say about thought was that it is free, he would indeed be saying very little. It is far more important for thought to be true than for it to be free, unless, of course, a condition for being true is that it be free. Of this latter Hegel was convinced,[68] but he was also well aware of the difference between a condition and a guarantee. At the same time he was convinced, both logically and historically, that thought more surely grasps the way things are the more it rids itself of dependence on what is not thought. In short, he was convinced that mind can grasp reality in a way that no other forms of consciousness can, and that purity of thought made for objectivity in a way that sense intuition cannot. This is but another way of saying that what reason says is true, no matter what other kind of evidence may seem to be against it. Thus, right from the beginning of his treatment of the history of thought Hegel will emphasize any movement he detects away from the sensible to the intelligible. This is evidenced in his interpretation of the material principles of the Ionians, which, he says, are objects of thought, not of sense perception. By the same token, we have seen,

---

[60] *Logik* II, pp. 217-18.
[61] *Geschichte* III, pp. 588-89.
[62] *Ibid.*, pp. 590-91.
[63] *Ibid.*, p. 615; cf. p. 618.
[64] *Ibid.*, p. 637.
[65] *Ibid.*, p. 653.
[66] *Ibid.*, p. 654.
[67] *Ibid.*, p. 662.
[68] To put this another way, Hegel was convinced that only when thought is fully autonomous is it truly thought and, thus, true thought.

the Eleatics are concerned with concepts rather than with imaginative representations of reality.[69] Parmenides recognizes true being in thought, not in the sensible,[70] and Zeno is the "master of dialectic," because he occupies himself with pure thought.[71] So true is this that Hegel will not recognize any sort of "*solvitur ambulando*" as an answer to *reasons* for denying motion—reasons can be refuted only with reasons, not with evidence of the senses.[72] Heraclitus, too, speaks of what reason demands : "Now, Heraclitus understands the Absolute itself as this process of thought, as dialectic itself."[73] Hegel, in fact, finds in Heraclitus nothing to which he himself cannot subscribe—and that in his *Logic*!—[74] not only because Heraclitus saw that the truth of being is in becoming,[75] but because he saw that only universalized consciousness is true.[76] In the proper sense of the term, then, philosophy begins with Heraclitus : "The beginning of philosophy's existence dates from him [Heraclitus]—it is the enduring idea which remains the same in all philosophers up to the present, just as it was the idea of Plato and Aristotle."[77] Even Leucippus conceived of atoms as objects of thought, in no way sensible, i.e. as ideal objects,[78] and Anaxagoras, with his concept of *nous* (which Hegel somewhat arbitrarily interprets as teleological),[79] took a big step toward making pure thought the basic principle of philosophy.[80]

It is, of course, the Platonic *eidos* which contains the recognition that reality is truly grasped in thought alone,[81] with the result that the most real (to ontōs on) is seen to be the ideal.[82] It is for this reason that, in Hegel's eyes, Plato is the first to make philosophy scientific : "With Plato philosophical science as science begins."[83] Plato, again, is the first to make explicit that not the sensible existent but only the universal determined in itself is true [84] and that this universal is not simply a thought present in the thinker

---

[69] *Geschichte* I, p. 296.
[70] *Ibid.*, p. 312.
[71] *Ibid.*, p. 318.
[72] *Ibid.*, p. 330.
[73] *Ibid.*, p. 344.
[74] *Ibid.*
[75] *Ibid.*, pp. 348-49.
[76] *Ibid.*, pp. 367-68.
[77] *Ibid.*, p. 362.
[78] *Ibid.*, p. 385.
[79] *Ibid.*, pp. 411-13.
[80] *Ibid.*, p. 397; cf. p. 408.
[81] *Geschichte* II (Glockner, 18), pp. 218-19.
[82] *Ibid.*, p. 224.
[83] *Ibid.*, p. 169.
[84] *Ibid.*, p. 199.

but is the very truth (substance) of being.[85] Along this line Hegel, in opposition to his contemporaries, looks upon Aristotle as the genuine successor of Plato [86] and not an "empiricist" in the commonly accepted meaning of that term.[87] Aristotle, too, finds the truth of being in the concept, and he is empirical only to the extent that he finds the concept in what he observes.[88] Only by a complete misunderstanding of the *"tabula rasa"* doctrine can interpreters make Aristotle say anything different; the writing on the blank page does not come from without but is the thinking activity of the mind itself.[89]

With Plato and Aristotle the primacy of the intellectual over the sensible was so well established that it suffered only minor setbacks in succeeding ages. What remained to be done, however, according to Hegel, was that thought become the universal principle in such a way that it would embrace the totality of reality, which is but another way of saying that philosophy was to become "system." For Hegel philosophy becomes that only with his own system, even though it was already implicit in Aristotle's thought. Why it should have remained merely implicit for so long or why philosophy had to wait for Hegel before achieving the unity toward which it had been moving all along, Hegel does not explain. In any event it was not until Spinoza posited substance, the *causa sui*, as the one unifying principle, that philosophy again took up where Aristotle left off.[90] Spinoza represents, so to speak, a new beginning of philosophy, in the sense that modern philosophy must proceed from the Spinozistic point of view : "In this regard it should in general be remarked that thinking had to adopt the standpoint of Spinozism; this is the essential beginning of all philosophizing."[91] Still, even though absolute substance is the true principle, it is not the completely true principle; it must also act, and this it does as substance which is also subject, i.e. as spirit.[92] In this process Locke and Hume, with their emphasis on the sensible, constitute negative moments, to be overcome,[93] whereas Leibniz saw that not sensible but intelligible being is essential truth,[94] even

---

[85] *Ibid.*, p. 200.
[86] *Ibid.*, p. 301.
[87] *Ibid.*, pp. 311-12.
[88] *Ibid.*, pp. 312-13: cf. pp. 340-41.
[89] *Ibid.*, pp. 386-87.
[90] *Geschichte* III, p. 372.
[91] *Ibid.*, p. 376.
[92] *Ibid.*, p. 377.
[93] Cf. *ibid.*, pp. 417-18, 495.
[94] *Ibid.*, p. 449.

though his intellectual world is left undeveloped, because his principle is absolute multiplicity and not absolute unity.[95] Kant sought to overcome the empiricist emphasis on sensibility by appealing to the self-validation of the intelligible,[96] whereas Fichte and Schelling sought to overcome the absolute multiplicity of Leibniz by insisting on the unity of the absolute subject.[97] All three (Kant, Fichte, Schelling), however, failed to achieve a concrete unity of the whole, because for each the ultimate unifying principle was merely formal.[98] This, however, brings us to another facet of the developmental process, the progressive identification of being and thought, which Hegel calls "concretization."

3. *The Identity of Thought and Being*

In his *Logic* Hegel tells us that the science of logic (philosophy) must begin with what thought first thinks, and this is being. Only gradually does it come to the realization that what thought thinks is itself and that, therefore the thought thinking and the being thought are identical. The same he will find progressively revealed in the history of philosophical thinking. Ostensibly being and thought are not only not identical, they are opposites : thinking stands over against that which is thought. In the dialectical thinking which Hegel espouses, however, it is precisely the function of thought both to engender and to reconcile opposition, as mind progressively recognizes that dialectical opposites must be said of each other, if they are to be true and not merely remain onesided abstractions. To return to the *Logic*, to think being and only being is to think an abstraction which must be complemented by its opposite, non-being. Both being and non-being as opposed to each other, are abstractions and demand concretization in becoming. By the same token, to think whatever is implied in the unity of being and non-being (the whole "Doctrine of Being") is to think of it as it is *in* thought, i.e. as opposed to its *mere* being (the "Doctrine of Essence"). To think the content of thought, however, as somehow other than thought is to remain at another level of abstraction which is to be completed (concretized) in the realization that to think at all is to think thought (the "Doctrine of the Concept"). If philosophy, then, can be characterized, as we saw before, as "thought occupied with itself,"[99] the history of philosophy will manifest the gradual realization that to think at all is to think thought and to seek to know any-

[95] *Ibid.*, p. 470.
[96] *Ibid.*, p. 558.
[97] Cf. *ibid.*, pp. 627-28, 683.
[98] Cf. *ibid.*, pp. 554-55, 637, 681.
[99] *Einleitung*, p. 83.

thing at all is to look for it in thought. To do this is to be genuinely "speculative," a quality which characterizes philosophical thinking more and more, as its concepts engender their opposites. Philosophical thinking is essentially speculative in the sense that from the very beginning it is in the process of becoming speculative.[100] It is not until Parmenides, however, that the sort of opposition which characterizes speculative thinking becomes explicit—even though Parmenides himself was not conscious that this was taking place : "Thus, with Parmenides the opposition of being and non-being is manifested more determinately, but still without consciousness."[101] Zeno makes even more explicit this movement of pure thought.[102] In Hegel's view, then, Zeno does not really deny movement; he simply seeks to show how it must be *conceived*.[103] The most clearly speculative thinker among the pre-Socratics, however, is Heraclitus, and the difficulty we find in understanding him arises precisely from this.[104] He it is who recognizes that being and non-being are mere abstractions, concretized only in becoming.[105] What is beginning to become apparent here is that only where there is opposition can there be harmony,[106] but the turning point in philosophy, where thought and being genuinely harmonize with each other, comes with Socrates : [107] "In Socrates there arose the consciousness that whatever is is mediated through thought,"[108] i.e. it is only *through* thought that being can be *said* of anything. The true greatness of Plato lies in the conscious way his thinking brings together the opposed determinations of the being it thinks.[109]

Characteristic of Platonic philosophy is its orientation to the intellectual, the supra-sensible world, the lifting of consciousness into the spiritual realm; such that the intellectual took on the form of the supra-sensible, the spiritual, which is proper to thought.[110] As a result the intellectual in this form becomes important for consciousness, enters into consciousness, and consciousness finds firm footing on this ground.[111] *To ontōs on*—"what in truth is

---

[100] Cf. *Geschichte* I, pp. 204, 213.
[101] *Ibid.*, p. 308.
[102] *Ibid.*, pp. 318, 320, 325-26.
[103] *Ibid.*, p. 334.
[104] *Ibid.*, p. 348.
[105] *Ibid.*, pp. 348-49.
[106] *Ibid.*, pp. 352-53.
[107] *Geschichte* II, pp. 122-23.
[108] *Ibid.*, p. 45.
[109] *Ibid.*, p. 237.
[110] *Ibid.*, p. 236.
[111] *Ibid.*, p. 170.

in and for itself" [112] is for Plato the ideal.[113] Aristotle makes this even more explicit by affirming the identity of concept and the substance of what is conceived : "Objects are subjectively thought by me; and then my thought is the concept of the thing, and this is the substance of the thing."[114] This is but another way of saying that the "substantial" (enduring) truth of reality is to be found in thought, not elsewhere. Aristotle's "ontology," then, is on the same level as Hegel's "logic,"[115] and Aristotle's logic is suited for the sort of science which is a function of finite understanding, not to Aristotle's own speculative philosophy.[116] This speculative philosophy of Aristotle culminates in the doctrine of the "unmoved mover," the *noēsis noēseōs* of *Metaphysics*, Book Lambda, which Hegel interprets as Aristotle's affirmation of the primacy of thought,[117] which alone permits philosophy to perform its most significant function of reconciling the finite and the infinite, i.e. the infinitizing of a being which in itself is merely finite : "That which alone is great in philosophy is the joining of the infinite and the finite."[118]

In all this, philosophy is gradually becoming aware that what is immediately present to consciousness is not true being; only what is present through the mediation of thought is true being. The immediate, as Hegel shows us abundantly in the *Phenomenology*, is inevitably bound up in contradiction, which only speculative thinking can resolve. Step by step post-Aristotelian philosophy became conscious of this. Stoicism, which is in general a mere formalism [119] did have the realization that immediate thinking does not yield the true; only a thinking which corresponds to the *logos* does, i.e. rational (speculative) thinking.[120] The mediation which rational thinking effects, however, is precisely the negation of the immediacy with which reality initially presents itself to consciousness. What is important to recognize, of course, is that this sort of negation is just as positive as is affirmation; it is that which determines the merely affirmative to be what it in truth is. Hegel credits Philo with having seen this : "Philo had the correct insight that the oppostie of being is just as positive as is being."[121] To recognize this is to think "speculatively," something which Hegel also finds

[112] *Ibid.*, p. 211.
[113] *Ibid.*, p. 224.
[114] *Ibid.*, p. 333.
[115] *Ibid.*, p. 319.
[116] *Ibid.*, pp. 413-15.
[117] *Ibid.*, pp. 328-30; cf. p. 391.
[118] *Ibid.*, p. 516.
[119] *Ibid.*, pp. 454-55.
[120] *Ibid.*, p. 447.
[121] *Geschichte* III, p. 25.

in Proclus;[122] it is another way of saying that what the mind necessarily thinks in thinking reality is so of reality. This, again, he finds in Plotinus,[123] and strangely enough, he finds more of it in Catholic thought inherited from the Middle Ages than he does in Protestant thought.[124] Not until Descartes, however, is the principle made explicit that only in consulting thought do we find what can be truly said of reality : "What is thought correctly and clearly is so. Thus is expressed that in thought man experiences what actually is true of things."[125] Unfortunately, the thought of which Descartes speaks is abstract, unable to concretize itself and, therefore, in need of experience to concretize it.[126] Spinoza, on the other hand, in recognizing that all determination is negation, a function of thought, saw thought as self-determining and, therefore, self-concretizing.[127] This permits him to unify all reality under the heading of absolute substance, a unity of opposing moments.[128] Significantly this absolute substance is "*causa sui*," i.e. has itself as its effect, and only thought does this.[129] The diametric opposite of this is to be found in Locke, who will not judge the validity of thought from its content but only from the manner of its derivation.[130] This, says Hegel, misses the point entirely : "It is entirely different to ask : is what is in us true. Whence it comes does not answer the question at all."[131] What deceives the empiricists—and here Newton is the paradigm—is their conviction that they are dealing with things, when in truth they are dealing with concepts.[132] What must be recognized is that not only the form of thought but also its content is the product of thinking,[133] and this is the realization, with which the *Phenomenology* has made us familiar, that reason is the consciousness of being itself all reality.[134] As Kant appears on the scene, then (Hume is historically important chiefly as providing the starting point for Kant)[135] philosophy is on the threshold of assuming its essential task, to

[122] *Ibid.*, p. 72.
[123] *Ibid.*, pp. 53-54.
[124] *Ibid.*, p. 259.
[125] *Ibid.*, p. 354.
[126] *Ibid.*, p. 364.
[127] *Ibid.*, pp. 374-75.
[128] *Ibid.*, p. 372.
[129] *Ibid.*, p. 379.
[130] *Ibid.*, p. 424.
[131] *Ibid.*, p. 428.
[132] *Ibid.*, p. 447.
[133] *Ibid.*, p. 481.
[134] *Ibid.*, p. 484.
[135] *Ibid.*, p. 493.

grasp (*begreifen*) the unity of thought and being : "The task of philosophy is determined to the point of making its object the very unity of thinking and being, which is its fundamental idea, and of grasping (*begriefen*) this idea, i.e. catching hold of the most interior necessity, the concept."[136]

Although Kant's contribution to the accomplishment of this task was enormous, Hegel is convinced that Kant's concern with the faculty of knowing rather than with what is known [137] led him to conceive of thinking as a process of *unifying* the manifold presented to it, in which the manifold and the form of unity supplied by the mind remain external to each other. Thus the true *unity* of being and thought is not yet achieved.[138] Because, for Kant, reason is not constitutive but only regulative of knowing,[139] it is dependent on an experience exterior to the concept in order to give the concept a content.[140] The result is that Kant does not succeed in reconciling the contradictions which a reality in process manifests in thought; he simply attributes the contradictions to the inadequacy of finite reason.[141] As we saw before, Fichte represents for Hegel an advance over Kant, in that his thought is more speculative; it calls for a self-development of the absolute concept,[142] permitting a unity of all thought and all being.[143] Still, since Fichte has the Ego progressively determine its objects in the process of thinking, he does not manage to bridge the gap between being and thought.[144] Schelling does take a step in the right direction by completely spiritualizing nature, thus making the whole of nature present in thought.[145] For Schelling "the truth of nature, nature in itself, is an intellectual world."[146] Thus, he presents a thinking whose content is more concrete, but he falls short of making the whole process one in which the concept need not go outside itself.[147] To show how this complete unity of reality is achieved in the concept is not the task of Hegel's historical treatment of philosophy. This is the work of Hegel's own *Logic*. The history he presents, however, does make clearer what the *Logic* is trying to do. Similarly, the process

---

[136] *Ibid.*, p. 535.
[137] *Ibid.*, p. 555.
[138] *Ibid.*, p. 558.
[139] *Ibid.*, p. 560.
[140] *Ibid.*, p. 561.
[141] *Ibid.*, p. 583.
[142] *Ibid.*, p. 615.
[143] *Ibid.*, p. 619.
[144] *Ibid.*, p. 637.
[145] *Ibid.*, p. 651.
[146] *Ibid.*, p. 683.
[147] *Ibid.*

of thought as subjective activity demands a progressive realization of just what subject is. This Hegel attempts in his *Phenomenology*, but again it is the *History* which helps to clarify what the *Phenomenology* seeks to do.

4. The Movement toward Subjectivity

Much of what has already been said regarding the historical development of philosophical thought obviates the necessity of a detailed exposition of Hegel's treatment of the question of subjectivity. In general it can be said that Modern Philosophy (beginning with Descartes) distinguishes itself from the philosophy which preceded it by its emphasis on the thinking subject rather than on the object of thought. Hegel, however, traces the gradual orientation of thought towards the thinking subject back to the ancient world; he in fact makes the increasing emphasis on subjectivity a condition for progress in philosophy.

He finds this movement already manifested among the Sophists who, in their concern for teaching, were aware that learning is a development that takes place in a thinking subject.

> To the turning back [on itself] of thinking, which is a consciousness that it is the subject who does the thinking, is linked another side, i.e. that the subject, therefore, has as its task to attain for itself an essential absolute content.[148]

To be aware that an object is necessarily an object for a subject is to recognize that somehow the criterion for the objectivity of thought is to be sought in subjectivity. Thus, the dictum of Protagoras, "Man is the measure of all things," can make eminent good sense, if it is speaking of man *as rational*.[149] In fact, all further progress in philosophy hinges on a realization that the goal of thinking is to be thoroughly rational.[150] It is Socrates, then, who summarizes all previous thought by turning explicit attention to the subject whose thinking contains all being.[151] Plato goes even further, in his awareness that being is available only in the mind.[152] "The source whence we become conscious of the divine is the same as it was for Socrates. Man's own mind is this source; it contains in itself precisely the essential."[153] Representations (*Vorstellungen*) of things come from without, but not the thoughts wherein they are universalized; these come from an acting subject, they are not the

---

[148] *Geschichte* II, p. 4; cf. pp. 3-5.
[149] *Ibid.*, p. 30.
[150] *Ibid.*, p. 31.
[151] *Ibid.*, pp. 42-43.
[152] *Ibid.*, p. 203.
[153] *Ibid.*, p. 202.

product of things acting on a subject.[154] Nevertheless, Plato's ideas were not adequately subjective; he came on the scene too early for that : "This lack of subjectivity is a lack in the Greek ethical idea itself."[155] Aristotle did not improve matters along this line, but he did contribute in his logic an account of the subjective activity, called thinking.[156] The stoics and sceptics, on the other hand, as we have already seen, pushed subjectivity so far that objectivity was lost. "The sceptics went all the way in their view of the subjectivity of all knowing; they universally substituted for being in knowledge the expression of illusion."[157]

Not until the advent of the neo-Platonists did the development we have been observing reach the point of a consciousness that only in mind does the world of reality express itself.[158] Here, then, the identity of the being of which we are conscious and the self of which we are conscious begins to take its place in philosophy : "More philosophically and more conceptually articulated (*begriffener*), however, the unity of self-consciousness and being emerges in the Alexandrian school."[159] For some strange reason Hegel does not seem to have been aware of St. Augustine's constribution to philosophy's consciousness of its own subjective character—despite the Augustinian overtones of so much of Hegel's own thought—and so he makes a lyric leap from the subjectivity of the neo-Platonists to the subjectivity of Luther, who turned men's minds drastically to that which came from within themselves.[160] Luther's question, of course, was the question of faith, but his realization that the content of faith is constituted as what it is in being believed [161] paved the way for the emphasis on subjectivity which characterizes philosophy from Descartes to Fichte. In this connection it is interesting to note how much attention Hegel gives to Jakob Böhme, primarily a mystical thinker, whom Hegel calls "the first German philosopher," whose principle was the Protestant one : "to place the intellectual world in one's own inner self (*Gemüth*) and to observe, know and feel in one's own self-consciousness whatever was otherwise outside."[162] It is with Descartes, however, that consciousness has within itself all it needs in order to philosophize : "With him [Descartes] we enter properly speaking into an indepen-

[154] *Ibid.*, p. 204.
[155] *Ibid.*, p. 294.
[156] *Ibid.*, p. 411.
[157] *Ibid.*, p. 538.
[158] *Geschichte* III, p. 4.
[159] *Ibid.*, p. 31.
[160] *Ibid.*, pp. 256-57.
[161] *Ibid.*, pp. 260-61.
[162] *Ibid.*, p. 300.

dent philosophy, which knows that it comes independently from reason and that self-consciousness is an essential moment of the true."[163] Philosophical thought can now justify itself,[164] and it is thinking in its universality which reveals the Ego as nothing else does.[165] Hegel sees no further advance along the lines of subjectivity until the advent of Kant, whose "Copernican revolution" is the most deliberate and emphatic turn to subjectivity yet witnessed. There is genuine knowledge only where there is necessity and universality, and the source of necessity and universality is the subject alone.[166] Unfortunately, however, in turning to the subject Kant finds only the subject;[167] not universal reason which is responsible for the very objectivity of its content: "The Kantian Ego, however, does not properly speaking attain reason, but again remains the individual self-consciousness as such, which is over against the universal."[168] Fichte, on the other hand is more thoroughgoing in seeking to *derive* the categories of being from consciousness of the self—a derivation which still separates consciousness of self and consciousness of reality.[169] With Schelling, finally, the correspondence of nature and spirit is complete, the "absolute unity of contradictions"[170] has been achieved. There has been a complete reconciliation of the empirical and the conceptual,[171] and there is a recognition that the concrete unity must be grasped as process.[172] Still, Schelling fails to work out the process logically,[173] and so, as Hegel tells us in the *Phenomenology*, the unity is one of indistinction, like "the dark night in which all the cows are black."[174] That subjectivity should have proved inadequate to its task all down the line was inevitable, precisely because individual, finite subjectivity is necessarily inadequate, and the process of universalizing the individual in a more than formal, abstract way had, again, to wait for the finishing touches supplied by Hegel's *Phenomenology*, then to be elaborated in his *Logic*. This reconciliation of the individual and the universal, however, also has its history, which consists in the gradual realization that, although each thinker

---

[163] *Ibid.*, p. 328.
[164] Cf. *ibid.*, p. 331.
[165] *Ibid.*, pp. 342-43.
[166] *Ibid.*, pp. 554-55.
[167] *Ibid.*, p. 554.
[168] *Ibid.*, p. 571.
[169] *Ibid.*, pp. 627-28.
[170] *Ibid.*, p. 659.
[171] *Ibid.*, p. 681.
[172] *Ibid.*, p. 646.
[173] *Ibid.*, p. 662.
[174] *Phänomenologie des Geistes* (6th Ed., Hoffmeister, Hamburg : Meiner, 1952), p. 19.

is an individual, and each thought is individually produced, still thought is thought only to the extent that its content is universal—with all that ultimately implies.

5. Synthesis of Individual and Universal

The process of thought's progressive universalization, strangely enough, could not get under way until the Greeks began to recognize the importance of the individual.[175] Until then the individual was swallowed up in the *an sich* universality of nature, and this could not be remedied until spirit began to dominate nature.[176] The shift is illustrated in the passage from the abstract, impersonal gods of the Orient to the individually personal gods of the Greeks.[177] If thinking is not individual it is not really thinking. If, on the other hand, it is merely individual it gets nowhere: it must be the thinking of spirit; initially the spirit of a people,[178] ultimately the universal spirit which embraces all men.[179]

The first significant step in this process comes when Socrates affirms his own individuality at its highest.[180] His *daimonion* which forbids him to acquiesce to the merely common opinion is precisely the affirmation of individuality in the midst of universality; it was Socrates who knew what he as an individual had to do in a given situation, no matter what the Athenians in general thought.[181] Essentially, then, the charge brought against him at his trial was correct; his god was not the god (or gods) of the Athenian people.[182] By appealing to his own conscience against the conscience of the people he was affirming a merely individual principle which had yet to become truly universal.[183] The process of fleshing out this principle, then, begins with Plato and his realization that thinking is not merely a property of the soul but its very substance and that thus the soul partakes of the universality which belongs to thinking.[184] The immortality of which he speaks in the *Phaedo* simply bespeaks the essence of the soul, i.e. the universality of thought, which cannot be confined to finite time.[185] The truth of being

---

[175] *Geschichte* I, p. 192.
[176] *Ibid.*, p. 190.
[177] *Ibid.*, p. 152.
[178] *Ibid.*, pp. 291-92.
[179] *Geschichte* III, pp. 691-92.
[180] *Geschichte* II, pp. 54-55.
[181] *Ibid.*, p. 95.
[182] *Ibid.*, pp. 106-107, 109-110.
[183] *Ibid.*, pp. 115-117.
[184] *Ibid.*, p. 208.
[185] *Ibid.*, pp. 212-13.

reveals itself in thought, and so thought is the work of the universal not of the individual.[186]

Aristotle once more stresses the significance of the individual,[187] who is subsumed, however, under the universality of reason.[188] Thinking, which for Plato was abstract, has with Aristotle become concrete, but not yet so systematic as to recognize the multiplicity of interrelationships that constitute reality.[189] Here again, throughout the vicissitudes of philosophy's development from Aristotle on, Aristotle remains unsurpassed, as one thinker after another stresses now the individual, now the universal, constantly failing to adequately reconcile the two. What gradually becomes clear, however, in the long period between Aristotle and Spinoza, who, as we have seen, is the first to take up where Aristotle left off, is that a reconciliation of individual and universal will be possible only if philosophy is oriented to a genuine knowledge of God : "Only philosophy is science regarding God."[190] Philosophy, then, must become theology, if it is to achieve its destiny as philosophy : "because philosophy is the knowledge of absolute being, i.e. is theology."[191] The theme which had been announced in the Introduction to the *Lectures*, echoed as it is in the *Phenomenology*, the *Logic*, the *Lectures on the Philosophy of Religion*, and the *Lectures on the Proofs for God's Existence*, is here reiterated in the context of the historical development of Aristotle's basic insight that God himself is thought thinking itself. For Hegel, religion and philosophy have the same identical content, the Absolute; religion under the form of representation, philosophy under the form most proper to the Absolute, i.e. thought.[192] Along this line, despite his multiple misinterpretations of Medieval philosophy, Hegel does credit the Scholastics (particularly St. Anselm) with having recognized the essential infinity of truth (here again his disregard of Augustine is puzzling), with presenting this infinite truth as spirit,[193] and with identifying the absolute which philosophy *knows* with the God who is theology's concern. Where the Scholastics went wrong was in their attempt to *prove* the being of God, on the basis of formal

[186] Cf. *ibid.*, p. 200.
[187] *Ibid.*, p. 302.
[188] *Ibid.*, p. 410.
[189] *Ibid.*, pp. 420-21; cf. J. Glenn Gray, *Hegel and Greek Thought* (Harper Torch Book, 1968), p. 71.
[190] *Geschichte* III, p. 151.
[191] *Ibid.*, p. 154.
[192] The present author has treated this subject at length in "Hegel on the Identity of Content in Philosophy and Religion," *Hegel and the Philosophy of Religion* (The Hague : Nijhoff, 1970), pp. 261-95.
[193] *Geschichte* III, p. 200.

logic, rather than to *grasp* (*begreifen*) that being speculatively.[194] When, in the Renaissance, the revival of humanism led to a renewed interest in antiquity, [195] the door was opened to an overcoming of the false Aristotelianism of the Scholastics [196] and a penetration into the God-idea as the true philosophical idea.[197] Once again, Spinoza is the high point in this development, but even he fails to reconcile the singular and the universal, since he sees the individual existent as essentially inferior to the universal of absolute substance.[198] His mistake was to begin with definitions (as one justifiably does in mathematics) and fail to probe the reality of thought's content.[199] In doing this Spinoza took his stand on the kind of knowledge available to understanding (finite) rather than reason (infinite),[200] which prevented him from grasping God as Spirit.[201] Although it is not presented adequately in the *Lectures*, Hegel's critique of Kant on this point is substantially the same as his critique of Spinoza: because Kant confines philosophical knowing to finite understanding, without going on to infinite reason, he cannot come to terms with the Absolute as the object of thought and must have recourse to *belief* in a God whom finite thought cannot grasp.[202] Neither Fichte nor Schelling, even though their thinking is more "speculative" than Kant's, succeed in bridging the gap between finite thinking and the Absolute which is the infinite content of thought. Fichte's absolute Ego somehow stands off from the developing concept as the content of its thinking,[203] and Schelling has recourse to an "intellectual intuition" which is not, properly speaking, thinking.[204]

Conclusion

The conclusion of all this is what we might have expected: philosophy does not show itself adequate to its own task, the thinking of the Absolute, until Hegel's *Logic* identifies the absolute thinking of absolute Spirit with

[194] Cf. *ibid.*, pp. 167, 203.
[195] *Ibid.*, pp. 213-14.
[196] *Ibid.*, p. 215.
[197] Cf. *ibid.*, p. 317.
[198] *Ibid.*, pp. 381-82.
[199] *Ibid.*, p. 384.
[200] *Ibid.*, p. 378.
[201] *Ibid.*, p. 408.
[202] For an extended discussion of Hegel's criticism of Kant's failure to recognize the infinity of reason, cf. Quentin Lauer, S.J., "Hegel's Critique of Kant's Theology."
[203] *Geschichte* III, p. 637.
[204] *Ibid.*, pp. 654, 662.

the absolute object of thought, the Idea. If the being which philosophy necessarily thinks is to be grasped adequately it must be seen as somehow the product of the thought which thinks it. Thinking, however, produces only thought, and thus, the being which is the object of thinking and the thought which is the product of thinking must be identified. But this cannot be, if thinking is no more than the activity of a finite thinking subject. It is not so much that the individual thinks thought—and, thus, being—but rather thought thinks thought and being in (and through) the individual. The perennial problem of philosophy has been the universalizing of a reason whose activity takes place in individuals but whose validity transcends the limits of individual reasoning. Whether or not Hegel has solved this problem may be a moot question; that he has drawn an impressive historical picture of the process whereby reason (or Spirit) has progressively transcended the bounds of finitude, thus revealing its infinity, can scarcely be contested.

THE HISTORY OF PHILOSOPHY
AND THE *PHENOMENOLOGY OF SPIRIT*

JOSEPH C. FLAY

The Pennsylvania State University

In this paper I shall be concerned with two problems in Hegel which are usually considered separately : the significance of the history of philosophy for the *Phenomenology of Spirit* and the question of the proper beginning of Hegel's system. The first problem has traditionally been approached by either interpreting the *Phenomenology* in terms of the history of philosophy, or indicating passages or sections in which an argument of some one of Hegel's predecessors is to be found. For the most part it has been a question of articulating how the history of philosophy, as an external form of the development of philosophy, is reflected in and reflects the *Phenomenology of Spirit*, the internally coherent organization of the same development. I shall be concerned with these aspects of the problem only in so far as they might contribute to an understanding of the beginning of Hegel's system.

The question of beginnings has usually taken one of two forms : either it has involved a dispute over whether the *Logic* or the *Phenomenology* forms the true and proper beginning of the system, or has been an inquiry into political or religious presuppositions for the system. Recently, however, in writings especially by Pöggeler and Kimmerle,[1] suggestions have been made that perhaps the history of philosophy itself has some bearing upon the problem of beginnings. Their researches into Hegel's Jena period have brought two facts to the attention of scholars. 1) Hegel's development at Jena involved as a central issue a struggle to find a proper beginning for a scientific system of philosophy. The first attempt to begin with logic itself had failed, and the issue was only resolved with the conception of the *Pheno-*

---

[1] See especially the following: Kimmerle, Heinz, "Zur Entwicklung des Hegelschen Denkens in Jena," *Hegel-Studien*, Beiheft 4, 33-47; *Das Problem der Abgeschlossenheit des Denkens* (*Hegel-Studien*, Beiheft 8), 301-312; "Dokumente zu Hegels Jenaer Dozententätigkeit (1801-1807)" *Hegel-Studien*, Bd. 4, 21-99. Pöggeler, Otto, "Zur Deutung der Phänomenologie des Geistes," *Hegel-Studien*, Bd. 1, 256-94; "Die Komposition der Phänomenologie des Geistes," *Hegel-Studien*, Beiheft 3, 27-74.

menology as a propaedeutic to *Logic*. 2) At the same time that Hegel was thinking out and composing the *Phenomenology*, he first presented lectures on the history of philosophy.

The occurrence of this resolution together with the first lectures on the history of philosophy may be understood as coincidental. I shall argue, to the contrary, that the history of philosophy is a presupposition for the beginning of Hegel's system, and that this beginning is to be found in the *Phenomenology*.

First, I will examine a distinction made by Hegel between two meanings of a beginning in order to clarify in what way the *Phenomenology* is the beginning of the scientific system and in what way it is not. In the second section I will examine the way in which the *Phenomenology* begins and how this beginning is necessitated. In the final section, I will show how and why the history of philosophy is presupposed by this beginning and briefly indicate two implications of this presupposition.

I

In the *Science of Logic* Hegel distinguishes between two meanings of beginning. In the first place, he is absolutely clear that the *Logic* itself is the first part of the system. In contrast to his first announcements describing the *Phenomenology* as the first part of the system, Hegel now claims that "it lies in the very nature of a beginning that it must be Being and nothing else."[2] This pure beginning with Being in the immediacy of pure knowing "simply takes up what is there before us."[3] But he is equally clear that this beginning presupposes a propaedeutic science which is to justify the standpoint and nature of the system, a science contained in his *Phenomenology of Spirit*.

In the *Phenomenology of Spirit* I have exhibited consciousness in its movement onwards from the first immediate opposition of itself and the object to absolute knowing. The path of this movement traverses every form of the relation of consciousness to the object and has the concept of science for its result. This concept therefore (apart from the fact that it emerges within logic itself) needs no justification here because it has received it in that work; and it cannot be justified in any other way than by this emergence in consciousness, all the forms of which are resolved into this concept as into their truth....The concept of pure

---

[2] Hegel, G.W.F., *Wissenschaft der Logik* (Hamburg : Meiner, 1934), I, 57. English translation *Science of Logic*, trans. A. V. Miller (New York : Humanities Press, 1969), 72. The English translation will be referred to hereafter as Miller.

[3] *Ibid.*, 54; Miller, 69.

science and its deduction is therefore presupposed in the present work since the *Phenomenology of Spirit* is nothing other than the deduction of it.[4]

The *Science of Logic* as the first part of the system, although it involves an immediate beginning in respect to itself, yet presupposes a previous science which justifies that immediate beginning in the *Logic*.

The passage just quoted continues with a brief, but precise account of how this preparatory science prepares us.

Absolute knowing is the *truth* of every mode of consciousness because, as the course of the *Phenomenology* showed, it is only in absolute knowing that the separation of the *object* from the *certainty of itself* is completely eliminated; truth is now equated with certainty and this certainty with truth.

Thus pure science presupposes liberation from the opposition of consciousness.[5]

The concern of the *Phenomenology* is to prepare us for this immediate beginning in the *Logic* by liberating thought from the opposition, contained in consciousness, between itself and its certainty on the one hand, and the objects of knowledge and their truth on the other. And this liberation is precisely the same articulated at the end of the *Phenomenology* itself as the consummation of that work.[6]

This is to say that although science begins on its own grounds and is self contained, nevertheless it is necessary first to achieve access to the standpoint or the domain in which scientific philosophy articulates the absolute truth. The point here is that we must make a distinction between the proper domain and content of a systematic and scientific philosophy and the access of the standpoint of that domain. If one is to enter into a scientific presentation of the truth, then one must first achieve access to its domain. In Hegel's discussion of the beginning of science as the first part of the doctrine of Being, he designates the immediate beginning of the *Logic* as the objective beginning, and the beginning of the *Phenomenology* which, when carried out, gives us mediated access to the domain of the *Logic* as the subjective beginning.[7]

In summary, the beginning offered by the *Phenomenology* is a subjective beginning, a beginning for the individual who would enter into philosophical *science*, in contrast to an objective beginning, one accessible only to those

---

[4] *Ibid.*, 29; Miller, 48-49.

[5] *Ibid.*, 30; Miller, 49.

[6] Hegel, G.W.F., *Phänomenologie des Geistes* (Hamburg : Meiner, 1952), 561-62. English translation *The Phenomenology of Mind*, trans. J.B. Baillie (New York : The Macmillan Company, 1931), 805. The English translation will be referred to hereafter as Baillie.

[7] *Logik*, 51-54; Miller, 67-69.

who have gained liberation from the schism of consciousness. Thus, far from there being a conflict between the beginnings of the two works, they complement each other. The subjective beginning is a necessary condition for there to be an objective beginning, and the objective is the *raison d'être* for the subjective. The latter is the true, immediate beginning and, when systematically carried out will grant us mediated access to the immediate beginning of the *Science of Logic*. In what follows I presuppose this distinction and consider the *Phenomenology* the proper beginning of Hegel's philosophy in the sense articulated.

II

Hegel's argument for the necessity of a propaedeutic science is based upon the claim that a difference exists between the domain of knowledge in which natural consciousness dwells and that of philosophical science. The former involves a schism between certainty and truth while the latter does not. If we are to be clear about what a subjective beginning entails, then we must understand how and why this difference necessitates the task of the *Phenomenology*.

In the Preface to the *Phenomenology* Hegel discusses two kinds of opposition with which a scientific philosophy, i.e., an *epistēmē*, is faced. One arises from philosophy itself at its then present historical stage, the other from natural consciousness. Both these sources maintain some form of the claim for the immediacy of knowledge, for a certainty which is always *in principle*, if not in fact, already established and on the basis of which secure knowledge can be acquired. Each criticizes the other, yet each claims what the other claims.

From the side of philosophy Hegel finds a contemporary demand for, and articulation of, a philosophy of intuition which seeks edification through a discourse which is to restore to self-consciousness a feeling, an intuition for existence.[8] The claim of this romanticism, according to Hegel, is that it has "immersed its self in the depths of Being, and philosophizes in all holiness and truth."[9] This philosophy, as well as the formalist dialectics of Schelling's idealism, finds for its beginning, without ever having established that beginning, a certainty of having achieved absolute oneness with Being. All that remains to be done is either to poeticize or to repetitiously formalize

---

[8] *Phänomenologie*, 12-13; Baillie, 71-72.
[9] *Ibid.*, 15; Baillie, 74.

the vision which has emerged from the supposed absolute vantage point of the immediate certainty. There is here no subjective beginning, but rather only an objective beginning. Access to the domain proper to truth has been presupposed.

When, on the other hand, natural consciousness confronts such claims for immediate knowledge, it rejects this form of immediacy on the grounds that this so-called "higher knowledge" is merely a perversion or an inversion (*ein Verkehrtes*) of reality. Hegel agrees with this rejection, but on slightly more determinate grounds : the individual natural consciousness has a right to be shown the justification for the claim of superior intuition in a domain other than its own.

> His right is based on his absolute independence which he knows he possesses in every form of his knowledge; for in all of them, whether recognized by science or not and regardless of their contents, the individual is the absolute form, i.e., he is the *immediate certainty* of himself....[10]

The justification for the rejection of a philosophy which begins with intuition, or which begins with an objective beginning, lies in the *fact* that immediate self-certainty is already a characteristic of natural consciousness. Consequently, all attempts of philosophy to claim for itself a higher knowledge of what-is appear as purposeless sophistry.

The crux of the matter is, then, that certainty appears to be *in principle* non-problematic both to romanticism and to idealism and to natural consciousness. And to each, the other appears to lack certainty. While Hegel agrees with philosophy that natural consciousness lacks certainty because in fact it involves a schism between certainty and truth, he agrees, on the other hand, with natural consciousness that intuitive, objective beginnings in philosophy are dogmatic and thus also lack certainty. He argues, therefore, that while each professes certainty, each lacks a warranted, i.e., deduced certainty; neither establishes his right to certainty, but merely presupposes it.

The precise need for a subjective beginning and the meaning and structure of that beginning are formulated by Hegel in terms of this dilemma concerning certainty and the dual attack upon a scientific philosophy. While maintaining that a philosophical science presupposes a liberation from the professed, but unaccounted for certainty of natural consciousness, and has for its domain one different from that of natural consciousness, at the same time Hegel recognizes the justice of the demand of natural consciousness to be shown both its own deficiency and the superiority of the philosophical domain as regards absolute truth. The objective beginning of philosophy

[10] *Ibid.*, 25; Baillie, 87.

can have no justification until such a subjective beginning is made, and that is to say, until natural consciousness is led to the domain and the standpoint in which the objective beginning can be made with a warranted certainty.

> Science has ... to unite this element of self-certainty with it, or rather to show that and how certainty belongs to it itself....This becoming of science in general or of knowledge is what this Phenomenology of Spirit displays.[11]

The first task for philosophy, if it is to be truly scientific, is to establish a warranty for its certainty, i.e., a proof that *its* certainty accords with truth itself, while that of natural consciousness does not. A *profession* of certainty is no valid substitute for the *establishment* of certainty. Thus, philosophy which purports to generate true knowledge must confront the claim for the immediacy of knowledge, i.e., the claim that certainty is *in principle* non-problematic.

The establishment of an absolutely reflexive certainty became the thematic of the *Phenomenology* of 1807. It is not only one theme among others, but the nexus of the work as a whole. The *Phenomenology* begins with the claim for the immediacy of certainty. The first chapter, "Sense Certainty," has for its primary subject matter "certainty," and not "sense-consciousness" as is most often supposed. The chapter is titled "sense certainty," and not "sense consciousness" or "sensuousness." The word 'sense' is adjectival in form and not substantive. The substantive content is certainty itself, that certainty which belongs to sensible beings. The phrase denotes the certainty to be found in "the knowledge which is at first or immediately our object," which "can be no other than that which is itself immediate knowledge, a *knowing* of the *immediate* or *what-is*."[12] The subjective beginning of philosophical science commences with the examination of this claim of immediate knowledge for a certainty which is non-problematic.

Hegel begins by attempting to validate the claim of immediate certainty by assuming, dialectically, the stance of being immediately in and toward the world in such a way that certainty is not problematic. After indicating that this claim implicates a knower and something known, both supposedly held together in a unity of certainty and truth, Hegel leads us to an examination of the possibilities for immediacy, which are three in number : 1) that the truth of which we are in principle certain lies in the entity alone, and certainty is achieved immediately by passively receiving this entity as it is; 2) that truth lies in the knower, and certainty is in principle achieved imme-

---

[11] *Ibid.*, 26: Baillie, 88.
[12] *Ibid.*, 79; Baillie, 149.

diately simply by intending what is meant; and 3) that truth lies in the total context of knower-known, and certainty is in principle immediately acquired simply by *being* within this context. But in each case an examination shows that the claim for the immediacy of certainty collapses on its own grounds and gives rise to a necessity for mediation between knower and known, and thus for the articulation of a mediated relation between certainty (which professedly belongs to the knower) and truth (which is to belong to that known, whether entity itself, intending consciousness, or the matrix formed by the immediate unity of the two). Thus, by proceeding dialectically, by assuming the validity of the claims made for the unproblematic nature of certainty, Hegel shows the invalidity of the claim that certainty is immediate, that is to say, he demonstrates that it *is* in principle problematic. Natural consciousness is thereby shown that its immediate self-certainty is not warranted, and thus the *Phenomenology* is given grounds for proceeding.

We cannot here further pursue in any detail the progress of this examination. But certainty remains the theme of the *Phenomenology*, a journey of despair which finds one possibility after another fall short of its own claims for warranted certainty. The thread runs uninterrupted to the end, where absolute knowing, the goal of the work, is defined in terms of the same quest for certainty which has been the process of development throughout.

Absolute knowing is spirit knowing itself in the shape of spirit, it is knowledge which comprehends through concepts. Truth here is not only *in itself* completely equal to *certainty*, but in addition also has the *form* of certainty of itself, or is in its existence, that is, for knowing spirit, in the form of knowledge itself.[13]

With the final achievement of a certainty certain of itself, and which is in a form not alien to that certainty, that is to say, with the completion of a subjective beginning which ends in a validated certainty, one is immediately confronted with the objective beginning of the *Science of Logic*, a standpoint now natural to the knower because validated, because deduced from the immediate self-certainty of natural consciousness. By following the course of the beginning of the phenomenological investigation into the problem of certainty, the individual's demand for a ladder to science has been satisfied.

In summary, then, the subjective beginning for philosophical science is necessary and finds its peculiar structure because of the professed certainty implicit in all finite modes of being in and toward the world. The objective beginning of science cannot be made until the nature and limitations of these various modes of professed certainty have been articulated, and the

---

[13] *Ibid.*, 556; Baillie, 798.

primacy of the certainty which belongs to scientific philosophy established. With this understanding of the claims and structure of the *Phenomenology*, we can now turn to the question of its relationship to the history of philosophy.

III

A closer look at the *Phenomenology* as this quest for certainty immediately reveals a problem. It is often noted by commentators that if it is to be accomplished under the given conditions, then the work must remain descriptive in character, that is to say, Hegel cannot, and by his own testimony does not, interfere with the process of the evolution of certainty. The process is to be one of self-limitation, such that each of the stances described, examined, and experienced of itself yields a progress. Yet, when we study the text, two facts seem to undermine this condition.

First, Hegel constantly makes a distinction between, on the one hand, the "we" who are being led to certainty and, on the other hand, the "they" or the "I" who has undergone or is undergoing the particular stances examined. For the latter there is no progression in the work, but simply one set of experiences beside others. For the former, however, there is not only an advance which leads to the standpoint of absolute knowing, but very often a prevision of the outcome of any particular stage in the quest. Secondly, it becomes clear from the very beginning that arguments and discussions are constantly appearing in the text which can be identified with one or another of Hegel's predecessors. Here we recognize Plato's argument from the *Theaetetus* concerning perception; at another place we find an argument of Locke or Leibniz or Kant. Hardly a figure from the history of philosophy does not show himself somewhere, and most appear many times.

Neither of these facts can be ignored or explained away; but if the philosopher is to add nothing, how can they be accounted for? A possible solution has been to say that Hegel and the "we" already occupy the standpoint of absolute knowledge when this subjective beginning is made. But this vitiates the force of the subjective beginning, and makes it only an *a posteriori* rationalization of the objective beginning, and thus either begs the question or makes a subjective beginning impossible. If the subjective beginning is to be authentic, then how can we explain the difference between the "we" and the "they" and the philosophical arguments "borrowed" from the history of philosophy? This question amounts to nothing less than a question concerning how the *Phenomenology* of 1807 makes a progress from the position of natural consciousness toward and into the domain of philosophical science, and thus the question of how a subjective beginning is to be made according to Hegel.

Recent scholarship has shown that the problem of subjective beginning and its relationship to systematic philosophy occurred to Hegel for the first time in 1803. Heinz Kimmerle has demonstrated that in the process of working out his first attempt at a system, a phenomenological crisis appeared.

> The question arose concerning how subjective consciousness which was made a theme of philosophy of spirit could be thought together with the concept of the absolute identity which was, in the earlier conception of the system, to accomplish the mediation between objective and subjective aspects.[14]

That this crisis was resolved with the writing of the *Phenomenology*, and even that a phenomenological crisis appeared was not, of course, a new discovery of Kimmerle's. But the relationship of this phenomenon in Hegel's career to his discovery of the history of philosophy is not something articulated by nineteenth century scholarship.

At the time of this crisis and its resolution, another change took place in Hegel's thought. In 1801 Hegel maintained that philosophy had no history. But in 1805 he lectured on the history of philosophy.

Unfortunately, the manuscript of these first lectures has disappeared. But we have reliable testimony that what we have today under the title *Lectures on the History of Philosophy* is *in substance* the same as the lectures of 1805-1806. Both Rosenkranz and Gabler inform us that no essential changes were made in later versions of the lectures; they were simply amplified. In addition to this testimony, the *Phenomenology* itself gives substantial evidence that Hegel had essentially developed his view of philosophy and its history by 1805. It is this latter testimony that I shall rely upon when I cite the *Lectures* as they have come down to us.

Simultaneously, then, two changes occurred in Hegel's thought. First, the subjective beginning of scientific philosophy became problematic; and secondly, philosophy came to be viewed as something with a history, and with a history, moreover, which led to a culmination in Hegel's own systematic thought. On the basis of these two facts, Kimmerle suggests that the problematic of a subjective beginning "was now thought together in a unique way with the thematic of a history of philosophy."[15] Kimmerle

---

[14] Kimmerle, Heinz, "Zur Entwicklung des Hegelschen Denkens in Jena," *Hegel-Studien*, Beiheft 4, 42.

[15] Kimmerle, Heinz, "Dokumente zu Hegels Jenaer Dozententätigkeit (1801-1807)," *Hegel-Studien*, Bd. 4, 83-84.

does not work out the "uniqueness" of this confluence, but we might ask whether or not his suggestion can lead us to a resolution of the problems we are here concerned with.

At the end of the *Phenomenology* Hegel makes a statement relevant to the relationship of the *Phenomenology* to the history of philosophy. History is identified as the succession of spiritual forms "from the aspect of their free existence appearing in the form of contingency." The *Phenomenology*, on the other hand, is the same progression of spiritual forms, "looked at from the side of their intellectually comprehended organization."[16] The inference often made, and in part supported by the historical introduction to the system in the *Encyclopedia*, is that there are available to us two ways of introducing the system, in Kimmerle's words, "on the one side an historical introduction, on the other however also a systematic laying of the foundation of the system of science."[17]

However, the Preface to the *Phenomenology* offers an interpretation of this relationship which does not leave them in external relation to each other as alternatives, and which will illuminate both the presence of a "we" and the presence of philosophical arguments of his predecessors in the body of the text. After posing the problem of the professed certainty of natural consciousness and of contemporary philosophy, and after announcing the *Phenomenology* as a solution to this problem, Hegel discusses the problem of leading the individual to the standpoint of absolute knowing. To do this, he says, we must consider both the particular individual and the general individual forms of spirit as they have come to be historically. The general forms constitute the substance of the individual; that is to say, the formed and effective world faced by the particular individual who is to be educated is *in fact* spirit which has developed through history and which contains at any given time as a result the confluence of this development. The uneducated individual, structured by natural consciousness, is unaware of this and considers this spiritual substance as an immediate object over against him. Although familiar with this world, he does not truly know it because he does not know it in its genetic nature.[18]

This description of the situation for natural consciousness contends decisively with the notion that simple natural consciousness can be elevated to the domain of philosophical science without further qualification. For it is precisely because of his natural certainty and attitude of immediacy

[16] *Phänomenologie*, 564; Baillie, 808.
[17] Kimmerle, Heinz, "Zur Entwicklung des Hegelschen Denkens in Jena," *Hegel-Studien*, Beiheft 4, 45-46.
[18] *Phänomenologie*, 19-28; Baillie, 80-91.

that the individual rejects philosophy. Something more, then, is needed if an individual is to proceed with the education of the *Phenomenology*. This "something more" turns out to be philosophy itself.

We know from the *Lectures on the History of Philosophy* that philosophy functions as a special moment in spirit, i.e., in that substance which individuals take to be their immediate world. Hegel tells us that in each epoch a people have "their institutions and forms of government, their morality, their social life and the capabilities, customs, and enjoyments of the same." These constitute their world as their own. But we are also told that "philosophy is one form of these many aspects.... It is the fullest blossom, the concept of spirit in its entire form, the consciousness and spiritual essence of all things, the spirit of the time as spirit present in itself."[19]

Philosophy therefore contains the essence, in any epoch, of the spiritual substance which constitutes world for a people. Furthermore, Hegel indentifies philosophy and the history of philosophy in such a way that there is but one philosophy in development, an historical-philosophical dialogue in which the participants engage in the pursuit of wisdom. From this it follows for Hegel that if one is to comprehend the philosophy of one's own time, then one must understand its place in the historical-philosophical dialogue which is its context and which gives it sense.

It is important that we understand, in itself, this notion of an historical-philosophical dialogue, if we are to see the relationship between the *Phenomenology* as a subjective beginning and the history of philosophy. But this view also has further consequences when related to what has been said of the relationship between philosophy and the other moments of the substance. It means that, given the relationship of philosophy to the rest of spirit, to comprehend the historical-philosophical dialogue is to comprehend the *essence* of the development of the substance, the general spirit which is the world for the particular individual. For the historical-philosophical dialogue is the *genetic essence* of the genesis of world-spirit. Thus it should follow from this view presented in the *Lectures on the History of Philosophy* that, if the task of the *Phenomenology* is to be accomplished, if the individual is to be shown the true nature of his substance, the world, and be led to certainty and philosophical science, then this should be accomplished by giving attention in some way to the history of philosophy.

If we now leave the *Lectures* and return again to the *Phenomenology* we find that Hegel maintains precisely this. After reiterating his point that a

[19] Hegel, G.W.F., *Vorlesungen über die Geschichte der Philosophie* (Frankfurt : Suhrkamp, 1971), Bd. I, 73. English translation *Lectures on the History of Philosophy*, trans., E.S. Haldane (New York : The Humanities Press, 1955), Vol. I, 53-54.

preparation is necessary for science and that this preparation means coming to know one's substance with a warranted certainty and as a confluence of its genetic development, he then *specifies* that our task must be accomplished through the office of the historical-philosophical dialogue.

Because the substance of the individual, because the world spirit has had the patience to pass through these forms in the long expanse of time,...and because it could not attain consciousness about itself with less labor, therefore the individual cannot comprehend his own substance with less than this; and yet he has less trouble because this is already accomplished in itself. The content is by now the actuality reduced to a possibility, vanquished immediacy, and the forms have been reduced to abbreviations and to the simple determinations of thought. Having already been thought, the content is the possession of the substance. No longer must existence be transformed into the in-itself; only the in-itself—which is neither raw any more, nor immersed in existence, but rather something recalled — needs to be transmuted into the form of the for-itself.[20]

This passage is crucial for an understanding of the *Phenomenology*. Here Hegel makes it clear that the task of the *Phenomenology* is not simply and didactically to indicate directly to the individual the nature of spirit which he calls world, but rather to *recall* to the individual the nature of the substance with which he is already familiar. The task of calling the subtance into intelligibility has already been accomplished in the historical-philosophical dialogue which is the history of philosophy. Now, according to Hegel, all that needs to be done is to *recall* what has already been called out of immersion in immediate existence by those who preceded him in the dialogue. Thus, there is nothing new in the *Phenomenology* except that sense has now been given to the historical-philosophical dialogue as a recalling of the essence of what has already been said.

To put the point in another way, Hegel has here specified the way in which the history of philosophy forms an integral part of the *Phenomenology of Spirit*. That history contains the essence of the genesis of the world spirit which is the substance of the individual who is to be educated. It is part of that spirit, and as such can be employed in the process of the development of the *Phenomenology*, not as something external to the objects which consciousness and finite spirit face, but as a moving force within it. Since, however, the *Phenomenology* is oriented toward and within the problem of the finite individual as he faces his world with professed certainty, the history does not appear in its pure form or in its own order of development, but as it is proper to recall it in the various stages of the development of the finite individual.

[20] *Phänomenologie*, 27-28; Baillie, 90-91.

For example, if it is being claimed by natural consciousness that perception is knowledge, that there is warranted certainty in perception, then there is present already in world spirit, the substance, a reflection upon this thesis, a reflection which shows the limitations of perception. This previous discussion, immanent in the world spirit itself, forms the heart of the comparison between the claims made for perception and the experience one actually has in perceiving the world. The critical or dialectical discussion, furthermore, not only illuminates the limitations of perception, but indicates to those following the *Phenomenology* what, in experience, might present a solution to the particular problems encountered in so-called perceptual knowledge, and thus leads to the next level for consideration, understanding.

Thus, we are not left with the problem of perception simply as it occurs immediately, but have already within our grasp as a part of the substance, a reflection upon and a conceptual grasp of the problem. The history of philosophy as an ordered sequence does not control the development of the *Phenomenology*, but rather the development of the latter determines the way in which the historical-philosophical dialogue is to be recalled. There is here, I think, an interesting parallel to a characteristic of the Socratic dialogues of Plato, where Socrates will say from time to time : "We must remember, my friend, what was said earlier concerning this matter." According to Hegel, the present stage of the historical-philosophical dialogue, the *Phenomenology of Spirit*, demands from its participants that something settled earlier be recalled in order that we might proceed.

The presence in Hegel's thought of this relationship between history and phenomenology resolves the two difficulties mentioned earlier. The *Phenomenology*, first of all, maintains its descriptive character because the recalling of what has already been accomplished in the history of philosophy is a recalling of something which belongs to the very substance in which certainty is being found. The substance already contains its own genetic essence, an essence which is necessary for a knowledge of the substance. The historical-philosophical dialogue is not external to the concerns of the *Phenomenology*.

Secondly, the crucial distinction between the "we" and the "they" is also clarified, and leads to the thesis of this paper. If the historical dialogue is to function effectively in the *Phenomenology*, then it must be recalled as a part of the substance, as the element of world spirit which contains its essence. But if it is to be *recalled*, then it must already be known : that is to say, one must already be immersed in the history of philosophy. Thus, the history of philosophy, in its temporal form, must be presupposed for the *Phenomenology*, not only in the sense that it exists before the *Phenomenology* but in the more radical sense that whoever forms the "we" of the *Phenomenology* must already have a familiarity with the content of that history. Without such a knowledge by familiarity, it could not be recalled, and if not recalled, the "we" would be reduced to the position of the "they" or the "I" undergoing one experience after another without any evidence of progress. Thus, "we" are already philosophers, that is to say, are already individuals who have become immersed in the history of philosophy and its quest for certainty.

If I am correct, then this resolves a dilemma concerning the *Phenomenology* which has stood from the beginning as a methodological threat, namely, that we must suppose that Hegel himself and the "we" are already at the standpoint of absolute knowing, thus making irrelevant the task and contradicting Hegel's own arguments against professed certainty. All that is necessary, I maintain, is that "we" and Hegel be already immersed in the dialogue of the history of philosophy. This presupposition neither vitiates the task of the *Phenomenology*, nor implicates us in a paradox. By literally comprehending the historical-philosophical dialogue in a speech which both attends to the problem of certainty and to previous speeches which deal with one or another aspect of this problem, the subjective beginning can be accomplished without manipulation of the content.

At least two things follow from this interpretation of Hegel, and I shall only mention them. The first is that the claim for a subjective beginning must be closely defined. The "philosopher" who approaches Hegel's system is given a subjective beginning; on the grounds of his *former* philosophical engagement, he is brought into the presence of the new epoch in which philosophy will be a science, knowledge and not just love of knowledge. On the other hand, this subjective beginning is not absolute, but relative. One who comes to the *Phenomenology* must already have made a beginning in the study of philosophy. Thus, if we wish to be complete in our analysis of a beginning, we cannot remain satisfied with this presupposition alone.

The second point is that there emerges here a clear sense in which the Hegelian system, including its propaedeutic science, is truly a circle, a completed whole. The system ends with philosophy according to the *Encyclopedia*, which is to say with the history of philosophy consummated. Hegel's system is the result of those preceding it and ends with a conceptualized and internally coherent grasp of the development of that history. Thus, the presupposition of a familiarity with the history finds its consummation in a knowledge of that history. The completion of the system brings the individual back to his starting point, but now with a total and complete comprehension of the historical-philosophical dialogue which was his starting point.

On my interpretation, then, Hegel's system involves both an openness at the beginning and a completeness within itself. The subjective beginning made by the individual presupposes his openness to this subjective beginning and thus appears to have no necessity as a beginning. But once this beginning is made, it is Hegel's contention that the subjective beginning and its presupposition in the history of philosophy find consummation in the completion of the system and therefore an enclosed circle constitutes systematic philosophical science.

HEGELIANISM AND PLATONISM

John N. Findlay

Boston University

I propose in this paper not so much to consider what Hegel *said* about Plato in that comparatively commonplace piece of work, his *Lectures on the History of Philosophy*, nor what he actually derived from his reading of the *Phaedo*, the *Republic*, the *Parmenides*, the *Sophist* and the *Timaeus* and other dialogues that he closely studied, as rather the essential affinity of his thought with Plato's, the degree to which Platonism and Hegelianism are, in my view, the same philosophy, with differences of emphasis and elaboration which make Hegelianism, all in all, its richer and more satisfactory version. I believe it is important to stress the extent to which all really deep-going philosophical systems converge in their ultimate findings, and how a great deal that occurs in one is no more than the transposition into another key of what occurs in the other. The same terrain is being worked over, though with a different approach and other instruments of search, and the differences which are very salient for followers or for commentators, interested in developmental stages and influences, fade into insignificance. In treating Hegel in this way, I am treating him much as he treated his historical predecessors. Thus in a passage from the *Science of Logic* that I was teaching from recently, Hegel shows how his notion of Being-for-Self was quite differently anticipated by the Greek Atomists, by Kant in his treatment of the Transcendental Unity of Apperception, by Spinoza in his view of the relation of Substance to its Modes, by Malebranche in his view of the relation of God to his own or anyone else's ideas, and by Leibniz in his imperfectly executed doctrine of monadic windowlessness. A philosopher who can smell out an identity between the Guillotine and the Categorical Imperative is obviously *capable de tout*, and how refreshingly different this is from the approach of those exact analysts who see a difference of concept in every change of phrase. To anyone sufficiently steeped in Hegelianism, Hegel *was* Plato as well as himself, as he was also about to be Russell and Avenarius and Whitehead and Wittgenstein *inter alios* with different degrees of close coincidence. I shall, however, drop these adumbrations of universal Identity-in-Difference, and shall first say something about what Hegel says about Plato and Platonism in his *History of Philosophy*.

Hegel in his *Lectures on the History of Philosophy* is as concerned as is Aristotle to read his own categories and his own dialectic into the thought of his predecessors : he seems, however, very often to ignore or underemphasize the points on which they most closely anticipated him. Thus in his brilliantly insightful account of pre-Socratic philosophy, and with deep knowledge of the available documents, he altogether fails to give due importance to the pre-Socratic philosopher whom above any other we feel to have anticipated the deepest inspirations of Hegel, Heraclitus, who believes in a harmony begotten from opposing tensions as in the bow or the lyre, or in a constancy of measures which preserves itself in flux, or in a shared rationality of dry spiritual life which contrasts with the damp spiritual isolation of drunkenness or sleep. To Hegel Heraclitus is the philosopher of absolute *Werden* and no more : he might have derived this picture from the Platonic *Cratylus* rather than from the accessible fragments.

Passing to Socrates and Plato, Socrates is seen by Hegel as a world-historical thinker who first brought conscious subjectivity to its own notice. The pre-Socratics thought deeply, but never thought of their thoughts as thoughts, the Sophists thought of thoughts as thoughts but only as belonging to the arbitrary variable subjectivity of the individual — Hegel again gets his conceptions from Plato. It was Socrates who first turned men's gaze upon the Universal, as something stable and objective and absolutely there, but also as something that can only make itself evident in and through the work of thought, a thought that each man must necessarily carry out for himself alone. Hegel emphasizes, as many admirers of Socrates have not sufficiently done, the tediously destructive sophistry of a great deal of his argumentation, of which the only positive outcome is a determination to persist in the good work of trying to replace Opinion by a Knowledge that never arrives. Socrates, he emphasizes, never reached nor thought he could reach that perfect analysis of the virtues to which he aspired, and to which complacent statesmen and teachers thought they had attained. His life rather than his doctrine realized the notional shape of virtue, and was on Hegel's account a classical work of art, *ein ruhiges, frommes Tugendbild*. And his irony had nothing in common with the arrogant, romantic affectation that went by that name in the writings of Schlegel and others : it was humble recognition of the inadequacy of any human analysis to that shape of what was honourable and right and suitable to the occasion, which he received as a correct opinion from his Daemon or from unexceptionable religious and social sources. Socrates did not wish to subvert that opinion, but to replace it by something that once and for all would lay firm hold on its elusive members, and render it impossible to slip from one's grasp. Hegel further recognizes the tragic rightness of the condemnation of Socrates by the Athenian authorities : the questing subjectivity which had broken the mould of the substantial, ethical life of the Greek city, and had begotten monsters such as Alcibiades and Critias, had necessarily to be condemned by that substantial, ethical city-life, even if this condemnation were later to be turned against that substantial, ethical city-life itself, which, conscious of its own inadequacy, allowed itself to be superseded by the new, individualistic life of the Christian west.

From the Socratic subjectivism Hegel passes to the Platonic : Plato, he says, saw the reality of everything in thought, but stood infinitely above the false idealism of modern times, which separates thought from reality, and which makes it be purely *conscious* thought, as opposed to the often unconscious thought which operates in Nature and History. Hegel, it is plain, gave to the Universals which govern our interpretation of the world an objective as much as a subjective status : they might attain their full deployment and self-conscious enjoyment in our thinking, but they also existed *an sich* in Nature or in the obscure forces of History before they made themselves evident to the thought of philosophers. This deep-set realism has something South Germanic about it, as opposed to the subjectivism which naturally assorted with Kant's Northeastern Baltic habitat and his perhaps Scottish ancestry, a subjectivism which Hegel simply shed once his thought had achieved maturity, being aided in this regard by his cooperation with Schelling in the development of a Philosophy of Nature, which was prepared to educe conscious subjectivity dialectically from unconscious Nature as a companion-piece to the transcendental deduction of Nature from the acts and structures of conscious subjectivity. This deep-set realism must also have been reinforced by Hegel's early immersion in the writings of Plato and Aristotle, an immersion far deeper than any that Kant or Fichte or perhaps even Schelling underwent. Hegel further connects Platonism with the faith in the super-sensuous which Christianity was to carry much further, a profound insight when one reflects on the almost completely Neoplatonic character of mediaeval Christian theology, regarding which Hegel was so inadequately informed.

Hegel, however, thinks it better that we should be largely dissatisfied with Plato's writings, than that we should read into them too close an approximation to contemporary truth, and he also deprecates that minute study of the text of the Dialogues, to the exclusion of any attempt to fathom their deeper drift, which was at that time starting its sinister career in the researches of Hegel's Berlin colleague Schleiermacher. As opposed to the earlier willingness to set an esoteric Platonism, set forth in unwritten discourses, alongside the confused testimony of the Dialogues, Schleiermacher preferred to be a render and not a maker of veils, and tried to see the whole message of Platonism transparently written out in the Dialogues. Hegel points out that all philosophy necessarily has an esoteric element, not in the least involving secret, privileged communications, but having its roots in the unphilosophical thickheadedness of the average interpreter and auditor of philosophy, who may even become a philosophical scholar simply because he cannot understand philosophy. Platonic interpretation in the XIXth and XXth Centuries has abounded in thickheaded expositors, and particularly so in very recent years, and Hegel is right in stressing that, while minute scholarship may be an inestimable aid to true philosophical understanding, it is merely a curse if pursued without it.

Hegel further takes the interesting and profitable line that, while the Platonic writings contain Pythagorean, Eleatic, Socratic and other deposits, Plato has effectively Platonized them all, and that it is quite unrewarding to try to determine precisely which elements represent earlier thinkers and which the superadded, transforming, Platonic note. He also points out, what surely requires no argument, that the Dialogues are not scientific works, and that they involve an ever-repeated, deliberate use of the *Vorstellung*, of picture-thought, behind which the *Begriff* or Concept lurks obscurely, and that such picture-thought, with its immense imaginative appeal, can be highly misleading and seductive. Much of Plato's most admired accounts of the dialectical or other approaches to the Forms are not, it is plain, actual approaches of the kinds in question : they are pictorial representations of such approaches. The *Republic*, e.g., is very vivid on the subject of Dialectic, but it offers us no specimen of the Dialectic it depicts. Plato, on Hegel's view, certainly thought of Universals as self-existent realities, far more substantial than the vanishing particulars that embody them, but such a substantialization did not mean as similating them to the intuitively given, vanishing things of sense, as Plato's metaphors might often suggest : it involved rather a transformation of our ordinary view of reality, so that not those vanishing sensuous things, but the Universals which gave them life and meaning, should alone count as substantially real. Hegel goes further, and holds that Plato, in according immortality to the soul, really meant no more than that its essence consisted in the purest Universality; which could take on itself any and every universal type or pattern rather than remain bound to one definite stereotype. The Soul is not a peculiarly long-lived pensioner precariously hobnobbing with an even longer-lived superior; its immortality rests on the fact that it is a functional form of that superior reality. In pushing the arguments of the *Phaedo* to this sort of consummation, Hegel is perhaps reading into Plato that subject-object identification which is far more explicit in the writings of Aristotle. Philoponus tells us that Plato is the person referred to by Aristotle in the *De Anima* who said that the Soul is the place of Forms, but such a doctrine is far from clear from the Platonic writings. Hegel, however, rightly attributes to Plato a belief in Ideas or Universals as real, active structures, more real than the vanishing instances in which they embody themselves, and constitutive of the thinking in which they are active rather than constituted by the latter.

Hegel divides his treatment of Plato into divisions which correspond to those of his own philosophy : the Platonic Dialectic corresponds to his own Science of Logic, the Platonic Cosmology to his own Nature-Philosophy, the Platonic theory of the Soul and Society to his own Philosophy of Spirit. He rightly bases his account of the Platonic Dialectic on such mature dialogues as the *Sophist*, the *Parmenides* and the *Philebus* which, in their freedom from myth and picture, represent the truly esoteric element in Plato. The Nature-philosophy is of course based on the *Timaeus*, which Hegel, following the theories of his period, believes to have been built around a neo-Pythagorean treatise falsely credited to Philolaus, rather than as providing the material for the latter. And Hegel's account of the Platonic *Geistesphilosophie* rests throughout on the *Republic*.

What Hegel has to say of the *Sophist*, the *Parmenides* and the *Philebus* is a little disappointing, though he sees their general tendency to anticipate his own doctrine. The *Sophist* is seen as teaching the doctrine of the identity of Being and Non-being : in having a built-in reference to Otherness, the Forms all are *not* as much as they are. On the whole Hegel approaches a deeper understanding of the *Sophist* than on the present interpretation according to which its message is to show that there really is no such thing as Non-being and Falsehood, that what seems to be such is really no more than the difference among entities of which all are comfortably real. (The message of the *Sophist* is not that there is no Non-being or Falsehood, but rather that it is hauntingly all-pervasive and full of positive content. Each form includes in itself, by being other than them, all the things that it is not, and that Sophists can induce us to believe that it is : Justice by not being the interest of the stronger, after a fashion is just this, and can be made to appear so by sophistic persuasion.) In the case of the *Philebus* Hegel approves of the Platonic identification of Goodness with Limit, and the affinity of its Infinite with his own notion of the Bad Infinite. The Mixture and the Cause of the Mixture have obvious affinities with his own True Infinite. In regard to the *Parmenides* Hegel's attitude is again disappointing. Though it has been described in the *Vorrede* to the *Phenomenology* as the greatest work of art of the antique Dialectic and an authentic expression of the Divine Life, Hegel is now hesitant to endorse such a view of its purport : it is thought to have a negative, rather than a positive outcome. He does not seize on it as exhibiting how the same content which, taken in itself, is utterly one and simple and abstract, none the less, in another regard, has any and every concept built into it, the very leading principle of his own Dialectic, nor does he seize on the superb last sentence of the Dialogue as exemplifying the reconciliations of seeming contradictions in speculative truth.

Of the *Timaeus* Hegel writes much as one might expect him to write : while slightly deploring its admixture of myth, he is somewhat more friendly to its at times arbitrary use of numerical notions. That the physical elements are arranged in a continuous geometric proportion, so that as Fire is to Air, Air is to Water, and Water is to Earth, he sees as anticipating his own ontological interpretation of the Syllogism, with the added correspondence that in the *four* terms of his continuous proportion Plato has recognised the broken or divided Middle Term which for Hegel is characteristic of the realms of Nature and of Essence. In the case of the Psychogony, Hegel is helped by the then current interpretation of the text which identified the being of the Forms with the Selfsame, and the Being of sensible things with Otherness, so that what is being asserted is the difficult union of Identity with Difference in which Hegel himself believed. I myself wish that the Greek could bear this traditional interpretation rather than the intricately curious meaning that now has to be put upon it. Hegel approves of Plato's unplausible colour-theory, as fanciful as his own and Goethe's and, he agrees in principle with what Plato says about divination and the liver.

In treating of the *Republic*, Hegel interestingly tries to regard it as expressing the *actuality* of Greek subjective and social life, rather than as the visionary ideal with which it has been thought to be concerned. The message of the *Republic* is (for him) that Justice and Morality are inseparable from the social institutions and organization of which they are the subjective expression, a view characteristic of the stage of ethical substantiality beyond which Greek political experience never went, and in which the individual was lost in the substance of state-life. This message has of course been outmoded by Christian interiority, but it presents itself as ultimate truth in the Platonic *Geistesphilosophie*. This philosophy is held to be defective only in not deducing political from spiritual, structure, and in its extraordinary, abstract provisions of community of property, liquidation of the family and external direction to a given social stratum, which Hegel seems to think applied to all the citizens of the Republic, and of which he deeply disapproves.

Plato is therefore taken by Hegel as anticipating Hegelian truth rather inadequately and confusedly, and much the same view is taken of Plotinus and Proclus, of both of whom Hegel betrays a remarkable, sympathetic study. He knows at least how much a Greek Plotinus was, and how little the *schwärmerische* Oriental of the common conception, and how even his ecstasy was a respectable version of the Aristotelian νόησις νοήσεως. He does not sufficiently stress the affinity of his doctrine of a necessary *Entäusserung* of the Absolute Idea in Nature and Finite Spirit to the Neoplatonic idea of a necessary irradiation from the Supreme Hypostasis to all lower manifestation : arguably the Neoplatonists had a profoundly logical and not at all pictorial an understanding of this concept as Hegel had of his, it being part of what it is to be a higher hypostasis that it should specify or instantiate oneself in lower ones. Nor does he sufficiently acknowledge the pervasive anticipation of his own notions of alienation and return, and of universal triadicity, in the thought of Proclus.

Having given an account of Hegel's treatment of Plato in his *History of Philosophy*, I now want to consider Hegel's relation to Plato in the actual history of philosophy. And I want to consider these two philosophers not merely causally, as particular beings one of whom transmitted influence to the other, but as differing expressions of an historic enterprise in which the same puzzlements made themselves felt, and the same expedients were adopted to appease them. I shall, in my treatment, describe Plato and Hegel as they have come to appear to me, an appearance in both cases singular, for the way in which I view each of them departs far from the traditional stereotype, and has in either case been deeply modified by the way in which I viewed the other philosopher. The singularity of my views lies in the fact that I believe in such a thing as philosophical truth, and that I measure this by the extent to which mere facts or unexplained surds are banished from a style of thought : I consider that both of my philosophers at least made an attempt to advance towards this goal, whereas one can say of philosophers like Aristotle or John Locke or Immanuel Kant that they did not dislike, or even positively liked, ultimate, inexplicable surds, or mere facts or ultimate dualisms. And in virtue of their determination to eliminate the scandal of mere fact my two philosophers necessarily converge towards common conclusions, whereas the other philosophers at many points remain far from one another. Hegel and Plato are both, in my view, thinkers who push their zeal for explanation so far that they not only do not admit mere immediacies of any sort, but that they also will not tolerate unexplained first principles, and therefore have to have recourse to principles that explain themselves, and in course of so doing also explain everything else whatsoever. I do not, in characterizing them both in this manner, mean that they do not allot a role to contingencies, to things that merely are the case and that might have been otherwise : they certainly do allow for such contingencies. But in their thought the presence of such contingencies is itself necessary and explicable, is such that we are able to understand just why it exists and how far it is possible for it to go. Now to credit Hegel with such an all-mediating, self-mediating programme is of course nothing strange : the complaint is only that he was unable to live up to it, that he makes many unjustifiable leaps of thought, that he covertly borrows materials from experience or other discreditable sources. But to credit Plato with any such programme is certainly a novelty, for nothing is more common than to ascribe to Plato unnumbered unsolved dualisms, the opposition of Being and Becoming, of Instance and Type, of Knowledge and Opinion, for which healing is not available or even conceivable. I believe, however, that this ascription involves a gross misunderstanding of the Platonic documents, largely due to Aristotle's genius for misunderstanding other thinkers, which fortunately did not prevent him from giving most revealing reports of what those whom he misunderstood really thought.

Hegel and Plato are at one, in the first place, in looking for something that is ontically ontic, or really real, beside which other things can be catalogued as being ontic or real only after a fashion ($\pi\hat{\eta}$), or in a qualified manner, or as in some manner depending for their hold on being on the way in which they depended on what was ontically ontic. Aristotle also believed that there was something that was ontically ontic, but he could never make up his mind just where it ought to be sought : the *Metaphysics* is the tortured document in which he dithered from one solution to another. One strain in his thought made him look for the really real in the concrete individual, the unity of matter and form, another in the specific nature that the individual embodied and that could in some cases exist separately and be an individual itself. He was, however, quite sure that it was not to be sought in the region of the generic or of the qualitative or quantitative or relational and so on. Plato and Hegel are, however, one in never doubting where what is ontically ontic is to be located : it is not to be sought in the region of vanishing particularity, accessible to sense-experience, but in the region of eternal meanings, thought-unities which emerged clearly in ideation and not in sense-perception, whose identity was that of Universals and not of particular instances. (In using the term 'thought-unities' I mean only 'unities accessible to thought', not unities constituted by, or dependent on thought.) And they both believed—though in the case of Plato we must have regard to the reports of Aristotle and not merely to the exoteric Dialogues—that some of these thought-unities had a prerogative over others, were more genuinely eidetic or *begrifflich* than various casually or arbitrarily or perversely combined nominal essences such as the notions of certain artefacts or hybrids or corrupt cases or nonsensical examples and so on. The ontically ontic realities were, moreover, not isolated from one another, but specified a certain ultimately ontic or supra-ontic source, a source from which they flowed in a necessary manner, so that all the specific forms of being were in a sense included in this supra-ontic source, which also determined their necessary relations to one another. (So strongly did Plato believe in the 'deducibility' of all species from their supreme generic source that he was led to believe that all notions ultimately permitted of a mathematical or numerical analysis : one can deduce all natural numbers and all geometrical configurations and establish their relations in a uniform, necessary manner, but one cannot hope to deduce the qualities of sense, such as redness, loudness and the like.) The belief, further, in a concrete Universal, a generic meaning which includes and sums up all its specific cases and which is in this sense self-specifying, is, of course, a well-known doctrine of Hegel's, but it is equally to be found in Plato, very clearly in such passages as that in the *Timaeus* where the Idea of Animal *in genere* is said to embrace all the *Eide* of specific animals. It was wholly unintelligible to Aristotle, and even to Plato's pupil Speusippus, who could not imagine how Animal Itself could survive diremption into, and could combine the properties of, Horse Itself and Man Himself.

Both Plato and Hegel are, further, at one in believing in the *real efficacy* of their specific and generic Universals : in the case of Plato this is made evident by the persistent protests of Aristotle that the existence of Ideas of Man, Horse etc. is *not* sufficient to produce cases of manhood or equinity —one requires in addition a cause of motion, i.e. an actual parent. Plato did not, however, deny the necessary presence of favouring mechanisms and conditions, but he asserted passionately that the only *true* causes of being and change were the ideal natures behind things which alone can make those things be or become what they are. Hegel similarly sees Notions everywhere at work in the world, though cunningly taking advantage of various contingencies and circumstances of fact. I think we must go further. Both Plato and Hegel believe that it is possible to reconcile the in-itselfness or cathauteity of their ideal natures with their authentic presence in and self-communication to their instances : such valid opinions as we can form regarding sensible things are entirely dependent on our discernment of operative Universals in and through them. The beginning of Hegel's *Phenomenology* builds throughout on the Platonic *Theaetetus*. The flux of appearances is as such unknowable and uncharacterizable : all that lends it substance and content are the identities of sense or meaning which filter through it. And though Plato, in the *Timaeus* and elsewhere, misleadingly talks of sensible instances as if they had some sort of being of their own, and as if they even had some sort of apartness from their informing Universals, he also makes it plain that they have only the sort of separateness from their Universals that a face glimpsed in a mirror has from the real face thereby indirectly glimpsed at, and that the mirror itself only exists in a manner of speaking, and can only be approached through spurious inferences and mutually contradictory metaphors. Neither Plato nor Hegel seriously believes that there *are* particular things or that we ever are acquainted with them, though particularity and particularization are, of course, necessary functions of what is universal. I agree with Plato and Hegel on both points. I do not believe that there are such entities as particulars, and I am quite sure that I have never encountered any. They are, I would hold, the products of a bastard reasoning, of a quest for unnecessary pegs on which to hang instantiated meanings.

It might, however, be thought that, in their relation to Subjectivity, to Soul and Spirit, Plato and Hegel are very different. For does not Hegel derive from Kant, and from Kant's reference of all categories and all categorized appearances to the functioning of the Transcendental Ego, and is Hegel's Absolute Idea not defined in terms of conscious subjectivity as 'the eternal vision of itself in the other'? And is the Idea not said to be concretely carried out in Absolute Spirit which is certainly something subjective? And is not Plato's Soul, looking towards, but not creative of the everlasting Ideas, in quite another position? I think, none the less, that we can show that subjectivity has a much more similar role in the thought of Plato and Hegel than has usually been supposed. It is important to stress, in the first place, that while Hegel's Absolute Idea can be taken to be the Idea *of* Absolute Subjectivity, to have Absolute Subjectivity for its content, it is in itself an Idea, an unrealized Form, and in no sense an actual subject. Hegel in fact explicitly says that if it were not in this sense abstract—there is of course nothing abstract about its content — if it were in fact an actual subject, the sort of actual subject that some suppose the Divine Mind to be, there would be no need at all for its alienation in Nature and for its return to self in Spirit. Hegel, in fact, makes the admission that the *Entäusserung* of self-externalization of the Idea rests on the fact that a merely abstract, notional filling out of what it is to be self-conscious, however perfectly carried out in the medium of pure thought, imperatively requires a *further* carrying out in the medium of sensuous particularity, and a further rising above the same, in order *fully* to be what it has in itself to be. And as to the Absolute Spirit which achieves complete actualization in Art, Religion and Philosophy, it is infinitely removed from the Transcendental Subject of Kant. The Transcendental Ego, by its acts of synthesis, schematization and what not, is responsible for the phenomenal world of Nature, while Hegel's Absolute Spirit, though it may be the goal of Nature, is its final cause, its ultimate consummation, rather than anything that consciously or unconsciously fabricates it. And while Absolute Spirit is always being achieved in the experiences of artists, devotees and philosophers, it is never stably and finally so achieved, at least not in any particular artist, devotee or philosopher. Hegel certainly did not believe that he was the walking or talking Idea. The conclusion is irresistible that Hegel's Absolute Idea, while it may be Absolute Subjectivity *as such*, is not an absolute self-conscious subject, but is as much beyond subjectivity *in its ordinary sense* as Plato's Idea of Good is beyond Being. And even when Hegel speaks of the Ego or the Subject as it is active in the finite thinking person, he does not follow Kant in identifying it with the formal unity of self-consciousness, which Kant was so grotesquely mistaken in regarding as the fountain and source of the categories, since it is as much present in learning a string of nonsense-syllables or in any inconsequent combination of items as in a well-categorized interpretation. Hegel identifies the Ego with Active Universality as such, with the *objective* synthesis which Kant had tried to deduce from its self-conscious unity : the thinking Ego becomes little more than the force of the Logical Idea, carrying out its interpretative activities in the focus of the individual mind. Hegel, in fact, made sense of the Transcendental Deduction by abolishing it : no trace of its exciting, utterly misleading constructivism is to be found in his writings.

Hegel, we saw, attributes to Plato his own view of conscious thought as Active Universality : it is, however, hard to believe that such an analysis quite fits the Platonic view of Soul as having an affinity with the eternal Ideas, and as being capable of apprehending them in its acts of pure thinking, and of being guided by them in the motions it originates in the world. There is, however, evidence in Plato of a view of Ideas of forms of psychic activity quite on a par with those of the objects of thinking : the form of Life, the pattern of all souls, occupies an important place in the *Phaedo*; the *Phaedrus* describes the souls as looking upon the Form of Knowledge

Itself; while the *Parmenides*, in one of its *aporiae*, connects the Absolute Natures of things with Absolute Knowledge itself, the sort of Knowledge that God might enjoy, and wonders how our instantial knowledge can find its object in such Absolute Natures. The *Republic* also studies the status of Conjecture, Opinion, Mathematical Ratiocination and Pure Thinking as ideal types on a par with their objects, and one is led to the conviction, supported by the strange position of the Demiurge in the *Timaeus*, the timeless fabricator of all temporal souls and minds, that Plato, like Plotinus, believed in an Absolute Mind Itself, correlated with all the Ideas and imperfectly instantiated in all souls, and as much the offspring of the Good as the objective Ideas with which it was correlated. On this view Plato's Ideal Order is not very different from Hegel's Absolute Idea : both include the Ideas of Consciousness and Self-consciousness though not their instantial carrying-out. Both, of course, are infinitely far from the travesty of the Ideas as thoughts in the mind of God, unless God is Himself regarded as an Idea, the Idea of the complete vision of everything ideal, including itself. I believe myself that Plato believed in such a God, a demiurgic Thinkingness, placed between the Good that was beyond Being and the Soul that was active in time, and that Aristotle travestied these beliefs in various ways which made Plato more and more reticent regarding them. Plato of course believed that Souls were the purveyors of motion in the realm of instantiation, and many believe that in Plato's later thought Souls took over the causal functions of the *Eide* and their principles. I believe nothing of the sort. It is yet another case of crypto-instantialism. Souls are sources of movement because they, and the movements they occasion, are alike parts of the zone of Becoming. But beyond all movements in the zone of Becoming lies Movement as Such, the eternal Kind studied in the *Sophist*, as well as the specific patterns of movement characteristic of certain celestial or terrestrial living creatures, and it is this pattern specified in all these patterns which is the ultimate source of movement in the cosmos, because it is the ultimate source of all souls.

There is yet another regard in which Hegel and Plato have a profound affinity : the close connection established in their thought between Being and Value, between notional patterns and species of goodness. Hegel believes that the true shape of anything is also the good shape of that thing, and that an instance that departs far from goodness, i.e. a diseased body or a corrupt political system, is also a 'low and untrue existence'. That the real is the rational, does not mean that everything that exists is as it stands rational, but that only such part of what exists as is rational is in the fullest sense real. Plato, likewise, conceives of his *Eide* as patterns of goodness of which their instances may in many ways fall woefully short : instantial units only aspire to be perfect units, instantial equals only aspire to be truly equal, and states only tend towards the ideal statehood whose pattern is laid up in heaven. This granting of a prime place to patterns of goodness goes together, however, with a willingness to accord a secondary, derivative or, as I like to call it, 'interstitial' place to deviant patterns of various sorts and even to the contrasting notion of complete formlessness. Plato accepts the Socratic principle that knowledge is always of contraries, and that if one knows how to be just one also knows how to be unjust in differing degrees down to the complete consummation of injustice. Hence beside the Ideas of Justice, Piety etc. go the attendant shadows of Injustice, Impiety etc., and sometimes Plato runs through a whole gamut of corruptions as in the remarkable account of deviant states in the *Republic*. Beside True Knowledge we likewise have arranged the shadowy declensions of Mathematical Ratiocination, Opinion and Sense-experience, ending up with that total Unknowingness which apprehends Non-being, and which is also probably the organ through which we are congnizant of the emptiness of Space. Patterns of disease are also elaborately considered in the *Timaeus* and ranged alongside of the patterns of health. But in all this study of the deviant and the totally disordered there is always the presumption that they are somehow parasitic upon the well-formed and regular, that they have being only as poor relations of the latter or as their total opposites—there is evidence in a passage in Sextus Empiricus and elsewhere, that Plato held a three-category doctrine of the Self-existent, the Relative and the Opposed—and that they are wholly subordinated to the well-formed and regular in the ideal zone, however much they may break loose in the zone of instantiation.

Having pointed to all these profound affinities of Hegelianism and Platonism, I shall now descant briefly on their differences. The main difference lies in the *necessity* of the descent of pure Universality into confused, deviant particularity, and its return to self in the conscious understanding of its own supreme role in being, which is the essence of Hegelianism, and which is only very underemphatically present in the treatments of Plato. Hegel believes that everything that is one and selfsame *must* call up a contrasting Other to serve as its foil, a contrasting Other which then 'repels itself' into a bad infinity of contrasting others, and that it must then gather together all the products of this its 'alienation', and must come to see itself in all of them. This development is not, in Hegelianism, something that just happens : it is essential to the being of the Absolute that expresses itself in it, and that simply is the negation of the negation, the cancelling of alienation and opposition in ultimate self-identity. Plato's Ideas and their Principle are much less emphatically wedded to alienation : it is not clearly said in the *Republic*, though implied, that the Good *must* specify itself in the total range of the Ideas, and it is only in the *Parmenides* (on an interpretation that I would push to the hilt) that an attempt is made to show that the notion of Unity Itself, which taken by itself is just itself and nothing more, none the less permits and demands every possible predication, and so can be said plainly to 'generate' the total range of the Ideas. What Plato is here doing is, however, so veiled that some have missed the serious intention of this, the most serious of all his works. And if the necessity of specification is not underlined, this is much more so in the case of instantiation. This is presented in the *Timaeus* rather as an act of unenvious graciousness than as a case of logical necessity. Plato very often talks as if it were not essential to Ideal Types to be instantiated or to be capable of instantiation, nor even essential to instances to conform to Ideal Types; before the Demiurge took the world in hand instances of a sort existed, though with every excess of irregularity. I do not myself believe that Plato believed in any such unregulated instantial being and that he only spoke of it for the sake of instruction. Instances are not ontically ontic, they owe all they are to the Patterns they instantiate, and to talk of them or the space in which they appear as entities of any sort is to talk with one's tongue in one's cheek.

Plato, we may say, was so supremely interested in what Ideal Patterns are in and for themselves that he failed to stress that it was of their essence, shown by the way in which we constantly make use of them in thought, and appeal to them in philosophy, to *have* instances, however imperfect, or at least to be capable of having them. It is, in fact, only in a well-known passage in the *Sophist* that he comes close to realizing that it is only in and through their instantiation in the zone of Becoming, including the instantiation of the modes of knowledge which have them for their objects, that Ideal Patterns have that Life and that luminous self-communication to actual consciousnesses which alone makes them things of value. On the whole he tends to speak as if the superiority of status of Ideas to their instantial embodiments were not at all dependent on the latter, and as if the ideal of thought were merely a dying to the instances of sense and a return to the ideality from which one has unfortunately deviated. Plato does not, like Hegel, clearly see particularity as a necessary mode of pure Universality, a mode in which the Universal must function in order to be what it is. A Universal cannot be a Universal unless there are divergent particularizations for it to gather together and pervade effectively, and the Universal's apartness from and superiority to its particularization goes together with its inclusion of them in itself as its dependent cases or expressions. Hegel has therefore perfected Plato by showing that the profound ontological gulf which separates Type from Instance, and which makes the former *be* what the latter only can exemplify, also brings Type and Instance into the closest mutual connection and, if you like, dependence, the Instance owing everything that it is to its share in the Type, and the Type's independence being also a dependence on the Instance, which however is nothing but an outlying form of itself. At the end of my talk I apologize for some of my metaphors which may to some seem undecipherable : I also apologize for the dogmatic way in which I have had to state my often eccentric opinions. To spell out all my metaphors and to justify or document all my opinions would, however, be impossible in a paper like the present. I can at best give you my sense of the main resemblances and differences between the two supreme philosophers I have been comparing.

ON HEGEL'S PLATONISM

Lucia M. Palmer

University of Delaware

Anglo-American students of Hegel owe a debt of gratitude to J.N. Findlay. Although on the Continent re-evaluation of Hegel's doctrines has proceeded continuously, fluidity of interpretation seldom characterizes the Anglo-American scholarship. In England Hegel has been made known and rejected through the great systems of Bradley and Bosanquet. That Hegel was a transcendent metaphysician, a subjectivist in epistemology, and a manic rationalist is a cherished idol in the English marketplace, and a story many times told. The fruits of Findlay's demythologization of Hegel are harvested in his various articles and volumes which have punctuated Hegelian scholarship over the past twenty years.

In the early Fifties to an audience which had just finished reading K. Popper's *The Open Society and its Enemies*, Findlay in equally passionate language emphasized the contemporary relevance of Hegel's philosophy to the analytic movement of the day. Findlay portrayed a Hegel whose metaphysics was immanent, whose epistemology was spiritualistic, and whose dialectic contained "a large amount of arbitrariness in the discovery of new notions and positions." Hegel's metaphysics, he argued, intended to describe what was "true" in experience, and not to revise its essential categories. On this view Hegel's enterprise was not dissimilar, ostensively at least, from G.E. Moore's conceptual and notional analysis. To the dismay of many analysts he found echoes of Hegel's method in Wittgenstein's dissolution of philosophical puzzles and further contended that the development of English philosophy in the middle of our century could be read as a "museum-specimen" of Hegelian dialectic.[1] While some of his remarks

---

[1] J.N. Findlay, "Some Merits of Hegelianism", *Aristotelian Society Proceeding* LVI (1955-1956), pp. 1-24. For a concrete example of the development of recent analytic philosophy in a Hegelian key see Richard Bernstein, *Praxis and Action* (Philadelphia, 1971), p. 24 n. 21.

tended to be apologetic, Findlay's interpretation of Hegelianism was clear and unobjectionable, and certainly familiar to anyone who had followed or belonged to the development of Hegelian scholarship on the Continent.

Findlay's treatment was set in bold relief by the accentuation of the concreteness of Hegel's system without drawing too extensively, or at all, on the early writings as many post-war Continental philosophers were doing. This recourse to the late Hegel caused embarrassment to the sober American scholars who found themselves incapable of placing Findlay on the right or the left, or even at the center, in the parliament of Hegelians.[2] For Findlay, in fact, Hegel's spiritualism, in its attempt to know and to overcome the natural order, of necessity, presupposes it. Thus Hegel's idealism was thoroughly imbued with naturalism, empiricism, and moderate realism.

Findlay's position on the philosopher's immanentism was reworked and developed at greater length in his *Re-examination* of 1958 and partly in yet another paper published in the following year. Then the thesis still rested on Hegel's relevance to contemporary thought, but with some marked variations from his previous arguments. Perhaps Findlay chose to consider more carefully the implications and output of Hegel's method in reply to critics who saw that he had minimized the strength and value of the dialectic in favor of the system. Using the model of contemporary semantic theories Findlay likened Hegel's dialectic to a series of notional transitions from first to second order concepts. Still he continued to argue that "Hegel's metalinguistic dialectic comments always involve the possible emergence of definite novelties of principles, things not formally entailed by what one has done at the lower level."[3] This quasi-probabilistic interpretation of Hegel's method, while it reinforced the richness and fluidity of its transitions, still failed to make clear the sense in which the dialectic is a series of improving definitions of the Absolute.

Shortly after he had published his phenomenological study *Values and Intentions* Findlay resumed the issue in a brilliant paper appearing in 1964.[4] His "Hegel's Use of Teleology" reiterated the metalogical features of the method, but also introduced the theoretical link which was missing from his past remarks on the dialectic. He endorsed Hegel's unquestioned debt to Aristotle and proceeded to show how Hegel's dialectical "comments" were always and entirely regulated by various forms of teleology. In the

---

[2] G. Kline, "Recent Reinterpretations of Hegel", *The Monist* 48 (1964), p. 45, p. 71 ff.

[3] J.N. Findlay, "The Contemporary Relevance of Hegel", Colloquium on Contemporary British Philosophy in London, 1959, reprinted in J.N. Findlay, *Language, Mind and Value* (London, 1963), p. 220.

[4] J.N. Findlay, *The Monist* 48 (1964), pp. 1-17.

Logic Hegel's concept of infinite teleology implicitly operated in the categories of Being and Essence, and attained its full and revealed explicitness in the category of Notion, the final step to the absolute idea. With Lasson, Mure, and Randall, Findlay acknowledged the affinity of the Notion to Aristotle's final cause. He parted company, however, and pointed out the difference in concreteness between the two fundamental versions of infinite teleology. This advance calls for no argument.

All this by way of preface to my response to the present paper whose argument on the problematic affinities of Plato to Hegel may puzzle anyone who has followed and savored Findlay's previous scholarship. To be sure, the road to Hegel from Plato is as plausible as a road from Aristotle, Spinoza or Kant. However, as many late nineteenth century scholars have shown, the Platonic path entails a Hegel whose holism is not empirical and a Plato whose Proclian and Plotinian identity is far from proven authenticity. Whether Findlay's idealization of Plato and Hegel will launch another re-examination in the Seventies remains to be seen.

Without anticipating what we hope to make clear in the course of our discussion, Findlay's novel re-examination is subtler than a mere change of philosophical perspective. He seems to let his "Hegelian" interpretation of Plato recoil on Hegel and to carry with it a Hegel who often seems ill at ease with the liberal humanism he defended in the Fifties. He makes two very general claims. First, Plato and Hegel are at one in their effort to make sense of our world of experience and in pushing their zeal for explanation so far as "to have recourse to principles which explain themselves." Consequently Platonism and Hegelianism are similar in both being equal to monism, rationalism, and essentialism. Second, the two systems differ in a relevant fashion. Their differences make Hegelianism a better version of Platonism.

Neither of Findlay's contentions is historical. He is not concerned with ascertaining the influences Plato and the Greek ideal made on the young Hegel. Nor is he interested in ascertaining affinities grounded on Hegel's assimilation of Classical and Christian doctrines. Rather, he wishes to present his views on Hegel and Plato in the same way Hegel treated his predecessors. He seeks to support his claims by analyzing first how Plato appeared to Hegel in the *History of Philosophy*, and then by presenting how both men "have come to appear to me" in the actual history of philosophy.

It goes without saying that the plausibility of Findlay's affinity-difference thesis rests on the persuasiveness of the second part of his paper. Findlay's assessment of Hegel's treatment of the Pre-Socratics and of Plato is accurately Hegelian. We are not, however, as disappointed as Findlay is with

Hegel's appreciation of Plato's later dialogues, whose theories Findlay considers most closely related to Hegel's. Nor do we believe that we should assent too hastily to Hegel's alleged underestimation of Heraclitus. Leaving aside questions of textual accuracy, Hegel's admiration for Heraclitus is clear. In words echoing the preface to the *Phenomenology* he praises Heraclitus for having discovered the dialectic of the objective world and for having demonstrated against the background of the Eleatics the fluidity of any content of experience. To be sure, for Hegel, Heraclitus is the philosopher of *Werden*, but in his ability to mediate being and non-being Heraclitus is also the discoverer of Hegel's very own category of becoming.

Perhaps Hegel's mistreatment of Heraclitus is not as relevant to Findlay's general thesis as is Hegel's blindness to the message that Plato's later dialogues should have conveyed to him. That message has been captured in various fashions by scholars as different as Maguire [5] and Brumbaugh,[6] and by Findlay [7] himself in this paper and elsewhere. Though Hegel does not recognize in Plato's *Parmenides* his own conception of the infinite or his own notion of specification, he endorses here as he did in the *Phenomenology* Proclus' interpretation of that dialogue. With this in mind we shall now turn to Findlay's main claim : the degree to which Plato and Hegel are similar in their unique effort to explain and bridge the gap between thought and reality.

No one would disagree with Findlay, not even Popper, that to be a Platonist and a Hegelian signify, among many other things, a commitment to the view that our world of experience is rational, intelligible, and explicable through and through. The rationality of the real as the theoretical characteristic of both Platonism and Hegelianism is an innocent assertion, innocent but also a lash with which to beat both philosophers. It can be embraced equally by right and left Hegelians as well as by pagan and Christian Platonists, whether or not they agree on beliefs and attitudes. It is only when one tries to unpack 'rationality' and 'real' that problems begin. In the case under consideration, the issue of the rationality of the real is more crucial for Plato than for Hegel, if one adheres to the Hegel who "appeared" to Findlay in the *Re-examination* of 1958. For it was one of the main virtues of that work to show that Hegel's successful effort to mediate between idea and fact did not commit his system either to a straitjacketed dialectic or to a supramundane self-sufficient realm.

[5] T. Maguire, *The Parmenides of Plato* (Dublin, 1882), pp. 1-21.
[6] R.S. Brumbaugh, *Plato on the One* (Yale, 1961), pp. 87, 112.
[7] J.N. Findlay, *Language, Mind and Value*, p. 149. But see also, *The Transcendence of the Cave* (London, 1967), pp. 108, 154.

Findlay is very much aware of the difficulites encountered by anyone who attributes to Plato the all-embracing, self-mediating program of Hegel. But to resolve these difficulties it is not enough to endorse, as he does, Hegel's monistic interpretation of Plato. Findlay must show that the "expedients" to which both philosophers resorted in order to satisfy their rationalistic fervor were similar. Findlay only partly succeeds in this effort and the differences he finds in both systems tend to minimize the success of his endeavor.

There can be little doubt that there is a family resemblance between Plato's ontology and that of Hegel. To the question as to what it is that makes the existent intelligible and rational they were at one in answering by appealing to universals, notions, ideal patterns, and, as Findlay calls them, "unities accessible to thought." But to impute to them an ontological kinship one must examine how the ontically ontic realities in which they both believed are structured among themselves and how exactly they are related to the instances they exemplify. Findlay takes several steps in that direction. He contends that their ontically ontic realities specified a supra-ontic source from which they flowed in a necessary manner. He finds similarities between Plato's generic universal in the *Timaeus* and Hegel's basic conception of the concrete universal, which Hegel first articulated and made unique to himself. He is convinced that both Plato and Hegel agree in assigning efficacy to their ontically ontic realities.

With each step Findlay takes and with each set of affinities he finds between Plato and Hegel, he offers insights into both philosophers, but he also tends to incriminate Plato and his Hegel. Let me explain by way of one example. Plato's attempt to organize his ontically ontic realities represent a stumbling block in his philosophy, as all his students know. We need but recall the *Republic* where the Good gives being and intelligibility to the entire world of ideas, and the *Philebus* where the Good is the supreme source of reality, and the *Sophist* where the great kinds are connected in a "Hegelian" categorical system through an element of non-being. Findlay endorses the questionable view that the Good and/or the One is the supra-ontic source from which the forms necessarily flow. The reduction of forms to numbers and Speusippus' interchangeability of the Good with the One are matters of legitimate controversy even without taking into account Aristotle's contentions in his *Metaphysics*. Aside from such textual problems, once Plato's ontic realm is conceived in the fashion proposed by Findlay, it casts a shadow on its affinities with Hegel's logical domain where mathematical deduction is hardly a characteristic of his logical categories.

All affinities in their objective ontologies tend to dissolve when we compare Hegel's philosophy of spirit, soul, and subjectivity with Plato's ambiguous and controversial notion of the soul that is akin to the form. Here Findlay imports Procrustes' bed to show a Platonic plausibility of a soul which is self-conscious spirit. For Findlay it becomes an instantiation of an absolute mind in which Findlay believes that Plato believed. In this sense, Hegel's absolute idea bears significant affinities to Plato's ideal order if indeed the latter were endowed with consciousness and self-consciousness.

In any work of comparative philosophy as the one Findlay has presented the differences among philosophers and their systems are often very crucial in throwing into relief how sound and plausible their similarities are; and so it is with Plato and Hegel. When the two philosophers are seen merely as "differing expressions of an historic enterprise," they are at one in their vision of a unified intelligible system. If one examines the "expedients" Plato and Hegel use to solve the issues which most concerned them, even this general statement of identity would have to be modified.

At the end of his paper Findlay briefly presents what he considers the main differences between the two philosophers. He closes by saying that it is the dialectic, the necessity of the descent of pure universality into particularity and its return to self-consciousness, which is the essence of Hegelianism and which, of course, is lacking in Platonism. This true statement seems to me an admission that Platonism cannot be a better version of Hegelianism because it is not Hegelianism at all. Findlay's assertion that Plato's ideal entities are not wedded to alienation is confession of failure. For it is to repeat Hegel's assessment of Plato's idealism as being not ideal enough or too abstract. Furthermore, it is to reiterate the Hegelian distinction between the form as *energeia* and the form as *dynamis*, and thus to reopen the gulf between fact and idea, thought and reality.

Hence if one is to look at the two systems of philosophy as an attempt to make complete sense of the universe, one has no choice but to be a Hegelian. As Findlay put it so neatly nine years ago, to understand the gist of Hegelianism completely is to stroll "on Main Steet" as if Main Street were the "Holy City." Plato, at least as I understand him, tried to give us a sketch of the immanence of infinity in the transient. If we are to attach to the *Timaeus* the significance which Hegel and Findlay accord it, Main Street and the here and now are bound to be a moving image of eternity.

Perhaps in the foregoing remarks I have involved myself in the truism that the difference between Hegel's idealism and Plato's idealism lies in the fact that the former is Christian and the latter is not. Although this appears to be a truism, I wonder whether it is not more accurate than saying that Hegel has absorbed those elements in Plato which are Christian.

CARTESIAN DOUBT AND HEGELIAN NEGATION

FREDERICK G. WEISS

The Citadel

> "There lives more faith in honest doubt,
> Believe me, than in half the creeds."
> Tennyson

In the *Meditations*, we find Descartes struggling to establish the true and real existence of self, God and world by a systematic application of doubt to the objects of experience. However "ingenuous" and "naive" the narration of his thoughts may have seemed to Hegel, Descartes' work is nonetheless given a place of prime importance in the *Lectures on the History of Philosophy*. "With him," Hegel remarks, "the new epoch in Philosophy begins," the *Cogito*, the first step in the grounding of all truth in self-thinking thought, being "the maxim on which may be said to hinge the whole interest of Modern Philosophy."[1] While Hegel's construal of Descartes and its importance for subsequent thought deserves comprehensive treatment, in this paper I propose simply to take an Hegelian look at some aspects of Descartes' struggle in order to clarify certain problems common to them both, and to all serious philosophy.

Descartes initiates his method of universal doubt quite simply because he has at times been wrong, and he wants to discover what is requisite for him to truly know, that is, to *know* that he knows. Not wishing to accept anything as true which is not beyond doubt, his initial problem is to locate a beginning in his awareness of things. I will "set aside" my opinions, he says, "and start again from the very beginning."[2] But what could constitute a *beginning* of knowledge, a beginning of truth? That is, how can *science*, the goal we are after, be said to have a beginning? Beginnings are always and everywhere gratuitous; they constitute an assumption which, as such, is incompatible with the notion of philosophic science, for the latter will not permit the limitation and therefore finitude which beginnings and their

---

[1] *Hegel's Lectures on the History of Philosophy*, tr. Haldane and Simson (New York : Humanities Press, 1963), v.3, p. 223, and *The Logic of Hegel*, tr. W. Wallace, 2nd. edn. (Oxford : Oxford University Press, 1892), p. 127, respectively.

[2] René Descartes, *Meditations on First Philosophy*, tr. Laurence J. LaFleur (Indianapolis : Bobbs-Merrill, 1960), p. 17.

concomitant and philosophically repugnant *ends* entail. And where shall we "set aside" our opinions? ³ If we are not misled by the metaphor, we shall see that the only way to set aside an opinion is to replace it with a truth. But *what* truth? The arguments from illusion, from dreaming, and from the hypothesis of an evil and deceitful spirit seem at first to eradicate any possibility of truth. Descartes says, however, that even if he cannot attain the knowledge of any truth, it is still in his power to "suspend judgment." But neither do we arrive at the truth of things simply by withholding judgment.⁴ If we say nothing about the world, we may prevent ourselves from falling into error, but we also preclude the possibility of uttering any truth. As it turns out, Descartes does not in fact suspend his judgment at all. He rather substitutes for the judgment that this or that is real a different judgment, namely that the earth, the sky, his hands, etc. are *un*real, merely "inventions of his mind." "I shall suppose," he says, "that everything that I see is false."⁵ Of course, "things" cannot strictly speaking be false; what he means is that he intends to deny the truth of his earlier *judgments* that these things, e.g. his body, are real, and since, at this point, "real" is for Descartes synonymous with "outside" or "independent of" the mind, denying their *ex*ternality results in affirming their *in*ternality.⁶ Sensible

---

³ "Was ich nur meine, ist mein." *The Logic of Hegel*, p. 38.

⁴ For Hegel, the examination of knowledge can only be carried out by an act of knowledge : "If the fear of falling into error introduces an element of distrust into science, which without any scruples of that sort goes to work and actually does know, it is not easy to understand why, conversely, a distrust should not be placed in this very distrust, and why we should not take care lest the fear of error is not just the initial error. As a matter of fact, this fear presupposes something, indeed a great deal, as truth, and supports its scruples and consequences on what should itself be examined beforehand to see whether it is truth. It starts with ideas of knowledge as an instrument, and as a medium; and presupposes a distinction of ourselves from this knowledge. More especially it takes for granted that the Absolute stands on one side, and that knowledge on the other side, by itself and cut off from the Absolute, is still something real; in other words, that knowledge, which, by being outside the Absolute, is certainly also outside truth, is nevertheless true — a position which, while calling itself fear of error, makes itself known rather as fear of the truth." G.W.F. Hegel, *The Phenomenology of Mind*, tr. J.B. Baillie. 2nd. edn. (New York : The Macmillan Co., 1931), pp. 132-3.

⁵ *Meditations*, p. 23.

⁶ *Here* is the logical birth of the notion of "finite" mind that haunts the whole of modern philosophy. See below, p. 91; also : "The peculiar quality of mind is to be the true infinite, that is, the infinite which does not one-sidedly stand over against the finite but contains the finite within itself as a moment. It is, therefore, meaningless to say : There are finite minds. Mind *qua* mind *is* not finite, it *has* finitude within itself, but only as a finitude which is to be, and has been, reduced to a moment." *Hegel's Philosophy of Mind*, tr. W. Wallace and A.V. Miller (Oxford : Clarendon Press, 1971), p. 23.

things may not be "real," but that they nonetheless *are*, in some sense, is later translated by Descartes into the *Cogito*—the claim that whether things be real (out there) or not, his awareness of and/or thought about them cannot be denied, and even the denial of the denial constitutes a judgment which he is powerless to relinquish. "I am, I exist, is necessarily true every time that I pronounce it or conceive it in my mind," he affirms. "Without doubt I existed if I was convinced or even if I thought anything."[7]

The usual question about this claim relates to whether "I exist" does or does not follow from "I think." This, however, is not the chief issue here, and Descartes disavows its being an argument at all. The question that needs to be asked is rather what basis Descartes has for the claim that he thinks. "I existed *if* I was convinced," he says. But if he will not allow that the judgments "I have hands," "I see the sky," etc. are true, why should he now assent to the truth of the judgment that he *thinks*? Descartes' answer, sometimes repeated almost verbatim by sense-datum theorists such as Price and Ayer, is that my mere thoughts, my ideas, my perceptions occupy a privileged position, in that *they* are what I *directly* experience in my (presumably complex) intercourse with the outside world. They may be merely subjective "mental" data housed in the privacy of my mind, but this very fact secures them for *me*, and confers upon them a quasi-objectivity. The very withdrawal of the immediate objects of experience from an external and remote existence brings them into a comforting realm of subjective certainty.

Descartes says: "I do really see light, hear noises, feel heat. Will it be said that these appearances are false and that I am sleeping? Let it be so; yet at the very least it is certain that it seems to me that I see light, hear noises, and feel heat. This much," he concludes, "cannot be false."[8] But what does it mean to say that "it is *certain* that I *seem* to see something?" I suggest that "seeming to see" or "thinking we see" amounts to nothing more than a doubt as to our certainty in the matter. Ordinarily when I say "I think I see X," I mean I'm not sure it *is* X; I want to qualify the judgment and allow for the possibility that it may *not* be X. If this is the case, then what sort of thing is it to say "I'm *certain* that I'm not sure?" The only way to be certain of our uncertainty in any *specific* case is to know what *would* constitute a true judgment in the matter.[9] It follows from this that the cer-

---

[7] *Meditations*, p. 24.

[8] *Ibid.*, p. 28.

[9] For example, in order to *know* I'm not sure that some object on the horizon is a ship, I must know beforehand what criteria such an object must satisfy if it *were*. See also footnote 4 above.

tainty of a specific uncertainty will not do as an absolute starting point, as it already presupposes prior knowledge of truth. The other alternative is to affirm that *nothing* is certain, and while Descartes mentions this at the start of the second Meditation, he does not at that point examine it critically. How can it be certain that *nothing* is certain? If nothing were certain, the very certainty of the claim would be nullified. Thus, if it were true, it could never be verified, a paradox, indeed. But Descartes does not fall into it; under the guise of the *Cogito*, he appears to take the position that "certainty that there is nothing certain" is self-contradictory, and therefore that "nothing is certain" is false. In other words, "If 'nothing is certain' were true it could never be verified" comes to mean "If 'nothing is certain' were true, it would be *un*true," thus the revealing contradiction, revealing in the sense that whether "nothing is certain" is true or false, *something* is certain.

This, I submit, is the best sense that can be made out of Descartes' claim above that "this much cannot be false," and it is also the logical basis of the *Cogito*. But this "something" is no being in particular (let alone Descartes), but the emptiest of all abstractions, Being in general, and the "self," the "I" which is thought is only the promise of complete unity or identity which must yet be mediated by a complex overcoming of each and every "other" confronting it. "Only when we discern," says Hegel, "that the content, the particular, is not self-subsistent, but derivative from something else, are its finitude and untruth shown in their proper light."[10] This involves mediation, he adds, and the only true content is one not mediated by an other, but self-mediated. But Descartes, and many of his successors and interpreters, particularly the empiricists, have constructed this abstract thinking into a subjective realm of which we are immediately or intuitively certain, giving it, in other words, a quasi-existence, and in turn set themselves the task of establishing relations between these internal, "mental" beings and those external realities which they in some way or other represent. Getting at the truth thus becomes the problem of freeing ourselves from our subjectivity, the abode of untruth or mere appearance.[11] Descartes' *Meditations* exhibit a variety of attempts to break out of this subjective realm to which what Hegel calls *Verstandesmetaphysik* has committed it. Indeed, the whole of modern philosophy is a battle with Descartes' and Locke's confounded *ideas*, a frustrated attempt to *know* the world and have it, too. Berkeley, for example, gives us the impression that he is transferring the objects of

[10] *The Logic of Hegel*, p. 137.

[11] Indeed, the finite "self" and all its "knowing" owes its existence to hypostatized uncertainty.

cognition from one "place," i.e. outside the mind, to another, i.e. in the mind, and the question then becomes how to endow (or *re*-endow) them there with that quality of truth or reality which was initially understood to consist in an *independence* of the mind, and yet maintain them *in* the mind, i.e. as *known*.[12] But when the old criterion of truth is removed, the problem of accounting for error remains.

Hegel, of course, equates falsity (not truth) with otherness or self-discordance, and holds that the true must in some way contain the false as a vanishing element in itself. His dialectic of *double* negation makes this possible by abrogating the hard and fast distinction between subject and object, idea and thing, which Descartes, endeavoring to philosophize at the level of *Verstand*, cannot free himself of. As long as the "inner" world of Cartesian ideas stands opposed by the outer as *other*, each becomes a mere abstraction, the whole business ultimately solidifying into dualism, with a *deus ex machina*, the greatest abstraction of all, providing the only hope of solution. The classical traditions of empiricism and rationalism after Locke and Descartes represent a kind of circus in response to the question: "If the 'real' is outside or other than the mind, and the known is inside or one with the mind, how can the real be known?" The empiricists and Kant turn the world's outside in, so to speak, and the rationalists turn the mind's inside out, but no solution in these terms satisfies, and in Hume, the Cartesian God, self and world all alike disintegrate in the unbridgeable gap between cause and effect.[13]

From an Hegelian point of view, appearances are not at all mental entities, nor do they occupy some internal place. Rather, they are, as such, uncertainties, which are really better characterized not so much as *un*truths but as partial truth, and they have been relegated by Descartes and some of his followers to a realm of subjectivity, itself a half-truth, because they claimed to be truer than they were.[14] I suggest, in other words, that Descartes' chief problem is what to *do* with untruth, falsity, error, otherness. In Hegel's eyes what he has discovered, knowingly or otherwise,

---

[12] From an Hegelian point of view, Berkeley's claim that sensible things exist "only in the mind" is quite contrary to the requirements of speculative idealism; their existence *qua* sensible is rather a measure of their *failure* to exist in the mind or to be known. There can *be* knowledge, i.e. a thing can be known, only to the extent that it has an identity; this identity is alone the proper object of knowledge. See below, p. 89.

[13] See G.R.G. Mure's account of "the magical vacuum cleaner" in his *Retreat From Truth* (Oxford : Basil Blackwell, 1958), pp. 55-6.

[14] Descartes' *Cogito* succeeds (in the sense set out above) because even sensible things, those perennial objects of doubt for rationalists, have a measure of truth, of selfhood or identity which, though it bathes in a reflected light, nonetheless must be given its due.

is that subjectivity, the "I", is *thought*, but thought is itself only the negation of every partial truth. It determines its objects, through language, as a system of relations, as *relata* rather than mere atomic percepts or ideas, reducing the claim on the part of any limited experience to be the whole truth, and demanding instead that the truth is the whole. I suggested earlier that Descartes actually has no right initially to claim possession of knowledge of any *particular* truth or thought, this because, as Hegel would say, truth *qua* particular or finite turns round into its opposite and becomes untrue. Descartes looks hard for a predicate to attach to his newly discovered subject, but he looks in vain. "What am I?" he asks, "I who am sure I exist?" A man? A rational animal? "Certainly not, for I would have to determine what an animal is, and what is meant by 'rational'; and so, from a single question, I would find myself gradually enmeshed in an infinity of others."[15] If thought were a real predicate, it would have to be this or that thought, this or that perception, this or that desire, etc. But each of these assertions of this or that particular predicate is doubtful, or could be doubtful, and so is inadmissable as sufficient evidence for self. But the fact that any assertion is open to doubt or some other challenge with respect to its truth does not make it false, nor does it unalterably lead to scepticism. Rather, it is the very *condition* for the possibility of its being true. Doubt challenges the claim on the part of any assertion to be the whole truth; it brings to bear upon that assertion its own "negativity" or limitedness, the recognition of which alone allows that truth to maintain its limited status as a positive function of a larger whole. The "falsehood" or otherness which characterized appearance is thus sublated (*aufgehoben*). The terms "true" and "false," Hegel says, and likewise reality and appearance, "must no longer be used where their otherness has been cancelled and superseded." Similarly

> The expressions "unity of subject and object," of "finite and infinite," of "being and thought," etc., are clumsy when subject and object, etc., are taken to mean what they are *outside* their unity, and are thus in that unity not meant to be what its very expression conveys; in the same way falsehood is not, *qua* false, any longer a moment of truth.[16]

For Hegel, therefore, genuine or philosophic truth is not some indubitable beginning, but a result which consummates rather than transcends the process of arriving at it; that is, the process must be construed as its *own*. Philosophic truth *is* genuineness, not the correspondence of one thing with another, of *our* idea with the thing (mere correctness), but the correspondence of a thing with itself, of its being or objectivity with its notion. Every

---

[15] *Meditations*, p. 24.
[16] *Phenomenology*, p. 99.

ordinary form of experience amounts to an approximation of this truth, and all sub-philosophical experience is only "abstract" to the extent that its form (the mode of apprehension) and its content (the object apprehended) do not fully penetrate and explicate each other. The merely phenomenal character of experience which so troubles Descartes is precisely this dissonance or incongruity in the subject-object relation. Thinking, Descartes' "doubt," begins in the wonder at this, and does not rest satisfied until it enters into and transforms the whole realm of appearance, and abrogates its mere show. This it does by reducing the various levels of experience (each of which exhibits both a unity and a difference) to what Hegel calls "ideal" moments of a developing whole, the relative absence of which at each such stage being at once what places it there and forces it beyond itself. Each moment or part lives only by participating in and eventually giving itself up to the whole in and through which it alone becomes a part. The "self" or identity which is given up, however, is only the claim on the part of a fragment to be the whole, *a* truth claiming to be truer than it is, a being which is not Being, which must reach out for another to support itself, thus affirming its own lack of a self-contained and self-sufficient identity. What it loses, therefore, is only its own initial state of being lost, its otherness and abstraction which the whole as its truth nullifies.

Self, i.e. thought, must be its own evidence, its own predicate, and that is exactly what Descartes' *Cogito* comes to. The self is not a first truth, the first brick in a structure of other bricks; in Descartes the doubt itself is his actual beginning, not some certainty reached by means of it. Not itself a truth, it is nonetheless the condition for the possibility of any and all truth. Thought, our innermost self, and the selfhood or identity of any being, is what Hegel means by absolute negativity, the double negation which is alone truly positive, which negates the immediacy of every finite "entity" and places it as a determination within itself.

Hegel sees Descartes as not fully in possession of his accomplishment. Although Descartes says toward the close of the second Meditation that "perceiving...speaking precisely, is nothing else but thinking," meaning that sensuous representations (*Vorstellungen*) are not *known*, do not become real objects except through the mediation of thought, he still takes "thought" in the abstract sense, as *Verstand*, as thought *about* objects, not thought *of* objects. Thus truth is also *about* objects, and cannot become the required truth *of* objects. Descartes' "thought," his subject, excludes the object, and the object is opaque to the thought. His analysis of the experience of a piece of wax results in the recognition that his understanding alone conceives it, that perception "is solely an inspection by the mind," and that, although we say we *see* the wax, it is our judgment which determines it in its true being.[17] But he never makes it entirely clear how thought, his abstract thought, brings this about, and the subject, the "I," tends also to solidify into a thing, preventing any real union of subject and object; knowledge is no longer a fact, but a problem to be solved. "Because subject and object are each a totality," says Hegel, "neither can bear a real relation to the other."[18]

Much of the remainder of the *Meditations* finds Descartes venting and exploring his overwhelming belief that his "ideas", from those of God to corporeal bodies, are caused by something beyond or other than them. But as the causes of a thing constitute its *raison d'être* and thus its very being, and as in Descartes they are not united with the thing but held to be beyond it, no satisfactory theory either of truth *or* being emerges; having arrived at doubt and having identified it with thought, Descartes' problem is that he does not know what to do with it. In an attempt to preserve the unstable integrity of sensible things, he abstracts their own tendency to come apart and makes it a function of *his* mis-apprehension. Hegel, on the other hand, sublates or develops this negation, puts it to work. His "*aufheben*" means at once to cancel or suspend, to raise up, and to preserve or maintain, but these three moments actually resolve themselves into a two-fold negation. The finite is *itself* the first negation, and the process of cancelling or abrogating this negativity, this lack of full identity or selfhood, this tendency to come apart, is the second. Hegel also speaks of "absolute negativity" by which he means the resultant, but not therefore static truth which is this double negation itself. It is this absolute negativity which is absent in Descartes. For Hegel, absolute negativity is alone infinite *self* affirmation, while simple negativity, i.e. finitude, rather represents self-suppression and self-abnegation. "The form of immediacy," Hegel says, "invests the particular with the character of independent or self-centered being. But such predicates contradict the very essence of the particular—which is to be referred to something *else* — they thus invest the finite with an absolute character."[19] This contradiction in things is the moving force of the world, the dialectic of Spirit, and the ceaseless but nonetheless devel-

---

[17] *Meditations*, pp. 30-31. These paragraphs compare with the chapter on sense-certainty in the *Phenomenology*, where Hegel argues that the first (sensuous) appearance of objects presents itself as the richest, but turns out, in truth, to be the poorest.

[18] *History of Philosophy*, p. 251. Hegel says this in connection with soul and body, but the same holds true for subject and object.

[19] *The Logic of Hegel*, p. 137.

opmental change the world manifests Hegel regarded as the process of Spirit's own continual doubting and re-affirming of itself.

For Descartes, only the denial of the real *qua* outside or other than self, the negation of the object's otherness or property of being not-self, is the first really positive truth, the first real self-affirmation. But this is not accomplished without the other, despite Descartes' wishing us to believe that it is, but in and through the other. "We make ourselves finite," says Hegel, "by receiving an other into our consciousness; but in knowing it, we transcend this limitation," and in this "transcendence" (*Aufhebung*), arrive at the selfhood which is the truth of both abstractions.[20] To the extent that the object is other or *not*-me, that is, to the extent that consciousness is not *self*-consciousness, to that extent is the object finite and external, and the consciousness merely subjective.

For Descartes, truth is something innate, revealed to him by God through the efficacy of clear and distinct ideas, which for him seem to be nothing more than analytical judgments. What Descartes fails to clearly realize is that his demand for a cause of his ideas, something other or external, is actually the need to find a place for, or rather give a role to the partial truth they represent. But the cast Descartes gives to his problem continually misleads. He takes error to mean "judging that the ideas which are in myself are similar to, or conformable to, things outside of myself," when they are not.[21] He repeats that the consideration of the immediate objects of experience *only as modes of his own consciousness*, with no reference to any "external" object, protects him from mistakes. But this is a frustrating gain, if a gain at all, because the real, the true, he conceives as lying outside his finite consciousness, and the problem becomes one of adequately relating these mere appearances to their causes; the problem of truth becomes for him that of locating the origin of his ideas.

From another point of view, we might construe error as privation of truth. But this still does not tell Descartes how to rid his ideas of their incompleteness, their privation. A "complete" idea is not one somehow linked to an external archetype. A complete idea is a true idea, and once we see that by "idea" Descartes means, or should mean "judgment," and not an hypostatized mental datum, the question of the origin of an idea shows itself to be the question "What makes any given judgment true?" The usual claim, of course, is that an assertion of fact is true or false in virtue of some existing state of affairs in the world. But Descartes has sacrificed any rapport

---

[20] *Philosophy of Mind*, p. 24.
[21] *Meditations*, p. 36.

with "existence" in arriving at his incorrigible first "truth." As he says, "Now as far as ideas are concerned, if we consider them only in themselves and do not relate them to something else, they cannot, properly speaking, be false; for whether I imagine a sage or a satyr, it is no less true that I imagine the one than the other."[22] But as Hegel remarks, "Since the criterion of truth is found, not in the nature of the content, but in the mere fact of consciousness, every alleged truth has no other basis than subjective certitude and the assertion that we discover a certain fact in our consciousness."[23] Likewise, a datum of sense, when cut off from a system of relations which thought and language provide, becomes an unspeakable something, ludicrously described as "certain." For Hegel, a true whole, a "complete" idea, is constituted of parts each of which, and in varying degrees, "mirror" that whole *negatively*; each is a microcosm, but not literally; that is, we do not have here the box-within-box thesis (which Hegel specifically repudiates). Rather, the whole is "there" by implication, in the sense that any attempt that is made to fully grasp the being of any part leads in the process to the whole which is its truth. The whole is thus, as it were, the *non*-being or negation of its parts : all determination is negation, but all negation is equally determination.

Descartes, however, continues to talk of an existence "outside" himself, which increasingly, like Kant's *Ding-an-sich*, takes on the characteristics of merely an ideal of perfect knowledge, rather than a concrete prototype. In the third Meditation, for example, he says :

I have often observed in many instances that there was a great difference between the object and its idea. Thus, for example, I find in myself two completely different ideas of the sun : the one has its origin in the senses, and must be placed in the class of those that...came from without, according to which it seems to me extremely small; the other is derived from astronomical considerations — that is, from certain innate ideas...according to which it seems to me many times greater than the whole earth. Certainly, these two ideas of the sun cannot both be similar to the same sun existing outside of me, and reason makes me believe that the one which comes directly from its appearance is that which least resembles it.[24]

Of course, Descartes has not at any point actually compared either of his two ideas of the sun with that "external" sun, and thus the difference he claims exists between his idea of the sun and the object itself never materializes. The difference actually presents itself as a difference between one idea and another. Furthermore, it is not resolved, that is, the truth of the

---

[22] *Ibid.*
[23] *The Logic of Hegel*, p. 134.
[24] *Meditations*, p. 38.

matter is not arrived at by a facing off against each other of the idea and some *de facto* existence. *Reason* makes Descartes affirm the truth of the judgment regarding the size of the sun derived from astronomical considerations. But what is reason? What Descartes says about it makes it either an *a priori* function of the "light of nature," or a formalized, mathematical mode of inference based upon the principle of non-contradiction. However, we get a better idea of the meaning of "reason" and the mode in which it determines the truth by paying attention to what Descartes does, rather than to merely what he says. In the case of the true size of the sun, it is clearly the frame of reference, the context of other judgments, which requires him to make the choice. The true meaning of "sun" is not "half-dollar sized burning hole in the sky," although it might well have been in another, earlier age, because a new theoretical context, a mathematically articulated celestial mechanics, requires us to "see" the sun in a new way. But as each judgment follows, not from some correct or mistaken comparison of idea and thing, but from varying theoretical contexts, the question of the truth of each judgment relates rather to its coherence in the context which gives it meaning. For Hegel, of course, this means that the "truth" is at once determined *and* limited by its context, and the true *per se* is the whole, where every determination, however limited and contingent in itself or in abstraction from that whole, is a necessary moment in the rational articulation of that totality.

For Hegel, thought is the manifestation of the negativity in things themselves, and dialectic is not a method applied externally, but the very pulse and life of reflective, self-critical truth. For Descartes, thought is something that goes on in his mind, and the relations developed therein are not determining relations within the thing itself. He must introduce God as the guarantor of his subjective judgments, and although there are in the *Meditations* some vague references to God's being the very law and order of nature, God is Himself a thing, distinct from both self and world. Descartes' difficulties are complex, and a full treatment is not possible here. We should see, however, that the work of the scientific or reflective consciousness only begins in the skeptical denial or negation of the immediate reality of finite experience. It continues in the search for a deeper ground in reference to which phenomena may be seen to have a mediated reality. Thought, properly understood, provides this deeper ground, but not the abstract thought of the understanding, which simply negates the presented object, and withdraws from it into a realm of abstract and formal "truth". Descartes seeks the truth too soon; for Hegel, "science cannot be the first, but only the final, state of knowledge."[25] The goal of the *Meditations* and the *Phenomenology*

[25] *Philosophy of Mind*, p. 98.

is the same—philosophic science, truth aware of itself, for Hegel, self-conscious Spirit. But Descartes' "voyage of discovery" is too brief, his vessel too slight to carry him through the turbulent waters of experience charted in Hegel's *Phenomenology*. The problem of truth, that full truth that alone can be the object of philosophic *Wissenschaft*, is the problem of error, the solution of which requires a confrontation with error far in excess of that found in the narrow confines of the *Meditations*, or for that matter, the whole of Descartes' philosophy.

This passage from the *Phenomenology*, while it contains no reference to Descartes, crystallizes Hegel's critique of the Cartesian method and sets out the requirements of his own.

Natural consciousness will prove itself to be only knowledge in principle or not real knowledge. Since, however, it immediately takes itself to be the real and genuine knowledge, this pathway has a negative significance for it; what is a realization of the notion of knowledge means for it rather the ruin and overthrow of itself; for on this road it loses its own truth. Because of that, the road can be looked on as the path of doubt, or more properly a highway of despair. For what happens there is not what is usually understood by doubting, a jostling against this or that supposed truth, the outcome of which is again a disappearance in due course of the doubt and a return to the former truth, so that at the end the matter is taken as it was before. On the contrary, that pathway is the conscious insight into the untruth of the phenomenal knowledge, for which that is the most real which is after all only the unrealized notion.[26]

Descartes' thought, nourished as it was by the abstract optimism of modern "science," was perhaps not designed to negotiate such a "highway of despair," nor to give up so much along the way.

---

[26] *Phenomenology*, pp. 135-6.

LEIBNIZ AND HEGEL ON LANGUAGE*

Daniel J. Cook

Brooklyn College, CUNY

1. Introduction

No two classical German philosophers have occupied themselves more with the problem of "teaching philosophy to speak German" than Leibniz and Hegel. Both, throughout their lives, and their writings, were also preoccupied with the broader problem of developing an adequate linguistic idiom in general (German or otherwise) for expressing philosophical truth. In Leibniz's case, these two endeavors, though motivated by the same search for universal truth and clarity which animates all his thinking, tend to diverge; he not only treats them as separate problems, but writes about them in separate works, in different languages and styles. His discussions about the need for the Germans to develop their own intellectual language are often written in German and have an exhortatory and homiletic style. On the other hand, his discussions on the need for philosophy in general to develop an adequate, universal language and symbolism are usually written in Latin or French, the international languages of the time, and have an intramural and erudite quality. This divergence in style and substance is understandable, given the nature of the respective problems and the different audiences to whom he was addressing himself.

With Hegel, however, these two endeavors, the development of a German philosophical language, and the more general problem of philosophical language, tend to converge. Hegel wrote virtually only in German, and his audience was primarily academic. He could, and often did, write in a popular fashion, but the main body of his work—certainly his own published works—is addressed to the intellectual community. There are obvious historical reasons why Hegel did not write, nor have to write, in Latin or French; by the beginning of the 19th century—thanks in part to Leibniz's

---

* A briefer version of this paper was given at the 2nd International Leibniz Congress at Hannover in July 1972.

own efforts a century earlier—German was an internationally accepted medium of communication. However, I believe that there are, as we shall see, internal philosophical reasons as well why Hegel's attempts at forging a German terminology for philosophy *and* his discussions on philosophical language in general, are treated as one problem, rather than as two different ones as in Leibniz.

The similarities between Leibniz's and Hegel's positions on the problem of the proper language for philosophy are as striking as the differences. In this paper, I would like to compare the views of Leibniz and Hegel on these two related problems. I believe that such an examination will generate an interesting and fruitful comparison, one which is perhaps relevant to our own philosophical situation today. In this connection, I will discuss Hegel's critique of Leibniz's notion of a Universal Characteristic, as found primarily in Paragraph 459 of the *Enzyklopädie der Philosophischen Wissenschaften*, although other important comments by Hegel in the *Wissenschaft der Logik* will also be cited. Hegel's *Auseinandersetzung* with Leibniz concerning the possibility as well as the feasibility of a Universal Characteristic —a formal or symbolical language for science and philosophy—enable us, finally, to understand several important aspects of Hegel's thought on language in general.

One other point should be noted : in dealing with the relations of thought or philosophy to language in Leibniz and Hegel, we are not dealing with a problem peripheral to the substance of their thinking, as would be the case were we to deal with Kant or Marx, for example. For Leibniz and Hegel, the problem of language in general and its role in philosophy are substantive questions. Both thinkers sought to establish a role for language *within* their respective philosophies, as well as being concerned with the role of language (German, Latin or the Universal Characteristic) for articulating the truths *of* these philosophies.[1] The views of Leibniz and Hegel on the nature of language in general and its role in philosophy directly influence

---

[1] Leibniz's most systematic considerations on the nature of language in general and its relationship to knowledge are found in Book III of the *New Essays Concerning Human Understanding*, entitled "On Words." However, there is much important material on these matters in his so-called German writings (*Deutsche Schriften*), especially his essays : "Von deutscher Sprachpflege. Unvorgreifliche Gedanken betreffend die Ausübung und Verbesserung der deutschen Sprache," and its companion piece, "Ermahnung an die Deutschen, ihren Verstand und ihre Sprache besser zu üben." Other relevant material is found in many of his fragmentary works on logic and language—most conveniently found in Franz Schmidt's edition and translation, *Leibniz' Fragmente zur Logik*. Some of this material is in Leroy Loemker's monumental translation and edition of Leibniz's *Philosophical Papers and Letters*.

their proposals and strictures concerning the development of an adequate philosophical language, and will therefore be referred to when appropriate.

I make this last point to obviate the objection, which might be made against my approach, that it is not very illuminating philosophically—except in some kind of simplistic "compare and contrast" fashion—to dwell on differing conceptions of philosophical language when they are underpinned by differing conceptions of philosophy itself. Better to concentrate, one might say, on the latter rather than merely on one of its superficial manifestations. It is for this reason that I want to stress the centrality of the problem of the relation between language and thought for both Leibniz and Hegel.

II. Leibniz and Hegel on the German Language

One of Leibniz's most common metaphors about language is that it is a true or clear mirror of the understanding ("*ein heller, ein rechter*," or simply, "*ein Spiegel des Verstandes*"). The intellectual level and quality of our language reflect the intellectual level and quality of our minds. Even more forcefully, Leibniz claims

> that languages are the best mirrors of the human mind, and that an exact analysis of the signification of words would show us better than anything else the workings of the understanding.[2]

Yet for Leibniz, our language does not simply passively reflect our thinking, but actively influences it as well. A clear, precise language will promote, as well as reflect, clear precise thinking. A language poorly developed in the proper intellectual terms, like the German of Leibniz's day, reflects a mentality which cannot deal with subtle abstractions, and which in turn reinforces such a cast of mind. Therefore, the average German lacks "a certain *esprit* and acuteness of thought, a seasoned judgment, a delicate sensitivity,"[3] that is found in certain foreigners. Picking up the mirror or glass motif once more, Leibniz says of the native language of such foreigners (e.g., either French or Italian) that each can be likened

---

Hegel's attempts at developing language into a meaningful category or concept *within* his philosophy (like, for example, labor or alienation) are found especially in his *Jena-Realphilosophie I* and *II*; the *Phänomenologie des Geistes* is also relevant in this regard.

[2] G.W. Leibniz, *New Essays Concerning Human Understanding*, tr. A.G. Langley (New York : MacMillan, 1896), III, Chapter vii, Paragraph 6, p. 368.

[3] G.W. Leibniz, *Muttersprache und volkische Gesinnung*, Vol. I of *Deutsche Schriften*, ed. W. Schmied-Kowarzik (Leipzig : Meiner, 1916), p. 14.

to a finely polished glass promoting keenness of mind and granting an illuminating clarity to the understanding.[4]

When the Germans wish to pursue scientific study, they must do so in a foreign tongue; in so doing they live and learn by the lights of others. Leibniz concludes by saying that the Germans can hope for no success, or esteem from others, "as long as we cannot utilize our own language in the sciences and other important matters."[5] Leibniz then exhorts his own people to develop proper abstract terms (e.g., for philosophy, government and law) in their native language. He sees nothing to prevent the Germans from eventually being able to express everything clearly in their *Volkssprache*. He also believed that if the proper native language is not developed for expressing such matters, the Germans will inevitably take on a foreign language (most likely French) and with it a foreign yoke. They will then lose not only their language, but their independence and identity as well—much as the Anglo-Saxons in England lost theirs.[6]

Leibniz's antagonist in these exhortations was the French or Italian languages (what the Germans pejoratively call "*Weltsch*"); for Hegel it was Latin. Though Leibniz did not think of Latin as a "living and popular language," he still saw the need for it as the *Vermittlungssprache* of the European intellectual world, as the "*lingua Europaea universalis ad posteritatem*."[7] Hegel, however, thought it particularly unsuited for expressing or appropriating the truths of modern philosophy. In this vein, he also attacked the predilection of his German contemporaries for Latin terminology for key philosophical terms when perfectly good German words were available : why not use "*Bestimmtheit*"instead of "Determination", or "*Wesen*" instead of "*Essenz*?"[8] Or why, for example, should "the expression '*quantitativer Unterschied*', appear more fixed than if we were to say : '*Grossenunterschied*'?"[9] Hegel thought it essential for the genuine appropriation of a science, especially philosophy, that one possess it in one's own *Muttersprache*. As Hegel sums it up,

---

[4] *Ibid.*

[5] *Ibid.*, p. 15.

[6] *Ibid.*, p. 30.

[7] *Ibid.*, p. XXII.

[8] G.W.F. Hegel, *Vorlesungen über die Geschichte der Philosophie*, III, Vol. XIX of *Sämtliche Werke*, ed. H. Glockner (Stuttgart : Fr. Frommanns, 1928), p. 476; *Lectures on the History of Philosophy*, trs. E.S. Haldane & F. Simson (London : Routledge & Kegan Paul, 1963), III, 352.

[9] K. Rosenkranz, *G.W.F. Hegels Leben* (Darmstadt : Wissenschaftliche Buchgesellschaft, 1969), p. 183.

...it is only when a nation possesses a science in its own language that it can really be said to belong to it; and in Philosophy most of all this is requisite. For thought has in it this very moment of pertaining to self-consciousness or of being absolutely its own; when one's own language is the vehicle of expression,...it is immediately present to our consciousness that the conceptions are absolutely its own; it has to deal with these at all times, and they are in no way foreign to it. The Latin language has a phraseology, a definite sphere and range of conception; it is at once taken for granted that when men write in Latin they are at liberty to be dull; ... [10]

Hegel, like Leibniz, saw a close connection between the intellectual liberation of a people, through its ability to think and speak in its *Muttersprache*, and its freedom. Hegel believed that the intellectual liberation of the German people began when it stopped praying, and reading the Bible, in Latin. It will be consummated only when it learns to think scientifically, i.e., philosophically, in German as well, for "to have one's own right to speak and think in one's own language really belongs to liberty."[11] Both Hegel and Leibniz even saw the use of Latin, rather than Gothic or German, script as affecting the political consciousness of the German people. Both, however, refrained explicitly from advocating any kind of linguistic purity, and were willing to use any foreign words if no appropriate German ones could be discovered or invented.

Both Leibniz and Hegel saw the ordinary German language as an excellent repository of words and expressions for developing a philosophical language. Both advocated, for example, the refurbishing of the language of the old German *Schwärmer* for theological and epistemological discourse. Nevertheless, it is in their differing notions as to exactly *what* elements constitute the strength and sources of the German language for philosophy that one detects their differing conceptions of the nature of philosophical discourse. Leibniz admired the German language especially for its richness in sense-oriented terms. Its wealth of vocabulary for concrete objects give the Germans an excellent foundation for future intellectual development. Though Leibniz bemoaned the existing lack of proper abstract terms in German, he nevertheless found this condition to be a definite advantage as well. For, along with a lamentable lack of *abstract* terms, there was a commendable lack of artificial and equivocal ones as well. In fact the present backwardness of the German language for doing philosophy is due to its inability to assimilate Latin and Latinisms, unlike French or Italian. Such a language and its constructions are simply incompatible with

---

[10] *Geschichte der Philosophie*, III, p. 476; Haldane and Simson, III, 351-352.
[11] *Geschichte der Philosophie*, III, p. 257; Haldane and Simson, III, 150.

good German. In a striking passage from the Preface Leibniz wrote to the works of Nizolius (1670)—worth citing at length—he strongly attacks the implication that German is therefore an inferior language for philosophy; indeed, just the opposite is true.

> ...in the daughter-languages of Latin, a term of barbarous Latinity can easily be converted into good French or Italian through a slight twist. Hence many terms of Scholastic philosophy have been retained in some way in French translation. But no one has attempted such a thing in German without being hissed by everybody. Whoever wishes to retain or to twist Latin terms into German will not be philosophizing in German but in Latin. And to no avail; he would not be understood by anyone ignorant of Latin, for unlike Italian and French, German is worlds removed from the Latin. The reason why philosophy has only more recently been dealt with here in the vernacular is that the German language is incompatible, not with philosophy, but with a barbarous philosophy. And since this barbarous way of philosophizing has only lately been rejected it is not surprising that our language has been slow to come into philosophical use... [12]

In other words, if properly exploited, the current backwardness of the German language, that is its lack of abstract terms and its abundance of *concrete* ones, can serve as a basis for proper intellectual development. For the Germans have a convenient touchstone (*Probierstein*) for detecting fiction and insubstantiality : namely, its intranslatability into ordinary, good German.

> ... I venture to say that no European language is better suited than German for this testing and examination of philosophical doctrines by a living tongue. For German is very rich and complete in real-terms, to the envy of all other languages.[13]

It is interesting that the above distinction between Romance and Germanic languages was noted by Marx in a footnote to the opening section of *Das Kapital*. After citing a passage from Locke, Marx continues by noting that even in 17th Century English (as a Germanic language), words of Germanic origin (i.e., "worth") are used to describe the actual or immediate object while words of Latin origin (i.e., "value") are used to express reflexive or abstract notions.[14]

The immediate connection of ordinary German with perceived empirical

---

[12] G.W. Leibniz, *Philosophical Papers and Letters*, tr., ed., with intro. by Leroy Loemker (2nd ed. rev.; Dordrecht, Netherlands : D. Reidel, 1970), p. 125.

[13] *Ibid.*

[14] "Im 17. Jahrhundert finden wir noch häufig bei englischen Schriftstellern '*Worth*' für Gebrauchswert und '*Value*' für *Tauschwert*, ganz im Geist einer Sprache, die es liebt, die *unmittelbare* Sache germanisch und die *reflektierte* Sache romanisch auszudrücken." Karl Marx, *Ökonomische Schriften*, eds. H.-J. Lieber & B. Kautsky (Stuttgart : Cotta-Verlag, 1962), I, 4.

reality gives a truth and clarity to popularly used terms that is lacking in other languages. When ordinary language is directly anchored in empirical reality, it is easier to determine one distinct meaning of a word in the language. In this way, the danger of equivocation and ambiguity are greatly reduced, since there will be a clearly defined (and hopefully easily perceived) relationship between each word and the object or concept it signifies. Ideally, each word would clearly correspond to one and only one idea and *vice-versa*.

Furthermore, if such a situation could in truth obtain, then the problem of the translatability of one natural language into another — or of the proper set of symbols (the Universal Characteristic) into a natural language—is greatly facilitated. Leibniz's later hope of developing an ideographic set of symbols (e.g., like Chinese characters or hieroglyphics) that could be "read off" or translated into any spoken language, is influenced by his belief that a definite perceivable relationship existed between many simple objects or concepts and our words (especially German words) for denoting them. I believe that Leibniz's ideal of such a universal written language with symbols isomorphically and congruently denoting natural objects or simple rational ideas (the totality of which exists in the mind of God) can in part be traced back to his long-standing belief in the naturalness and primitiveness of certain languages, in particular Greek and German. Lengthy sections of Part III of the *Nouveaux Essais* are devoted to showing the natural. primitive relationship (for example, onomatopoeia) between certain concrete objects or actions and certain German root-words.

I mention this curious side of Leibniz's thought only so that one may see that Leibniz's conception of the German language's relation to the reality it is describing or expressing is, in part at least, a natural and not a conventional one. In other words, for Leibniz, key elements in the vernacular German language or Germanic languages, and hopefully all elements of some future universal characteristic and language could be expected to reveal knowledge about the nature of the human mind, and physical reality itself. The true primitive language (cf. Boehme's notion of an Adamic language, which Leibniz occasionally refers to), of which German retains many traces, is natural and not conventional. Though, as we shall soon see, Leibniz eventually abandoned any hope that an ordinary language could become the vehicle for philosophical knowledge, he continued to do research into the origins of words, I would speculate partly in the hope that he could discover further natural or real words or characters whose very oral/aural configurations would reveal something about ultimate reality—both physical and mental. In this connection, it should not be forgotten that Leibniz saw the foundations of the Universal Characteristic not only deciphering the book of nature, but as equivalent to demonstrating the existence of God as well.[15]

Whereas Leibniz sees the intellectual forte of the German language in its concrete and direct expressions, Hegel finds it in the abstract and equivocal terms of ordinary language. German is fortunate that it has so many purely abstract, yet familiar words of its own that it has no need for Latin or foreign terms to philosophize.

> "*Sein*," "*Nichtsein*," "*Eines*," "*Vieles*," "*Beschaffenheit*," "*Grösse*," and so forth are such purely abstract forms (*reine Wesen*), with which we nevertheless "keep house" in our everyday life.[16]

Hegel believed that in using such words, we become alive to certain contextual implications and etymological resonances that impart a vividness and "movement" to the ideas which these terms are meant to denote, thereby avoiding a static, formalistic interpretation of reality, "whereby the spirit and life of the matter itself (*der Sache Selbst*) disappear."[17] Even such colloquial phrases as "*an (und für) sich*" can prepare us for the perspectives we must progressively adopt to attain finally the speculative viewpoint.

Hegel also thought that the German language had the advantage that some of its words had the peculiarity

> of having not only different but opposite meanings so that one cannot fail to recognize a speculative spirit of the language in them : it can delight a thinker to come across such words and to find the union of opposites naively shown in the dictionary as one word with opposite meanings, although this result of speculative thinking is nonsensical to the understanding. Philosophy therefore stands in no need of a special terminology... [18]

The best known example of such a word for Hegel is "*aufheben*," which expresses one of the most important notions of his philosophy. The dictionary cites both the negative (to cease, to finish) and the positive (to keep, to preserve) meanings of "*aufheben*"; Hegel finds this use of one word for two opposing meanings striking and quite congenial to speculative thinking.

Another well-known ploy of Hegel's is his playing on the etymologies of certain German words in order to make the reader aware of the speculative or dialectical elements resident in ordinary language. I mention only one—his playing on various tenses of the verb "to be" (*Sein*) to illustrate

---

[15] P. Wiener, "Notes on Leibniz's Conception of Logic and its Historical Context," *Philosophical Review*, XLVIII, 6 (1939), 568, n. 4.

[16] *Hegels Leben*, p. 183.

[17] *Ibid*.

[18] G.W.F. Hegel, *Wissenschaft der Logik I*, ed. G. Lasson (Hamburg : Meiner, 1967), p. 10; *Hegel's Science of Logic*, tr. A.V. Miller (London : Allen & Unwin, 1969), p. 32.

the transition from Being to Essence in the "*Logik*." Being (*Sein*) "is" and "is not," i.e., has been (*gewesen*). Essence (*Wesen*) is therefore transcended Being (*Sein*).[19]

What is important for us to note in these examples is the *type* of words that Hegel finds conducive to his ends — simple, but abstract words, purely German (that is, non-Latin), that are vague and often equivocal. Furthermore, the word "language" for Hegel always refers specifically to such words, phrases or sentences as occur in ordinary language. He never uses the word "*Sprache*" to refer either to artificial or logical languages or to metaphorical "languages"—like the "language of Nature."

III. Leibniz on Philosophical Language

Given the different views that Leibniz and Hegel had on the aspects of the German language worth cultivating for philosophy, it should not be surprising that they hold radically differing notions on the nature of an adequate philosophical language in general. Leibniz imputes most of the confusion and disagreement among men to the imperfections of language,[20] that is, to its ambiguities and unclear words and expressions. If we can make the meaning of our words clear and precise — at least in the sciences and philosophy—we can "destroy the tower of Babel" [21] which now separates and confuses mankind. Though Leibniz found clarity and precision in a natural language such as German or Latin, he apparently came to realize that the degree of precision necessary for philosophy could ultimately be found only in some sort of Universal Characteristic, a written language (which could also be sounded) where each particular mark (either figural signs, letters or numbers—Leibniz seriously considered all three of these possibilities; he even toyed with the idea of using musical sounds or colors as the basis for his Characteristic) would unequivocally denote one particular idea. The analysis of composite signs or groups of signs, or the synthesis of particular signs, could properly be executed according to

---

[19] *Wissenschaft der Logik II*, p. 3; Miller, p. 389. Hegel notes that occasionally the German language expresses certain conceptual abstractions which not even Latin possesses. For example, the above distinction between being and "having been" (and therefore "not being") — between Being (*Sein*) and Essence (*Wesen*) — which is preserved in German is not present in Latin, a language usually praised for its precisely reflected distinctions. "... das Ens begreift sowohl *Sein* als *Wesen* in sich, fur welchen Unterschied unsere Sprache glücklicherweise den verschiedenen Ausdruck gerettet hat." *Wissenschaft der Logic I*, p. 46; Miller, p. 63.

[20] *New Essays*, III, Chapter ix, Paragraph 21, p. 375.

[21] *New Essays*, III, Chapter ix, Paragraph 9, p. 373.

certain principles of calculation, which hopefully could be applied in a strict mechanical fashion.

Summing up the advantage of such a characteristic over natural languages, Leibniz says that although the latter are very useful to thinking, they have countless ambiguities which do not make them amenable to the principles of calculation,[22] since the identical word or expression of a natural language can have different equivalents. On the other hand,

> only the signs of the arithmetician and algebraist perform the truly admirable service whereby all thinking occurs through the employment of characters and an error in thought is simply an error in calculation.[23]

In this brief paper, we cannot enter into all the details (or difficulties) of Leibniz's notion of a Universal Characteristic, or rather notions, since he never espoused, or even clearly formulated, one definite theory about its nature or function. What is of importance to us is that even those aspects of a natural (i.e., German) language which Leibniz prized for philosophy were not, and could not be, sufficient for an adequate philosophical language. It is Leibniz's later apparent rejection of ordinary language for philosophy which I wish to highlight here. It is instructive to note that Leibniz's view that the essential "qualities of philosophical discourse [,] ...of speech seeking certainty are clarity and truth",[24] was invoked early in his life (1670) in connection with his discussion of the positive role that ordinary language can play for philosophy! Whether the rejection of a natural language (with all its unavoidable ambiguities and varied connotations) in the quest for clarity and truth is compatible in any way with advocating its further development for philosophy, as Leibniz apparently thought it was, is a question that many of our colleagues, especially in Anglo-American circles, must ask themselves. In any event, Leibniz was among those, not uncommon in the 17th century, who, as one writer has recently put it,

> we find...offering new signs modeled on the principle behind Arabic numerals, algebraic notation, and even hieroglyphics or Chinese characters...[and] hop-[ing] that such signs might eventually become the only vehicle for philosophical knowledge.[25]

---

[22] G.W. Leibniz, *Fragmente zur Logik*, selected, tr. with notes by Franz Schmidt (Berlin : Akademie Verlag, 1960), p. 111.

[23] *Ibid.*, p. 112.

[24] *Philosophical Papers and Letters*, p. 122.

[25] H. Aarsleff, "Leibniz on Locke on Language," *American Philosophical Quarterly*, I, 3 (1964), 166.

IV. Hegel on Leibniz and Philosophical Language

Hegel's answer to this question is clear and unequivocal. He would accept no such ultimate distinction between a technical philosophical language and ordinary German. To be sure, scientific philosophy for Hegel is not merely the distillation of common sense and language. Hegel did believe that philosophy had to develop a terminology of its own, but he thought that a natural language should serve as the source and medium of philosophical discourse. Space does not permit me to detail Hegel's position on the nature and role of philosophical language,[26] but we can get some idea of it by examining his attack on Leibniz's notion of a Universal Characteristic. Hegel's *Auseinandersetzung* with Leibniz on this matter might be generally characterized as a defense of spoken natural language as the medium for philosophy [27] against those, such as Leibniz, who believed that only some sort of formal mathematical or symbolical language was adequate for the task. I will begin with Hegel's discussion of such a language, found in Paragraph 459 of the *Enzyklopädie*.[28]

In this paragraph and in a parallel section of the 3rd Course of the *Philosophische Propadeutik*,[29] Hegel addresses himself at length to the insurmountable practical and pedagogical problems of developing and transmitting a comprehensive *written* symbolism for any Universal Characteristic. I will pass over the details of Hegel's critique, and possible responses to it, but I mention it to show that his interest in the problem was not only theoretical. His theoretical objections to Leibniz's ideal for a philosophical language are what concern us here today.

Hegel begins Paragraph 459 by noting that signs *qua* signs exist only as "*aufgehobene*," as a given in space whose original meaning has been negated by consciousness. He continues by noting that the true self-transcending

---

[26] For a full treatment of this topic, see the author's *Language in the Philosophy of Hegel* (The Hague : Mouton, 1973).

[27] J. Hyppolite, *Logique et existence : Essay sur la Logique de Hegel* (Paris : Presses Universitaires de France, 1961), p. 61.

[28] G.W.F. Hegel, *Enzyklopädie der philosophischen Wissenschaften im Grundrisse* (1830), eds. F. Nicolin and O. Pöggeler (Hamburg : Meiner, 1959), pp. 369 ff.; *Hegel's Philosophy of Mind*, tr. W. Wallace with *Zusätze* tr. A.V. Miller (Oxford : Clarendon, 1971), pp. 213 ff.

[29] "Einer allgemeinen philosophischen Schriftsprache, wovon Mehrere den Gedanken gefasst haben, steht die unbestimmtbar grosse Menge von Zeichen entgegen, die nötig wäre, besonders zu erfinden und zu lernen." *G.W.F. Hegel : Studienausgabe in 3 Bänden*, eds. K. Löwith & M. Riedel (Frankfurt : Fischer Bücherei, 1968), III, 186-187, Paragraph 161.

quality which a sign has for the intellect is better seen when it is given an ideal existence through a sounded, temporal sign which disappears as soon as it is uttered.[30] Vocal, rather than written language is primary, both chronologically and philosophically, since the former relies upon the *temporal* nature of sound, while the latter is based upon spatial configurations. Hegel defends at length an ordinary alphabetical language, as opposed to a formal type of sign-language, in which each simple idea would be represented by a simple sign.

Hegel called a sign-language, such as Leibniz proposed, a hieroglyphic one, since it used simple signs or figures to represent (often with pictorial similarity) simple ideas. Such a language presupposes an atomistic view of reality and thought. It assumes that one can analytically reduce the various *Vorstellungen* and abstract thoughts present to consciousness to a particular set of simple signs, representing simple ideas, and also (re)produce such *Vorstellungen* out of the total set of logically simple ideas or terms.[31]

Hegel claims that such an analytic, atomistic approach to the problem of human expression fails to recognize the basic role of language as a system of conventional (in themselves meaningless) signs, i.e., names, designed to refer as pointers to certain mental objects which are being entertained or communicated. The true role of language is to present as directly and immediately as possible the various mental intuitions and constructs present to consciousness. Therefore, Hegel thought that such an analytical approach resulted in individual signs being viewed as definitions and pictorial representations rather than as arbitrary signs conveying their meanings only when synthesized with the actual experience of the speaker or auditor. With this goal in mind, the necessary qualities for a language are ideally present in its spoken, and next best in its alphabetical form, viz., having those characteristics which stress that language serves only as an external medium which immediately points beyond itself to a nonsensuous universal world of meaning. The most adequate forms of expression concentrate themselves into temporal moments, rather than spatial ideograms, thereby gaining their true existence only in the stream of memory and the interrelating power of thinking consciousness. In an alphabetical language, the ultimate purpose of a language as a set of intrinsically self-transcending phonograms is most apparent. In such a thoroughly conventional mode of writing, such as an alphabetical one, the visible (i.e., written in space) stands in proper relation to the audible (i.e., spoken in time), because the

---

[30] *Enzyklopädie*, p. 369; Wallace, pp. 213-214.
[31] *Enzyklopädie*, p. 372; Wallace, p. 217.

visible language relates itself to the sounded one only as a sign, [for] the intellect expresses itself immediately and unconditionally through speaking.[32]

Hegel's conception of language is based largely on the qualities resident in language as a spoken, temporal medium.

Furthermore, the dialectical nature of knowledge requires that such signs or names be understood as pointing to notions or ideas that are not always the same or rigidly determined, but depend for their meaning on their contextual relations, that is, on the character of the knowing activity which redintegrates them according to its own level of experience and knowledge. Even when our ideas are "broken down" and analyzed into a composite of symbols and signs, thinking organically relates them to a concrete, specific context, and reunites them into a single thought.[33] Thus Hegel rejects, as he says elsewhere, the

pet idea of Leibniz, embraced by him in his youth, and in spite of its immaturity and shallowness not relinquished by him even in later life, the idea of a *characteristica universalis* of notions—a language of symbols in which each notion would be represented as a relation proceeding from others or in its relation to others — as though in rational combination, which is essentially dialectical, a content still retained the same determinations *that it possesses when fixed in isolation.*[34]

Improper use of an hieroglyphic, as Hegel calls it, reflects an erroneous view of the nature of the truths of philosophy, their interrelationships and expression. One does not arrive at an understanding of the nature of philosophical truth (of the Notion, or *Begriff*, in Hegel's terms) by seeking

to fix it by spatial figures and algebraic signs for the purpose of the *outer eye* and an *uncomprehending, mechanical mode of treatment* such as a calculus.

Rather,

Since man has in language a means of designation peculiar to Reason, it is an idle fancy to search for a less perfect mode of representation to plague oneself with.[35]

It should be obvious that Hegel's conception of language is worthless to someone, like Leibniz, who thinks that the primary purpose of language is to remove all possible vagueness and equivocality by narrowing down and analyzing all ordinary terms of speech into a form, artificial or otherwise, which would allow for the univocal designation and expression of particular ideas or images and their respective components. It should be

---

[32] *Enzyklopädie*, p. 374; Wallace, p. 218.
[33] *Enzyklopädie*, p. 373; Wallace, p. 217.
[34] *Wissenschaft der Logik II*, p. 332; Miller, p. 685.
[35] *Wissenschaft der Logik II*, p. 259; Miller, p. 618.

just as obvious, however, that for Hegel, the primary purpose of language as a philosophical tool is to make use of the equivocality and flexibility of meaning and expression present in ordinary language.

Only in its natural form could language serve as the "means of designation peculiar to reason," and as the external manifestation (*Dasein*) of Spirit itself.

Though Leibniz and Hegel both saw ordinary language as a source for developing a language of philosophy, Leibniz ultimately rejected such a medium as inadequate for the task for almost the *same* reasons that Hegel found it conducive to his endeavors. I have tried to show that Leibniz's growing belief in the need for distinguishing between an ordinary language, and a technical one for philosophy—and Hegel's rejection of such a distinction—should not be explained simply on historical grounds, but arises out of their differing conceptions of the essential role of language in the pursuit of philosophical truth, and indeed in the very different conceptions each had of that very truth itself.

HEGEL'S CRITIQUE OF KANT*

JOHN E. SMITH

Yale Uuiversity

One of the problems to be faced by anyone seeking to understand and to evaluate Hegel's treatment of other philosophers is that he never seems to regard their thought as having any tenure beyond the framework of his own philosophical account of the history of philosophy.[1] All philosophical standpoints and systems are understood by him in terms of his own comprehensive philosophy of spirit. To a large extent, of course, every philosopher proceeds in this way; how else are we to interpret and assess a given position except in terms established by our own view of what is real and what is true? But in Hegel's case which is, admittedly, extraordinary because of his having made history decisive for philosophy, one feels both the presence and the force of his philosophical vision to a peculiar degree at just those points where he considers the thought of others. His treatment of Kant is no exception, and, in fact, he sees Kant as most penetrating in his understanding at precisely those points where he most nearly approximates Hegel's own position. For example, according to Hegel, the singular merit of Kant's *Critique of Judgment* is that in his treatment of the Ideas of nature and freedom, he approached genuinely "speculative" thought, in contrast to criticism, and at the same time caught a glimpse of the Idea as a self-determining reality. Or again, he claims that Kant was, in his treat-

---

* This paper appeared earlier in *The Review of Metaphysics*, Vol. XXVI, No. 3 (March 1973), and is reprinted here with permission of the editor.

[1] References to Hegel's *Geschichte der Philosophie* are found in *Werke*, ed. Hermann Glockner (Stuttgart, 1959), vols. 17-19; the corresponding English references are found in *Hegel's Lectures on the History of Philosophy*, edited and translated by E.S. Haldane and F.H. Simson, 3 vols. (London, 1896). The text of the *Logik* which forms the first part of Hegel's *Enzyklopädie* is found in Glockner, vol. 8; references are to the numbered sections in the original and the corresponding English references are found in *The Logic of Hegel*, trans. W. Wallace (2nd ed., Oxford, 1892). References to *Glauben und Wissen* are to the Felix Meiner edition. All references to Kant's *Critique of Pure Reason* are to the Kemp-Smith translation.

ment of the categories, closest of the truth when he grasped their interrelationships and attributed their triadic arrangement to the fact that the third category results from the application of the first category to the second, which, if we take the unity, plurality, totality triad as an example, means that as we proceed in the analysis of something from unity to plurality, we must understand its totality as the unity of the plurality which resulted. It is clear that Hegel approved of Kant's account because it is in accord not only with his own self-reflected triadism, but also with Hegel's persistent attempt to develop the categories from each other based on his demand that they not be accepted from without "as they are classified in ordinary logic."[2]

I am calling attention at the outset to Hegel's procedure in interpreting the thought of others not to suggest that he simply failed to represent their views, but rather to indicate that he invariably sets them down in the midst of his own systematic idealism and judges them in accordance with the adequacy of their response to questions posed by his own position. One consequence of this approach is that Hegel views a philosophical position not primarily in terms of its own unifying intention, but from the standpoint of the Idea and his own logic of the Notion plus the assumption that this logic is working itself out through the history of thought. If we apply this principle to his treatment of Kant, it becomes clear the the central point of Hegel's critique must be that Kant failed to hold fast to the actuality of reason and the force of the Idea because he opted for the primacy of the understanding and its knowledge of finite reality over all speculative thought. In short, Kant was attacked for subordinating what Hegel made paramount. In this sense the ultimate validity of Hegel's critique of Kant is made to depend on the viability of Hegel's own system.

---

[2] *History of Philosophy*, Glockner 19.567; English trans. Haldane, 438.9. It is worth noticing on this point that despite Kant's claim of completeness for the table of categories (B 105-107), there is very little indication in the *Critique* as to how one would even go about answering the question, "Why these categories and no others?" Hegel, on the other hand, although we may find fault with his particular results, does propose to answer this question through the "labor of the notion," i.e. by "showing" through the actual development of the categories from each other in the dialectical attempt to think Being, how the totality of Being is actually articulated through those categories and no others. In the end, of course, the argument takes the form of claiming "this or nothing" and, on his view, anyone who objects then has the task of providing an alternative "this," that is, an alternative system of categorial articulation. But in any case the actual working out of a consistent and coherent, all-encompassing scheme with a set of categories does provide some ground for answering the initial question; one can say, "Look, we have articulated the whole with these categories and no others are required because there is nothing more to include."

Hegel's examination of Kant's philosophy is spread over many of his writings starting with *Glauben und Wissen*. Major comments are found in *Phenomenology*, the *Encyclopedia*, in the *Lectures on the History of Philosophy* and in the *Philosophy of Right*. I shall have to limit myself and, therefore, I have decided to confine attention to the treatment of theoretical reason and to exclude the moral philosophy, not because that criticism is not also instructive but rather in view of the fact that it follows largely from principles developed by Hegel in his analysis of Kant's theory of knowledge based on the distinction between understanding and reason. Moreover, in the interest of focusing issues for discussion, I shall not attempt an historical account of the development in Hegel's treatment of Kant from beginning to end. The central points stand out in the later writings through repetition, although it is clear that certain points much emphasized in *Glauben und Wissen* such as the identification of the transcendental imagination with "reason itself," do not figure largely in Hegel's later discussion of Kant's thought.

In what follows, three basic issues will be presented and, while in the nature of the case, they are not independent of each other, they can be given separate treatment. *First*, there is the matter of Hegel's understanding of Kant's enterprise including the question whether there can be a critique of knowledge and, if so, how it is to be carried out. *Second*, there is Hegel's criticism of the "thing-in-itself" doctrine and the consequent charge against Kant of "subjectivism," which Hegel sometimes expressed in the thesis that the Kantian categories are "meaningless" (*bedeutungslos*) apart from the materials of sense. *Third*, there is the examination of the grounds upon which Kant opted for the priority of the finite knowledge of the understanding over the claim of reason, which at the same time raises the question of the relation between experience and the transcendental ideas. Limitations of space do not permit an equally detailed account of all these issues, but each is important and must figure to some extent in any discussion of Hegel's critique of Kant.

I

One of Hegel's most fundamental criticisms of Kant concerns the basic enterprise of making a critique of the cognitive faculty itself as distinct from, in Hegel's language, proceeding at once to think the Absolute.[3] It has been suggested that what divides the two thinkers can be summed up

---

[3] See *Glauben und Wissen*, Meiner edition, p. 14.

by saying that Kant believed in the priority and necessity of *criticism*, whereas Hegel did not and consequently was forced to proceed with his own system in a fashion which, in Kant's view, could only be described as *dogmatic*. This summary is not entirely correct; a more adequate expression of the relation between the two positions on this head would make it clear that both believed "the forms of thought must be made an object of investigation,"[4] but that they differed considerably in their conceptions of the manner in which the investigation should be carried out. And since the two alternatives they manifest reflect a fundamental division in modern philosophy, some consideration of this issue will at the same time call attention to the contemporaneity of both thinkers.

In the *Lectures on the History of Philosophy*,[5] Hegel credits Kant with having taken an important step forward in focusing on knowledge as a subject for analysis. And he expresses a similar view in the long *Zusatz* to Section 41 of the *Encyclopedia*, commending Kant for making the concepts through which the old metaphysics was expressed the subject of criticism. Hegel, therefore, was by no means opposed to the aim of making thought and its categories the object of critical scrutiny. But, as was suggested previously, everything depends upon how this is to be done. "In particular," says Hegel, "he [Kant] demanded a criticism of the faculty of cognition as preliminary to its exercise."[6] But, he continues, there at once arises the "misconception of already knowing before you know," since on Hegel's terms the analysis of knowledge and the faculty of cognition must itself constitute an instance of cognition. This point is, of course, crucial for the Kantian program; what, it may be asked, is the logical status of criticism, and, more specifically, of the conclusions arrived at by transcendental philosophy with regard to such issues as the relation between the categories and the sensible manifold, the relation between understanding and reason, and, finally, the limitation of reason's legitimate employment to the empirical sphere? Although Kant regarded criticism as proceeding with certainty because its problems can be stated and resolved from the standpoint of the rational faculties themselves, it is curious that there are not many passages in the *Critique* where its pronouncements are specifically referred to as "knowledge." And, indeed, he must have been aware that critical philosophy itself does not locate itself within the confines of either of the two bodies of thought — mathematics and general science of nature —

---

[4] *Encyclopedia* 41; Wallace p. 84.
[5] Glockner, 19.556; English trans., p. 429.
[6] *Ibid.*

which stand for him as the paradigms of actual knowledge. Critical philosophy, presumably, is on another level from that occupied by the knowledge which stands in need of justification,[7] and its own justification must rest in the end on the claim that it marks out those necessary conditions without which there could be no experience at all. Kant could reply to Hegel's charge that we are seeking to know before we know in the Kantian enterprise by saying that this preliminary "knowing" represents a peculiar mode of cognition *vis-à-vis*, for example, knowing a proposition describing the behavior of a physical system or knowing that a given geometrical theorem can be deduced from Euclid's axioms. The peculiarity would consist in the fact that the critical knowing purports to specify the conditions requisite for all knowing. But Hegel insists that the knowing involved in the examination of knowledge, whatever particular form it may take, be an actual knowing and not merely a propaedeutic to actually knowing.

The dividing line between the two thinkers, however, need not be drawn at the "knowing before you know" issue; more important is Hegel's objection to the *separation* of the activity of criticism from what might be called the "first order" knowing which is the subject of criticism. This, I take it, is Hegel's more fundamental objection to Kant's procedure. He interpreted Kant's analysis of judgment and of the table of categories derived therefrom as an attempt to find the ground of knowledge in universal and necessary conditions which are, in the nature of the case, abstract and separated not only from their content, but from their *activity* in constituting what we have called "first order" knowing as well. Hegel, by contrast, claimed that criticism and the knowing which is under criticism must be together in a dynamic process of development. The point is well expressed in the same passage of the *Encyclopedia* to which we have referred:

So that what we want is to combine in our process of inquiry the *action* of the forms of thought with a criticism of them. The forms of thought must be studied in their essential nature and complete development: they are at once the object of research and the *action* of that object. Hence they examine themselves: in their own *action* they must determine their limits, and point out their defects. This is that *action* of thought, which will hereafter be especially considered under the name of Dialectic, and regarding which we need only at the outset observe that, instead of being brought to bear upon the categories from without, it is immanent in their own *action*.[8]

---

[7] There is, of course, a problem involved in speaking of "justification" since Kant did not regard mathematics as standing in need of a certificate from philosophy (B 199ff.), but it is clear that, in the case of knowledge involving the dynamical categories, he thought otherwise.

[8] *Encyclopedia* 41, Wallace, pp. 84-5. Emphasis added.

Hegel's fundamental complaint, then, is that Kant analyzed the categories as functions of thought, not when they were functioning in actual knowing, but only in their status as necessary conditions for knowing contained in the formal structure of the understanding for the purpose of providing the ground upon which objectivity is based. Hegel wanted to see the categories at work, as it were, in the determination of what is to be known, whereas on his view, Kant considered them only when they were "idling" in the understanding as conditions for the possibility of experience without exhibiting themselves as operative in actual knowing.

Criticism, for Kant, had a positive and a negative side; on the positive side it meant the transcendental determination of those a priori elements which guarantee objectivity in knowledge by virtue of the fact that nothing can be thought as an object except through the one universal and necessary set of categories which structure the faculty of understanding possessed by the transcendental subject. On the negative side, criticism has to set the limits of knowledge and of the employment of human faculties and also explain satisfactorily how it happens that reason finds itself inevitably asking questions which it is unable to answer in a cognitive form. Kant clearly regarded criticism as a preliminary to the further exercise of our rational faculties in knowing what is other than themselves and this point is established by his claim that in transcendental philosophy we consider questions "obliquely" and are not directly concerned with knowledge of objects, but rather with the relation between an idea and an object insofar as it can be thought a priori. For Hegel, on the other hand, criticism is no preliminary, but an immanent affair in which the meaning, scope and validity of a category are to be determined by discovering what feature and how much of reality it can express in relation to other categories through the actual process of knowing the world. The difference between them is quite fundamental and presents itself as a gulf which seems impossible to span. Kant, not unlike Descartes, is a *foundationalist* who demands criteria and wants to establish knowledge on the universal and necessary, albeit in transcendental terms, which means the argument to the conditions rather than any appeal to the intuitively self-evident. By contrast, Hegel looked to *outcomes* and *results* so that for him the emphasis in criticism falls not on the structure or contemporaneous pattern of cognitive faculties, but rather on the action of thought in actually interpreting reality and in expressing its intelligible structure. In the former case one looks not to the particular content manifested in some actual process of knowing, but to formal and transcendental criteria which are meant to define knowing as such. In the latter case, one starts with particular determinations of things for the purpose of discovering, through a critical analysis of the interrelation between the categories involved, just what and how much of reality these categories actually express. An atomistic philosophy, for example, has, from this standpoint its element of truth, but its inadequacy and relative abstractness is brought to light only when it is forced to face the task of expressing the whole of reality including actual togethernesses of things which manifest the organic feature of existence. The Kantian type of criticism focuses on the entrance requirements to the arena of knowledge, the Hegelian type on the critical examination of actual interpretations that have already been entered.

The truth in the Kantian approach is that no philosophical position can remain naive and avoid the exposure and critical examination of either its fundamental categories or its basic program. The Kantian insight exposes the error of those who claim that they are just "doing" philosophy and who stare in amazement at anyone who asks for a critical account of what they are doing or of what they assume. But the chief difficulty of the Kantian approach is the risk of never reaching the discussion of actual philosophical theses, since all the dialectic is devoted to consideration of the preliminaries in the form of what you would, could, might mean or know if you were to propose any such theses — which you often do not. The truth in the Hegelian approach is that it sees the necessity of proceeding directly to *die Sache selbst*, since there is no presuppositionless philosophical preliminary which is neutral with respect to the question of the nature of knowledge or indeed of anything else. The problem posed by this approach is that it may fail to make explicit the existence of immanent criteria — concreteness, consistency, comprehensiveness — which are indeed invoked by the system, and were this not the case, there would be no ground for judging the *outcome* of a process of thought.

Another facet of Hegel's treatment of the critical philosophy as a program is represented by his persistent lumping of it together with the epistemology of Locke and describing both as "empirical psychology." Hegel was, I contend, mistaken in this view, even if it is true that Kant retained some of the assumptions of the classical empiricism he aimed to attack. In *Glauben und Wissen* [9] Hegel describes Kant's task as identical with Locke's, namely, to discover the limits of understanding so that it will not become hopelessly involved in matters which it does not have the power to resolve. Moreover, throughout the exposition of Kant in that work, Hegel calls his position "psychological" idealism. Much later in the *History of Philosophy*,[10] Hegel

---

[9] Meiner edition, p. 15.
[10] Glockner, 19.561; English trans. pp. 432-33.

was still claiming that Kant proceeds "psychologically, i.e., historically, in describing the modes of the knowing faculty."[11] And in reference to Kant's categories, Hegel contends that Kant accepted both the forms of intuition and the categories "in an empiric way." [12] Still further on in the discussion of Kant's treatment of reason, Hegel claims that Kant is still following the "psychological method" and that consequently he comes upon reason by the merest chance as if it made no difference whether it were a reality or not.[13] Exactly the same point is made in Introduction to the *Encyclopedia*, but there the emphasis falls on the order of Kant's exposition of the a priori elements of thought; this order, Hegel claims, "is solely based on psychological and historical grounds." [14]

Now it is obvious that no full scale account of what it is to be a transcendental philosophy as over against a "psychological" theory is possible here, but several crucial points may be made which will serve to place Kant's unique enterprise in proper perspective. Despite the force of current attacks on the viability of transcendental arguments, it cannot be denied that Kant had hit upon an ingenious and entirely novel approach to the nature of knowledge in terms that go beyond and between an ontologically rooted position like that of Leibniz and Spinoza, and a psychologically oriented approach like that of Hume and Locke. In seeking to delineate what Paton has called a "metaphysic of experience," Kant was defining knowledge in terms of a validity furnished by a priori elements without which there could be no experience at all. The approach is not to be confused with a genetic account and it is erroneously called "psychological" as was made clear by Kant in the statement, "though all of our knowledge begins with (*anheben*) experience, it does not follow that it all arises out of (*entspringen*) experience." [15] The key question concerning the a priori synthetic, moreover, points to the uniqueness of the Kantian position in attacking the dogma, based on a complete disjunction between reason and experience, that what is necessary cannot be empirical and what is empirical cannot be necessary. The idea that experience may have a necessary structure to be possible at all is not something which occurred to Kant's predecessors and it has been persistently misunderstood by many of his successors because they have tried to understand the purport of the "transcendental" in terms merely

---

[11] Hegel's description harks back to Locke's "plain, historical account" of knowledge in terms of a literal tracing of ideas to their origins in both sensation and reflection.

[12] Glockner, 19.567; English trans. p. 439.

[13] Glockner, 19.573. English trans, p. 443.

[14] *Encyclopedia*, Section 41; Wallace, p. 84.

[15] Bl; cf. B 166.

of some dyadic distinction between the "logical" and the "empirical," or even worse, between the "factual" and the "linguistic." The mark of this confusion coincides with the conflation of "a priori" and "analytic" which at once reduces to nonsense Kant's fundamental question. No justice can be done to Kant's position if it is approached on the basis of a dyad; a triadic distinction is necessary involving (a) material of sense, (b) formal logic represented by the principle of contradiction and (c) the transcendental elements which one hesitates to call "logic" because of possible confusion. The crucial point is that (b) and (c) must neither be confused nor lumped together. The best way to clarify the special character of the transcendental approach is to point out that the concepts "object" and "object of knowledge" [16] do *not* properly occur within the framework of formal logic as conceived by Kant. Formal logic is a necessary condition for all thought, but it is *not* a sufficient condition for determining what is meant by an "object" in the quite fundamental sense which the term assumes in the Kantian theory of knowledge. The entire transcendental apparatus of the esthetic and analytic is meant to be definitive of what it is to be an object. This apparatus cannot and must not be put down merely to the "logical" side in contrast with the sensible material taken as "empirical," because the analysis of being an object issues at the same time in the delineation of the general shape of experience, and that is not a matter of formal logic alone. Kant's deduction may be declared invalid, the transcendental approach may be rejected, but the fact remains that Kant's attempt to mark out the necessary conditions which must be met if there is to be any experience at all, not only distinguishes his view from all "historical" or genetic accounts, but it also defies legitimate interpretation in terms of a simple "logical"/"empirical" dichotomy. The necessary conditions are transcendental which means that they are neither purely "logical" in the sense of past or present formal logic, nor again are they "empirical" in the sense of sensible material. It is not clear that Hegel fully appreciated Kant's unique conception of the transcendental [17] as fitting neither into the "logical"/ "psychological" dyad nor the "logical"/"empirical" disjunction, and, therefore, he was content to describe Kant's approach as "psychological" and "historical." Such a characterization, however, does not do justice to the Kantian position. Perhaps the explanation is that Hegel was less concerned with the justification of empirical knowledge as such and more interested

---

[16] It seems clear that for Kant the two concepts must ultimately coincide.

[17] Hegel seems also not to have grasped the force of the *problem* to which Kant was addressing himself when he insisted on the synthetic character of mathematical judgments. Hegel accepted them as analytic without extended discussion.

in criticizing Kant for having acknowledged the unity of reason as an idea at the same time that he denied its actuality.

If, however, Hegel's description of Kant's view as "psychological" and "subjective" is seen as a fundamental rejection of the thesis that knowledge is confined to "appearance," that is another matter and the issue should be discussed without turning Kant's theory into something other than itself. For the peculiar fact about the doctrine of appearance in Kant is not only that the conditions for appearance are said to be universal and necessary, but the object of knowledge (B 236) is defined by him as that in the appearance which determines that it will be apprehended (i.e., judged) in accordance with universal rules. The point is that Kant's domain of appearance does not have to do with bent sticks in the water or with round coins which "look" elliptical from a certain perspective. In short, Kant's view on this head should not be discussed in the context of Locke and Hume and Hegel had a tendency to interpret Kant in that way.

II

That Hegel was opposed to Kant's doctrine of the thing-in-itself and his consequent limitation of human knowledge to the sphere of *Erscheinung* is well known and has often been repeated. The limitation in question forms the basis of Hegel's repeated charge of "subjectivism" and his claim that, for Kant, knowledge fails to include the things of the world. Hegel was, in this regard, a thorough-going realist: what we know is the things themselves, their properties, unities and relations. For Hegel, the real is not "behind" or "beyond," but actually *present* in what we apprehend. From this essentially Aristotelian vantage point, Hegel declared Kant's domain of *Erscheinung* insubstantial and subjective. The charge is familiar and does not need to be labored.

There is, however, an aspect of Hegel's criticism with regard to Kant's treatment of things which has not been given the attention it deserves. When, says Hegel, Kant proposed to interpret knowledge of an object in terms of an identity of consciousness and sensible appearance, he in fact failed to include the things themselves because in attributing to consciousness the properties of the thing, the thing itself is reduced to a mere abstract form of unity. But, Hegel contends, the properties are as essential to the thing as the unity. "It is more reasonable," says Findlay representing Hegel's view, "to treat the 'I' of self-consciousness as a self-reflected unity indifferent to what it cognizes, than to do so in the case of the thing and its properties."[18] Although Kant was undoubtedly correct in insisting on the spontaneity exhibited by the experiencing subject in contrast to those accounts of experience which reduce the knower to a passive recipient, there is reason to believe that he exaggerated what appeared to him as a clear asymmetry in the subject thinking the object. The subject judges the object in accordance with the a priori categories of the understanding and the unity, identity and objectivity of the object thought is established through the transcendental unity of apperception. The subject, in short, *thinks* or judges, and the object—is *thought* or judged. While, however, it is true that the object does not "think" the subject, it is also true that *only through thinking the object does the subject apprehend itself as a unified thinking subject* capable of exercising the functions represented by the categories in the formation of judgments. The subject, according to Kant, cannot legitimately think of itself as an object, but only as subject—a point on which Hegel in many places expressed agreement with Kant—and it is able to grasp itself as subject only to the extent that it finds that very subjectivity reflected in the transcendental analysis of the subject thinking or judging an object. Hegel's point is that a mutual or reciprocal relation should be acknowledged in which there is due recognition of the "I" of self-consciousness as a *self-reflected unity* which comes to light in the thinking of the object, whereas Kant placed all the emphasis on the unity bestowed on the object in virtue of its being thought by the subject. The unity of the subject for Kant, the unity of apperception which, as he says, is higher than the category of unity, is in fact a reflected unity apprehended solely through transcendental analysis. A proper regard for this fact, on Hegel's view, would have enabled Kant to do greater justice to the things themselves, both their unity and their properties, precisely because the spontaneous activity of the subject would then be counterbalanced by a recognition of the role played by objects in bringing the reflected unity of self-consciousness to light. When, moreover, undue emphasis is placed on the one-way relationship of the subject thinking the object, the relations of *the things themselves to each other* are likely to fall from sight and these relations form an important means whereby the unity and properties of the things become manifest.

Another feature of Hegel's indictment of the Kantian position as "subjectivism" is expressed in his oft repeated claim that the categories are "meaningless" (*bedeutungslos*) apart from the sensible manifold to which they are applied. Whereas I find myself in agreement with much of Hegel's critique of Kant, I do not believe that Hegel was entirely correct in this

---

[18] Findlay, *Hegel, A Re-examination* (London, 1958), p. 202.

charge and I am prepared to break a lance in Kant's behalf even if it becomes necessary at the same time to defend Kant against himself. For what complicates the situation is that Kant provided some of the evidence to be used against himself when, at times, he described the pure concepts of the understanding as "purely logical" (or as *sinnlos* apart from the empirical manifold) when he should have written "transcendental." Let us begin with Hegel's own statement from the *Lectures on the History of Philosophy* :

> For their own part, the categories are empty, unfilled, and they belong to thought. In order for them to be filled, material is required. They have content (*Inhalt*) only through the given manifold material of intuitions...and they have meaning (*Bedeutung*) only through their combination with this material.[19]

The principal question to be raised is whether Hegel means to assert that meaning is identical with reference or with the existence of the sensible content to which the category is applied. It would seem more plausible to say that for Kant, while the category is "empty" without intuition, it is not thereby meaningless, as if its meaning were indeed identical with the existence of the sensible content.

In B 284 Kant draws a clear distinction between the "formal conditions of experience" and some particular perception for the purpose of explaining that whatever is in agreement with these conditions is possible, whereas the actual requires, in addition, a connection with perception. We need not concern ourselves here with problems peculiar to the modal categories; the important point is that there is no warrant for supposing that the "meaning" of the elements expressing the a priori conditions — the forms of intuition and the categories—is uniquely furnished by the singular perception as if these elements had no meaning apart from their instantiation. Again, in B 252 (= A 207) where Kant is discussing the second analogy, he distinguishes the *form* of alteration from a specific content. He writes, "But apart from all question of what the content of the alteration, that is, what the state that is altered, may be, the form of every alteration...can still be considered a priori according to the law of causality and the conditions of time." From this it would seem clear that the concept of causality is not "meaningless" apart from its application to particular, actual forces. And, indeed, were this not the case, it would make no sense to distinguish, as Kant did at many points, between *thinking and knowing* an object (e.g., B 146, among many). Though no sensible intuition were actually given, we can still think and understand the general form or shape of experience. To adopt an example suggested by Russell, we do not know whether in

---

[19] Glockner, 19. pp. 568-69.

the year 2000 there will be any people in London, but if there are and any three of them stand in a row, one of them will be "between" the other two. This assertion is perfectly intelligible quite apart from reference to actual individuals standing in that relation. The meaningfulness of the pure spatial concept is *not* identical with the intuitional material which instantiates it on some actual occasion.

On the other hand, it must be admitted, there are passages in Kant which seem to point in the opposite direction. In B 298 Kant says that, with regard to every concept,[20] we grasp its "logical form" and consider the possibility of its having an object. Referring to the concept, Kant says, "In the absence of such object, it has no meaning (*Sinn*) and is completely lacking in content (*Inhalt*)."[21] Further along in the same discussion, he points out that the categories, apart from intuition, "have even less meaning (*Bedeutung*) than the pure sensible forms."[22] The category, understood as a mode of combination by the understanding, Kant declares, "signifies nothing at all" (*gar nichts bedeutet*), when no manifold is given.[23] Here Kant confuses meaning and reference,[24] and writes as if the "meaning" of a category is identical with its reference to an object, but surely he cannot mean to assert this identity, since apart from the sensible manifold, the a priori conditions of both sense and understanding retain their meaning as expressing the necessary shape of experience. Without the sensible manifold, the categories may be "empty," but they are not on that account meaningless. Kant does greater justice to his position when he writes, "The pure categories, apart from formal conditions of sensibility, have only transcendental meaning."[25] But it is precisely this meaning which defines the generic structure of experience.

When Hegel declared that Kant's categories are "meaningless" in the absence of the intuitional manifold, he was correct only if he meant that the categories under those circumstances are empty. If, however, he meant

---

[20] B 300 makes it clear that categories and principles are involved along with empirical concepts.

[21] B 298.

[22] B 306.

[23] *Ibid.*

[24] It is difficult to find terminology which will not be misleading. The particular version of the *Sinn/Bedeutung* distinction offered by Frege and familiar to us, was, of course, not available to Kant and we must not assume it.

[25] B 305; cf. B 166 n. where Kant wants to stress the point that "for thought" the categories are not limited by the conditions of sensible intuition; it is the "knowledge" claim that requires limitation to intuition. "In the absence of intuition," he continues, "the thought of the object may still have its true and useful consequences ...."

to deny their transcendental meaning in calling the empty categories meaningless, he was mistaken.

It would, however, be unfair to Hegel on this point if we did not take into account the curious section 43 of the *Encyclopedia*, where the question of the nature of the categories is central. There the categories are said to be both the means by which the perceptions of sense reach objectivity, and unities of consciousness which have "nothing of their own" because they are conditioned by the material given to them. In the *Zusatz*, however, Hegel writes : "to assert that the categories taken by themselves are empty can scarcely be right, seeming that they have a content at all events, in the special stamp and significance which they possess." [26] This content is not perceptible since it belongs to thought, and Hegel goes on to describe a book or a speech as "full of content" in proportion to the number of "thoughts and general results" contained in it. The categories, it would appear, have "content" in being thoughts which unify data. On the other hand, Hegel can then go on to write : "it is not altogether wrong...to call the categories of themselves empty, if it be meant that they and the logical idea, of which they are the members, do not constitute the whole of philosophy, but necessarily lead onwards in due progress to the real departments of Nature and Mind." [27]

On the basis of these comments, it is not altogether clear that Hegel appreciates the uniqueness of Kant's idea that the significance of the categories as such consists in their helping to define the transcendental shape of experience. Hegel was preoccupied with the fact that, for Kant, the categories stand related to a content which is heterogeneous, given from the outside, and not to be developed from these categories themselves. For if the categories are "empty" in the sense of needing to be filled by the "real departments of Nature and Mind," it would appear that, for Hegel, having "content" means developing the content from the categories themselves rather than coming into possession of a content "originally foreign" to the categories. Hegel should have taken his own advice; on numerous occasions he claimed that Kant asked the wrong question—that, for example, he did not ask for the *Begriff* of space and time, but only whether they are subjective or objective. Hegel should have been less concerned to brand Kant's categories as "subjective" [28] and more concerned to discover their *Begriff* in Kant's thought, i.e., that they contribute to defining a metaphysic

---

[26] Glockner, 8.132.
[27] Wallace, p. 91.
[28] Cf. *Encyclopedia*, 42; Wallace, p. 90.

of experience which is basically misunderstood if it is taken either as a Lockean psychology or a Leibnizian ontology. Moreover, it will not do to say—even if Kant sometimes puts it this way himself—that the categories apart from the sensible manifold have only a "logical function" because this language is likely to obscure the transcendental meaning which goes beyond the general or formal logic to the concept of an "object," a concept which does not occur at the level of formal logic. No criticism of Kant should be allowed to obscure the concept of transcendental meaning; it was his unique contribution.

III

Kant himself raised with admirable clarity the question concerning the relation between the transcendental idea and experience which is at the heart of Hegel's fundamental criticism. In his discussion of the cosmological antinomies (B 517-18), Kant writes :

We have said that in all these cases the cosmical idea is either too large or too small for the empirical regress, and therefore for any possible concept of the understanding. We have thus been maintaining that the fault lies with the idea, in being too large or too small for that to which it is directed, namely, possible experience.

Having declared that the fault is with the idea, Kant goes on to ask whether he might not have opted for the opposite position, finding fault not with the idea but with the empirical regress as providing an empirical concept which is always too small for the idea. Kant's answer is clear, though Kant was probably not fully aware of the gravity of his choice in determining which of the two — the idea and the empirical regress — exists for the sake of the other. "Possible experience," he says,

is that which can alone give reality to our concepts; in its absence a concept is a mere idea, without truth, that is, without relation to any object. The possible empirical concept is therefore the standard by which we must judge whether the idea is a mere idea and thought-entity, or whether it finds its object in the world.

Here, it is clear, Kant chooses finite, empirical knowledge as that to which the idea must adapt itself. If, as in the half-humorous case of the ball which cannot pass through the hole, no priority is established, it makes no difference whether we say that the ball is too large or that the hole is too small. But, to use Kant's other example of the man and his coat, we do not say that the man is too tall for the coat, but that the coat is too short for the man, implying, of course, that the coat exists for the man and not vice versa.

Having established the priority of the empirical concept over the idea on the ground that possible experience is the only standard for determining the truth of any concept, Kant can say that the fault lies with the idea in being too large for what the understanding can furnish. But it is precisely the establishment of this priority which Hegel contests on the ground that it represents a dogmatic preference for understanding and empirical knowledge over the claims of reason. Why, Hegel asks, may we not maintain the validity of the idea while at the same time pointing out that it cannot be exhibited in the world of sense? The purported "object" of the cosmological idea is obviously not to be found "in the world" which, according to Kant's statement above, is where it would have to be found if the idea is to be other than a mere thought-entity. And, we must add, Hegel is not without help from Kant's own doctrine in advancing his criticism. For had Kant not allowed as legitimate the demand of reason to seek the unconditioned? Had he not claimed that the transcendental ideas "necessarily" arise as the result of reason's demand on the understanding? Moreover, had Kant not said that the ideas can be *thought* even if they cannot be *known* to denote realities? On all these heads, Kant is on shakier ground *vis-à-vis* Hegel's position than are classical empiricists and positivists who, armed with a sense-bound criterion of meaning and a proper *disrespect* for the "demands of reason," [29] can simply declare the Hegelian philosophy of spirit and the notion to be meaningless. This Kant on his own terms could not do because, though he severely restricted the scope of theoretical reason, he nevertheless recognized its reality above and beyond sense and understanding. Having done so, however, he was forced to absolutize the understanding, thereby establishing mathematics and natural science as the paradigms of knowledge in order to restrict reason to its purely regulative function. Hegel's claim is that if the reality of reason is once acknowledged as Kant had indeed done, the only way in which it can be deprived of its proper status and function in philosophical thought is through the dogmatic claim that understanding and empirical concepts have priority over the idea. Nor is Hegel satisfied with reason being confined to a regulative function since that once again makes it thoroughly subordinate to understanding. Findlay has expressed this point precisely and forcibly in his critical comparison of Kant's and Hegel's treatment of the Idea. "But while he [Hegel] agrees

---

[29] See Strawson's critical treatment of Kant's dialectic in *The Bounds of Sense* (London, 1966), pp. 157 ff. This sort of criticism serves to point out the precariousness of Kant's position in allowing, on the one hand, the legitimacy of reason as a source of ideas and principles and as a demand for completeness while on the other hand claiming that reason as such has no cognitive reach beyond the sphere of what intuition can supply.

with Kant that the Idea has no full expression in sense experience," says Findlay, "he refuses to treat it as a merely regulative conception, something which it is profitable to aim at, but not possible to reach." "The Idea," Findlay continues, "is in fact what all things *truly* are, and to the extent that sensible things fall short of it, it is they, not the Idea, which are defective in 'truth' and reality." [30] In Hegel's early critique of Kant expressed in *Glauben und Wissen*, he claims that an understanding which knows things only as appearance, is itself only an appearance and nothing in itself (Meiner, p. 23.). He takes Kant's position, however, as implying precisely the opposite; he writes : "But the understanding which knows discursively becomes, on the contrary, something in itself and absolute and the knowledge of appearances is dogmatically considered to be the only mode of knowing, while rational cognition (*Vernunfterkenntnis*) is denied" (Meiner edition, p. 23). Hegel's aim here is to expose the presence in Kant's view of a selective and differential philosophical claim which might not be identified and evaluated as such because critical philosophy is supposed not to be treating issues directly and "objectively," but obliquely in terms of the pre-conditions for the legitimate exercise of our faculties. "That, however, the understanding is absolute with regard to the human mind," says Hegel' "is something about which Kant never appeared to have the slightest doubt; on the contrary, understanding is the absolutely fixed, not to be transcended finitude of human reason" (Meiner edition, p. 23). Further along in his examination of Kant's position in *Glauben und Wissen*, Hegel emphasized again the choice (*Wahl*) manifested by Kant when, after acknowledging the *necessity* of the idea of an intuitive understanding, he set it aside in favor of a faculty of cognition which knows only appearances wherein possibility and actuality are separated. What troubled Hegel in all this was Kant's repeated acknowledgment of the necessity of the idea of reason, on the one hand, and his denial, on the other, that this necessity has any force in determining the real. "Here," he writes, "Kant has both before him, the idea of a reason in which possibility and actuality are absolutely identical, and the appearance of reason as a faculty of knowledge in which the two are separated. He finds in the experience of his thinking both thoughts; in the choice between the two, however, he scorned his disposition to think the necessity, the rationality, of an intuitive spontaneity and simply decided for the appearance" (Meiner edition, p. 34.). And, according to Hegel, Kant had no other ground whatever for making this choice but "experience" and "empirical psychology."

[30] J.N. Findlay, *Hegel*, p. 253.

It is clear that in referring to Kant's position as a "choice," Hegel was pointing to a problem at the heart of a critical or transcendental philosophy. At times Kant described the critical tribunal of the first *Critique* as marking out a standpoint from which "all disputes of pure reason" can be adjudicated. And Kant made strong claims for this tribunal. In B 512 we are told that critical questions can be resolved with "complete certainty;" in B 697 it is asserted that "the highest tribunal" which is the critical standpoint cannot possibly be the source of illusions and deceptions; and in B 779 the superiority of this tribunal is said to consist in the fact that it is not itself involved in disputes "which are immediately concerned with objects." Criticism, in short, enjoys advantages denied to reason in its supposedly dogmatic employment.

From these claims it seems clear that Kant was taking transcendental philosophy as occupying a standpoint above and beyond any standpoint from which differential, "dogmatic' metaphysical theses would be advanced. If, for example, someone were to assert with Leibniz that there must be simples because there are complexes, Kant would take that assertion, coming as it does without the benefit of prior "criticism," as a prime illustration of a dogmatic thesis directly concerned with objects. And he would regard it as incapable of being established on the basis of our human knowing apparatus.[31] But it is clear that while Kant was viewing dogmatic philosophical standpoints as hopelessly involved in making transcendent claims about the nature of things, he was also regarding his cirtical standpoint as immune from criticism. Transcendental statements about the nature of knowledge, it would appear, somehow escape involvement in any dialectic, and they exist in another dimension than that of the metaphysics which it was the aim of the *Critique* to examine. And here Kant exhibits in his own thought what must be regarded as a major paradox in the development of modern philosophy, a paradox of which Hegel was fully aware because it is represented in his criticism of Kant from beginning to end. The variety of epistemological examinations of reason which we associate with the Enlightenment and aimed at the determination of the nature, scope and limitations of man's rational capacity, all come together in one point. From different standpoints and on different grounds the Enlightenment philosophers set forth the limits of reason as coinciding with the bounds

---

[31] I am assuming here, of course, that in the discussion of the question of simples (or any others) in the Antinomy, Kant was manifestly not attempting to resolve the antithetic problems in an "objective" way, but rather to illustrate his thesis that this cannot be done which is why the discussion of the antinomies does no more than illustrate "the natural dialectic of human reason."

of sense and confidently challenged the validity of the great philosophical systems of the rationalist tradition. But somehow the form of thought operative in these critical enterprises themselves managed to escape judgment and remain unaffected by the sceptical conclusions thus attained. The critical philosophies, in short, asserted the limitation of reason without limitation. And this was possible because of the assumption not clearly recognized that the analysis of thought, understanding, reason represents a peculiar case quite different from what is involved in first-order knowing of things and events. The official conclusion of such epistemology is that reason has limits, but this assertion itself was put forward as a certainty that is without limit. It was the merit of Hegel's critique to call attention to this outcome, and in two principal respects. First, he pointed to Kant's introduction into the critical philosophy itself of his choice of the appearance of reason in the faculty of cognition which knows only appearances, over the idea of the intuitive understanding, a choice which can be justified ultimately on no other ground than the doctrine of possible experience which in turn presupposes that knowledge is confined to mathematics and natural science. It is Hegel's thesis that in making this claim, critical philosophy assumes a dogmatic stance which absolutizes the understanding. Second, Hegel called attention to the problem implicit in determining the cognitive status of the thesis that the unity of reason is merely subjective and assumes the form of a postulate. He was unwilling to accept this thesis merely as part of a prolegomenon which aims at knowing before one knows. Instead, in *Glauben und Wissen*, he inquired into the nature of a postulate as a means of understanding what the subjectivity of reason amounts to in Kant's thought. Before attending to that section, it is important to notice that Hegel is not here appealing to the well-known and formal argument that to have knowledge of a limitation is *ipso facto* to be "beyond" that limitation. Here he is concerned rather with the purported knowledge and the ground upon which the limitation itself is asserted. At the end of his discussion of Kant in *Glauben und Wissen*, Hegel commends Kant for remaining within the limits of his postulates as, so Hegel claims, Fichte did not. But Hegel wants to know more precisely what is meant by a postulate, particularly with regard to faith and subjectivity. Hegel's analysis is clear and expresses the heart of his criticism. The entire passage is well worth reproducing:

> According to Kant himself the postulates and the faith they involve are something subjective; now the only question is how this subjectivity is to be taken. Is it that the identity of infinite thought and being, of reason and its reality, is something subjective, or is it only the postulation and the faith in it [which is

subjective]? Is it the content or the form of the postulate? It cannot be the content because its negative content is at once the cancellation (*Aufhebung*) of all subjectivity; therefore it is the form and this means that it is something subjective and accidental that the idea is only something subjective.[32]

As was pointed out previously, Hegel is directing attention exclusively to the basis upon which Kant declares the subjectivity of reason, and he came to the conclusion that the ground of Kant's position consists entirely in his having opted for understanding and possible experience over the claim of reason, despite the fact that he saw the necessity of that claim in the idea of the intuitive understanding. Hegel's conclusion at that point is that if the subjectivity of reason depends in the end on a choice and a postulate, it cannot be as well-founded a thesis as the critical tribunal is supposed to deliver.

---

[32] Meiner edition, p. 39.

KANT AND HEGEL ON PRACTICAL REASON

Peter Laska

The University of Arizona

Introduction

For Kant it was the fate of human reason to fall into contradiction when it attempted to transcend the limits of empirico-scientific knowledge as formulated in the first *Critique*. These limits are the epistemic consequences following from the application of the model of mechanistic materialism to the objects of human experience. Under this paradigmatically but ahistorically restricted conception of experience, nature appears as a uniform causal chain of externally related events. Freedom of thought and decision transcend this mechanistic system generating therein a dialectic of reason in the form of an antinomy of freedom and necessity. For Kant this contradiction is a permanent feature of human reason conceived as a set of formal categories imposed on an "originally foreign" given content. Professor Smith has described how this notion of an "originally foreign" given is central to Hegel's theoretical objections to Kant and lies therefore at the core of the controversy between them on the actuality of reason. In this paper I shall try to add to the discussion of the controversy from the practical side where the question is the actuality of reason in moral and social practice. Before discussing Hegel's dialectical "resolution" of the problem, I shall sketch just enough of the Kantian background to be able to demonstrate the way in which Hegel is responding to the antinomies of bourgeois thought which the Kantian critique develops in systematic form.

I

Kant argued that if man as he appears under the conditions of empirico-scientific knowledge is man as he really is, then the idea of human freedom can have no legitimate application. Human behavior in so far as it consists in an objective series of events, would be ruled in its entirety by the "law of natural necessity." That is, in all his behavior man would stand under conditions of past time, and spontaneity in human conduct would be inconceivable. Kant's answer to the problem of free causality was to deny that man's conception of his own agency is limited to what is available in sense-experience. Given the paradigmatic hold of the model of mechanistic materialism, the possibility of a free-causality can be conceived only by employing concepts for which there can be no sense-intuitions (for example, the concept of a spontaneous beginning). Kant, therefore, in order to preserve the actuality of human freedom declares that human self-knowledge within the limits of the mechanistic model cannot be a complete account of human nature. Beyond this empirical self-knowledge, he argued, there is in man a transcendental consciousness of an *intelligible* character.

In the *Foundations of the Metaphysics of Morals*, Kant says, "If we abstract from a personal difference of rational beings and thus from all content of their private ends, we can think of a whole of all ends in systematic connection, a whole of rational beings as ends in themselves," as distinct from thinking of them in terms of the particular ends which each may set for himself.[1] This latter system of ends constitutes the "system of happiness" which is founded on the principle of self-love. The former, on the other hand, constitutes an "ethical system" founded on the principle of morality. Thus Kant distinguishes the intelligible from the empirical, the strictly moral from the merely prudential concern. Through the former man finds his freedom under moral law; in the latter he is caught up in a system of natural necessity. Here we meet with the classical opposition of universal and particular which Hegel sought to overcome in his dialectical development of the rational will.

Although Kant holds that man is capable of viewing himself as a member of an intelligible realm (i.e. as a rational being and an end in himself), he is careful to add that the adoption of this point of view in no way increases his knowledge. The concept of an intelligible realm is, he says, "only a standpoint which reason sees itself forced to take outside appearances, in order to think itself as practical." [2] For Kant the practical aspect of reason consists in "the determination of the subject and its volition," or in other words, a determination of the will.[3] The will is a "faculty" or human power "through which an object can be made real by making a rule of reason

---

[1] *Foundations*, Academie ed. 433; Beck trans. Lib. of Liberal Arts, p. 51.
[2] *Ibid.*, 548; p. 78.
[3] In a somewhat disguised reference to the will in the first *Critique*, Kant says,
(If) reason can have causality in respect of appearance, it is a faculty *through* which the sensible condition of an empirical series of effects first begins. For the condition

into the motive of an action." [4] Thus the intelligible aspect of human action centers on the free act of adopting a "rule of reason" as the motive of action. Kant sees in this "act" the creation of a fundamental character or attitude of will (*Gesinnung*). To say then as Kant does, that morality is a matter of character is also to say that morality is concerned with the intelligible aspect of human action.

Kant's theory of the moral will is primarily an attempt to vindicate the possibility of an "intelligible cause," a free causality of reason, in the face of the mechanistic Newtonian world-view. This attempt leads Kant to develop the notion of an "intelligible act" consisting in the adoption of a fundamental principle of reason (i.e. a "supreme maxim") as the basic principle of conduct.[5] The individual moral agent who carries out this intelligible act achieves what Kant calls "a revolution in character." [6] In this "revolution" the individual masters his sensuous nature by determining the conditions of its expression in accordance with a principle of reason. This principle is, however, a purely formal one. It derives from pure reason alone and contains nothing originating in the material of experience. As a guiding condition of the will, therefore, it can only function as a formal end, a moral form for the will. For Kant an intelligible act consists in the adoption of a formal principle of reason as the fundamental rule by which to regulate one's material ends (i.e. one's particular desires and inclinations).

In so far as the individual is capable of this intelligible act Kant holds that *pure reason can directly determine conduct*. Through this intelligible act reason is constitutive. It is constitutive not of experience of an object but only of the moral form of our purposes and intentions in action. Thus in practice reason directly determines only the form of an object of will and not its content which is determined by sensuous nature. The creative activity of the rational will extends, therefore, only to the moral form which we

---

which lies in reason is not sensible, and therefore does not itself begin to be (A 552 = B 580).

The "faculty" referred to here is that of the human will. It is the power whereby reason becomes practical, that is, whereby reason *determines* practice.

[4] *Critique of Practical Reason*, Academie ed. 60.

[5] If the act of adopting a fundamental principle of choice is, as Kant says, "an original act, such as can by itself bring about what did not exist before," then, Kant holds, it is not an act to be found in the empirical series of appearances. Therefore, this "original," free act will have no empirical criteria for its completion. This is what Kant calls an *intelligible* act, and it is what he is referring to when he speaks of the intelligible aspect of human reason.

[6] *Religion within the Limits of Reason Alone*, Greene & Hudson transl., (Harper), p. 43.

can impose on our future manner of conduct by resolving to seek a purely rational end. It does not determine any particular ends of desire but only the universal manner in which we ought to satisfy them.

Thus the practical and moral problem for Kant is a problem of the individual will. The individual must struggle against his particularistic natural inclinations, bringing them under the control of the universal principle of pure reason which, by an intelligible act, he has made the form of his own will. That reason is practical means for Kant that the individual can bring a moral form to his will and therein give to his own particular system of ends the character of an "ethical order of incentives." However, by Kant's own admission, this autonomous act of moral self-determination lacks a theoretical justification. Because of its intelligible or supersensible character, there can be no empirical criteria adequate to establish its completion. Although he does attempt a "practical proof" of its possibility,[7] Kant nevertheless concludes that

Reason's ability to master all opposing motivating forces through the bare idea of a law is utterly inexplicable... [8]

Faced with the unresolved antinomy of rational freedom and natural necessity, Kant acknowledges the limitations on his account of the will. Pure reason is affirmed as practical but the relation between pure reason and practice remains inscrutable.[9]

This unresolved antinomy between the freedom of human reason and the natural necessity of the "given" in human desires and inclinations underlies Kant's pessimistic assessment of the human condition. The life of the human individual is one of unceasing conflict between his commitment to duty on the one hand and his selfish interests which are the obstacles to its fulfillment on the other. The individual's pure reason is free but his natural inclinations are "blind and slavish."[10] Thus for Kant the ethical order is not a possibility contained within the natural passions themselves. On the contrary, the "bare idea" of the moral law stands opposed to "the despotism of desires." [11] The impulses of nature must be subdued under an abstract moral law of pure reason. Each individual accomplishes this task

---

[7] Kant's practical proof rests on the assumption that "ought" implies "can," that nothing binds us morally beyond our capabilities. Given this premise, the proof is valid, at least for those who experience a categorical moral command.

[8] *Critique of Pure Reason*, A 803 = B 831.

[9] *Religion, op. cit.*, pp. 17, 17n., 20, 34n., 129, 179.

[10] *Critique of Practical Reason, op, cit.*, 118; p. 122.

[11] *Critique of Judgment*, § 83; Bernard transl. p. 282. Although Kant often speaks of the "tyranny of desire," he argues that through moral education the individual can learn to affirm his power of self-determination over the natural forces of instinct.

privately and immediately in an intelligible act which has no empirical correlate.

Because this external control of natural desire by reason is necessary, the practical consequence of the Kantian critique is an internalized master-slave relation as the means to a moral life and moral community. The possibility of an individual moral life and the possibility of a universal ethical community rest on the selective repression of self-seeking ends by the internal moral authority, the consciousness of duty. If human individuals repressed their worst aggressive impulses and performed their duties to others even when they lacked the benevolent inclination to do so, then Kant thought a universal moral community was possible, at least as an ideal that one could approach asymptotically. Without this moral repression of the individual's natural sensuous life, Kant holds,

The inconsistency of his own natural dispositions drives him into self-devised torments and also reduces others of his own race to misery, by the oppression of lordship, the barbarism of war....[12]

The inconsistency Kant speaks of is a conjunct of the irreducibly irrational component in human life which his ahistorical positing of a material given originally beyond the categories of all rational thought forces upon the theory. Reason is practical only in the restricted sense that it can give a moral form to individual volition. Kant has conceptualized moral freedom subjectively and individualistically and therefore in abstraction from concrete social life.

The theoretical correlate of this restriction lies in the severe limitations which Kant's theory places on the possibility of human self-knowledge. Kant does not succeed in justifying the possibility of a science of psychology in anything other than a physiological sense, and a science of society makes no appearance at all. Given the ideological presuppositions of bourgeois thought this did not appear to Kant as a defect in his program. The "artificial" social institutions of feudalism are replaced in bourgeois ideology by the "natural" institutions of market society. The social relations by which wealth is accumulated are then seen as part of the system of laws of physical nature. Human social relations themselves are not seen as something humanly produced but rather as something *given* in conformity with universal natural laws. Therefore, it does not appear to be a theoretical lack that a socially practical reason has been ruled out, even though reality and idea, sensuous nature and reason remain in opposition and cannot be reconciled and unified in experience. Within the limits of the Kantian critique, no more can be asked of the "valid employment of reason."

[12] *Ibid.,* § 83; p. 280.

II

In order to resolve these fundamental oppositions Hegel must transcend the limitations of Kantian thought. These limits have their roots in the Kant critique where the possibility of scientific knowledge is limited to a system founded in part on the category of *natural* necessity in the sequence of events. Hegel attempts to overcome these restrictions by denying the given timeless status of the forms of conscious unity constituting objective experience, thereby opening up the possibility of developing the category of *rational* necessity as the basis of an ethico-scientific knowledge of self and society. By incorporating contradiction and the transcendence of contradiction into the process of knowledge Hegel hoped to show that the idea of reason could overcome the antinomies of bourgeois thought systematized in the first *Critique*.

The incompleteness of the Kantian theory of practical reason is for Hegel the unresolved confrontation between the rational will with its abstract commitment to a universal moral form, on the one hand, and the natural will embodying the content of the individual's particular desires and inclinations on the other. The timeless status of the Kantian categories and the unresolved opposition between reason and nature, between the intelligible and the empirical, leave Kantian epistemology in the grip of a crisis as far as the possibility of ethical self-knowledge is concerned. Since for Kant the category of freedom includes the element of spontaneity, an element which cannot appear in human experience without jeopardizing the possibility of objectivity, freedom in any aspect of experience must fall outside the scope of scientific knowledge. Thus, morality, history, psychology and the study of societies, for example, cannot be included within the scope of science except insofar as they can be purged of their ties to a free causality and reduced to a system of natural causal relationships. The freedom of the moral will, therefore, is not an object of scientific knowledge for Kant. Rather, the free act is conceived only as an intelligible act which cannot be known under empirical conditions. It is for this reason that Kant makes the startling assertion in the first *Critique* that "Right can never be an appearance;... it represents a property (the moral property) of actions, which belongs to them in themselves." [13] It is only "in themselves," that is only in their intelligible aspect that human actions could exhibit the property of moral right. Since it has no empirical correlate, the intelligible aspect cannot be experienced under conditions that make scientific knowledge

---

[13] *Critique of Pure Reason*, A 44 = B 61.

possible. And for this reason the freedom of the moral will cannot be an object of knowledge for Kant.

To admit 'moral right' which embodies the category of freedom into the objective domain of scientific knowledge would, according to the Kantian critique, generate a contradiction, an antinomy of freedom and necessity which Kant himself was able to avoid only by restricting natural necessity to 'appearances' and the spontaneity of freedom to the intelligible realm of the thing-in-itself (or in this case, an end-in-itself or person). He attributed the appearance of this antinomy only to the irrepressible urge of human reason to transcend the limits of its own valid employment. Thus, in a sense, human reason generated its own difficulties which it could also avoid by emasculating itself in the way the Kantian critique proposed. Kant's mistake, according to Hegel, lay in attributing the source of the antinomy to activity on the part of reason. Against this Hegel argued that the appearance of the antinomy of freedom and necessity was not the fault of human reason but the fault of the world that did not yet reflect the demands of that reason. For Hegel the defect lay in the incomplete historical development and actualization of reason. The contradiction could be overcome only through the historical process of the rationalization of nature in and through human self-development. The overcoming of the opposition of freedom and necessity is conceived as the outcome of a dialectical development of human history whereby human social relationships are transformed, and the freedom of reason no longer appears in positive form as external constraint. It was Kant's argument that each individual creates himself *morally*, through an autonomous "intelligible act" of self-determination which lacks an empirical correlate and therefore falls outside of scientific knowledge. Only in this way was pure reason conceived as practical. Hegel takes the necessary step beyond this individualistic moral self-determination, not by rejecting its possibility, but by demonstrating that its possibility rests on an expanded conception of practical reason.

True freedom for Hegel is freedom under the moral laws of reason. On this crucial point he follows Kant. But Hegel goes on to argue that under this conception "the antithesis of freedom and necessity disappears." [14] Kant could not take this final step because he could not conceptualize the unity of the subjective freedom of reason with the objective necessity governing man's appearance in nature. For him their unity lay in some inscrutable ground. Consequently, he could not transcend the opposition between the moral law which controls the form of the individual will through the con-

---

[14] *Reason in History*, Hartman transl. p. 53; Suhrkamp Verlag, 12, p. 57.

sciousness of duty and the natural passions which make up the actual content of the human will. The moral disposition in conflict (*die moralische Gesinnung im Kampfe*) remained always the central focus of Kant's work.[15] It is from this point that Hegel's own work goes beyond Kant. Throughout his writings Hegel argues that the natural human passions are potentially rational, that the natural will is potentially a rational will in which the opposition of freedom and necessity is overcome. On the practical side the crucial difference between them lies in Hegel's dialectical and historical attitude toward repression. For Hegel repression, no matter how selective, is self-defeating in ethical life if it does not actualize a free individuality. Self-mastery, therefore, is merely negative without self-fulfillment. The Hegelian conception of practical reason is expanded to include the actualization of free individuality within a historically developed social totality.

For Hegel "reason" and "rational" have both an historical and a trans-historical meaning. In the latter case, the rational refers to the theoretical Idea of reason in which oppositions have a *final* reconciliation. Hegel finds this Idea expressed metaphorically in Christianity as the final re-union of man with God. Up to his own time, he claims, this Idea of reason was conceived *only as an ideal*, that is, only as something to be realized *beyond* human worldly existence (as the Christian religion taught) or to be approached asymptotically but never actually attained in human life, as Kant held. Against these views Hegel argued that "reason" and "rational" have also a concrete, historical meaning, and that in the process of human history the distinction and "opposition" between reason as ideal and reason as imperfect historical reality, between reason as theoretical ideal and reason as actual social and moral practice, has a final resolution.

Hegel's account of this resolution trades heavily on what he calls "the cunning of reason." "The universal," Hegel argues, "must be actualized through the particular,"[16] the rational will must be developed from the material of the natural will. This actualization of the universal through its opposite the particular is for Hegel "the cunning of Reason" (*die List der Vernunft*).[17] Reason in the sense of the universal rational community (i.e., the Kantian Kingdom of ends) is realized in the concrete world of human history as a result of individuals pursuing their own particular interests rather than consciously pursuing this Ideal. He sees it as part of the notion of the cunning of reason that human civilization has not advanced through conscious intent, but rather in spite of it:

[15] *Critique of Practical Reason, op. cit.*, 152; p. 147.
[16] *Reason in History, op. cit*, p. 35.
[17] *Ibid.*, p. 44; Suhrkamp, p. 49.

The passions of man satisfy themselves; they develop themselves and their purposes in accordance with their natural destination and produce the edifice of human society. Thus, they fortify a structure for law and order against themselves.[18]

Spiritual or social development, then, is a process that goes on "behind the back of consciousness." [19] The "cunning" in the "cunning of reason" is that the human individual acts freely (i.e. spontaneously) in his own interest but in doing so actualizes a "universal," a rationally necessary constraint on his power of arbitrary choice. This "universal" of rational thought attains objective existence in the institutionalized relationships of human society, that is, in what Hegel calls the "spiritual" or cultural aspects of human life.

Apparently in direct opposition to Kant's restriction of rational principles to the intelligible sphere, Hegel asserts *that right is an appearance* and therefore a possible object of scientific knowledge. As a result of free self-interested activity on the part of individuals, Hegel tells us, a universal of reason achieves objective existence. His term for such an objective existence of reason is "right" : "An existent of any sort embodying a free will, this is what right is." [20] Hegel identifies the cultural restraints of religion as the first forms of the objective embodiment of rational freedom. The difference between religion and fetishism, according to Hegel, lies in the failure of the latter to give rise to any existence embodying a free will. A fetish or magic piece is an existent embodying nothing more than abritrary choice. It is not an instance in which a universal of reason (i.e. right) is actualized because there is absolutely no bond, no restraint upon that arbitrary will or choice; the will remains in its natural or savage form. The fetish, Hegel says, is nothing but "the fancy of the individual projecting itself into space...." [21] The self's power of arbitrary choice remains supreme, and for this reason no universal of rational thought, no form of right, can attain objective existence.

For Hegel the rational principles which structure human conduct constitute the forms of social life within a given historical community. Within this community the possibilities for any individual's self-development are limited. Thus, a given society presents the developing individual with a system of social practice, whether in conscious or unconscious form. The system is not abstract, but has concrete existence by virtue of the fact that

---

[18] *Ibid.*, p. 35; Suhrkamp, p. 42.
[19] *Phenomenology of Mind*, Suhrkamp, 3, p. 80.
[20] *Philosophy of Right*, Knox transl. p. 23; Suhrkamp, 7, p. 80.
[21] *Vorlesungen über die Philosophie der Geschichte*, Suhrkamp, 12, p. 123; Sibree transl. p. 151.

the forms of right are the historicallly developed categories constituting human interaction within that totality.

The historically conditioned limitations on individual self-development constitute the basis for the experience of alienation and generate in bourgeois thought the antinomy of freedom and necessity which the Kantian critique formulated but could not transcend. In order to gain an identity and objective existence as an individual outside the family, one restricts one's natural freedom and spontaneity upon entering bourgeois society and submits to a system of necessary constraint : e.g. a life of specialized labor. Without this systematic repression one cannot gain the power by which to establish oneself as person, i.e., develop one's bourgeois individuality through the accumulation of capital. To resolve this antinomy Hegel begins with the proposition that the "immediate" or natural will of the developing individual is inherently rational. From this postulate it follows that if the social substance (viz. the historically developed forms of right constituting a society) to which the individual must conform is a fully rational system, then the alienation of his natural will is at the same time the actualization of his rational potential. Alienation will then coincide with full self-determination, and the antinomy of freedom and necessity will have been overcome dialectically in a new form of unity.

The problem of human history then is to actualize this new form of social unity. The possibility of its final actualization is established by Hegel in his postulate that the natural human passions are implicitly rational, that the passions are by no means always opposed to morality but (through the cunning of Reason) actualize the universal. Hegel's account of the process whereby arbitrary choice is limited and rational freedom or right is actualized is at the same time his account of reason in history. To locate reason in history is to identify the historical forms of these objective restraints on their own arbitrary wills that humanity has wrought. Collectively, they constitute the body of "right," in which human subjectivity (i.e. freedom) appears as an object. Historically, they represent the attempts of a people or nation to actualize their freedom as a system of reason, a moral whole. The imperfection in a given historical system of right, the contradiction it contains between the possibility of a life of freedom under universal moral law and the repressive forms of social relation that succeed one another in human history, is for Hegel the negative force which propels human civilization forward to a final actualization of reason in the form of the state. The rational state, then, is the completely developed ethical or moral whole in which the antinomy of freedom and necessity is overcome.

The Hegelian conception of practical reason is one in which the actualization of rational freedom is achieved through the subjection of individuals to an alien repressive authority. The actualization of rational freedom is the dialectical result of this alienation. In the *Lectures on the Philosophy of History*, Hegel makes the point epigrammatically when he says that it is not so much *from* slavery as *through* slavery that mankind is emancipated.

On the theoretical side alienation is overcome in the scientific knowledge of nature. Nature remains an "alien existence" only because it remains outside conceptual thought, and something "in which spirit does not find itself." [22] In scientific knowledge rational understanding replaces superstition. For the society that actualizes the freedom of reason, nature becomes an intelligible order of phenomena. Just as rational understanding replaces superstition on the theoretical side, rational self-determination replaces arbitrary choice or "caprice" on the practical side. In this final "reconciliation" (*Versöhnung*), the arbitrary character of the natural will has become a system of rational freedom, freedom under necessary and universal moral laws. Hegel's expanded conception of practical reason then is that of a society or state in which each individual is fully self-determining; that is, a self "conscious of itself as the controlling necessity (*Schicksal*) of what is essential and actual." [23] In such a social system the experience of an alien necessity or external constraint on individual freedom would disappear. The freedom of reason (i.e. *right*) would no longer appear in positive form as an external constraint. In this manner Hegel's thought transcends the external relation of rational freedom and "natural" necessity in the conception of a dialectical unity of these opposites, the rational society or state.

Concluding Remarks

For Hegel the human passions are natural forces whose conflict presents the historical picture of a life and death struggle. But inasmuch as they are postulated as the alienated form of the rational Idea, Hegel can say that they are implicitly rational. Out of this struggle there develops a system of "right," that is, an objective system of social relations. These systems of right are the objective existence of rational freedom, so far as humanity has been able to embody it under given cultural and material conditions. The freedom of reason develops dialectically through historical forms that imperfectly realize it as a universal right, and it was Hegel's speculative judgment that history reveals the progressive actualization of this ideal.

[22] *Philosophy of Nature*, A.V. Miller transl., p. 3.
[23] *Phenomenology of Mind*, Baillie transl. p. 687; Suhrkamp, 3, p. 496.

Hegel's advance over Kant is, in sum, his historicization of the process of rational self-determination. Against Kant, Hegel argues that the opposition of freedom and necessity appears to be unresolvable only because it is viewed ahistorically and individualistically. Against Kant's individualism, Hegel makes reason practical through the active spirit of a people in erecting a system of right within a social totality. In this expanded conception of practical reason then freedom is not restricted to an abstract moral consciousness whose "intelligible act" has no intelligible relation to the empirical world of appearance. Human nature (freedom) is not hidden within the "thing in itself" but makes its appearance in human history, fully developed as the morally necessary and universal laws of the state.

With the dynamic or developmental concept of reason, Hegel can say that Kant has made a wrong choice in giving priority to empirical reality over the rational idea. On the contrary, he claims, what is truly real is the idea of reason developing itself in the world. In saying this, however, Hegel loses his advantage over Kant and is forced into a position inconsistent with his own criticism. For if the idea of reason, developing itself in the world is *what is truly real*, then the irrational and contradictory turns out to be illusory, a form of false consciousness. Thus Hegel does not conceptualize a solution to the problem of an irrational empirical reality since the problem is never really faced.

Given the application of the mechanistic model to bourgeois society, in the form of the "natural" functions of the market, the freedom of reason has no role to play except in an abstract moral sphere whose relation to the empirical world of the market is left unexplained. Hegel's critique of Kant is a reaction to this unresolved antinomy between moral freedom and "social" necessity. By historicizing the problem of rationality, Hegel transcends the dualism in Kantian thought. However, since this is done only by extending idealism into spiritualist ontology, Hegel fails to confront the ground of this dualism and therefore is unable to establish the possibility of a complete development of reason. Like Kant, Hegel ends with a form of the master-slave relation. Side by side with his conception of the ethical development of individuals in a rational totality, there remains the undigested stone of bourgeois society whose irrational forces must be controlled externally by means of a bureaucratic state.*

---

* Editor's note : For a fuller discussion of this conclusion, see Hofmeister's paper in this volume, especially pp. 155-158.

MORAL AUTONOMY IN KANT AND HEGEL

HEIMO E.M. HOFMEISTER

The American University

I

One can only be surprised to learn that Hegel in his *Lectures on the History of Philosophy* [1] did not devote even six whole pages to the presentation and critique of Kant's ethics.[2] His *History of Philosophy* comprises three volumes, totally nearly 1700 pages, and Hegel himself stated once that the Kantian philosophy is the foundation and starting point of modern German philosophy. The general influence of the Kantian works and in particular the influence of Kant's ethics on Hegel's *Philosophy of Right* is well known, and Hegel himself recognized it. This discrepancy between Kant's influence and Hegel's overt recognition of it was first pointed out by Karl Ludwig Michelet, the editor of the *Lectures on the History of Philosophy*. He justified it with a hint about how this book was written: there were additions to the introduction and main text which became more and more extensive and which did not leave Hegel at the end of the semester with sufficient time to cover the period beginning with Kant.[3] Although Hegel's elaboration of Kant's ethics is linguistically elegant, it is not philosophically detailed, and if one wishes to shed light on it, he will not be able to do so without the help of certain passages from his other writings, especially from the *Phenomenology of Mind* and the *Philosophy of Right*.[4]

---

[1] All references to Hegel refer to vol. and p. nos. in the edition of H. Glockner: G.W.F. Hegel: *Sämtliche Werke*, Jubiläumsausgabe, Stuttgart — Bad Cannstatt, Friedrich Fromman Verlag. The page number in parenthesis refers to the English translation of the *Phenomenology of Mind* by J.B. Baillie (New York and Evanston, Harper & Row, Publishers, 1967). Since the *Philosophy of Right* is subdivided according to paragraphs and their additions (ad) and will be quoted accordingly, there is no need of giving the page number of an English translation. I used the translation of T.M. Knox. Quotations based on the before mentioned translations are occasionally modified.

[2] Hegel, 19,588-593.

[3] Hegel, 17,13 f.; preface by K. L. Michelet.

[4] Hegel, 2; Hegel 7.

II

Both Hegel and Kant are concerned with the problem of human freedom, although it must be said straightaway that the concept of freedom plays a more far-reaching role for Hegel than for Kant. Indeed, as Edward Gans [5] has shown, this concept not only grounds but also permeates the argument of Hegel's *Philosophy of Right*. In Kant's ethics, freedom operates in every human action as a fundamental conditioning principle (*principium*) which because of its transcendental character is thought to resist every kind of description. The *Philosophy of Right*, on the other hand, attempts to comprehend the system of right as the "realm of freedom made actual," [6] and by exhibiting this system Hegel is trying to show concretely what freedom means. Kant taught that "what is essential in the moral worth of action is that the *moral law* should directly determine the will." Accordingly he had to distinguish between legality and morality.[7] Hegel on the other hand viewed morality as only one moment in the process of the unfolding of human freedom, for freedom has its fullest realization within what he calls Right as right, as morality, and as ethical life. Hegel takes up the Kantian distinction and systematically weaves it into the fabric of the philosophical science of right, which he defines as the doctrine of the "Idea of right," that is, the doctrine of the "concept of right together with the actualization of that concept."[8] Hegel posits that freedom must not be restricted to the realm of thought but must find its realization within the history of man.

Because Kant held that morality refers only to the agreement with the

---

[5] Hegel, 7,7; preface by E. Gans.

[6] Hegel, 7,50, § 4.

[7] Kant, V, 71; and VI, 219 : "The mere agreement or disagreement of an action with the law, without regard to the incentive of the action, is called *legality*; but, when the Idea of duty arising from the law is at the same time the incentive of the action, then the agreement is called the *morality* of the action." In the *Critique of Practical Reason* Kant writes on the same topic (V, 71) : "If the determination of the will occurs in accordance with the moral law but only by means of a feeling of any kind whatsoever, which must be presupposed in order that the law may become a determining ground of the will, and if the action thus occurs not for the sake of the law, it has legality but not morality." All references to Kant refer to vol. and p. nos. in the Edition of the Prussian Academy of Sciences (Berlin, 1902 et. sequ.). Since L.W. Beck's translation of the *Foundations of the Metaphysics of Morals* and of the *Critique of Practical Reason*, J. Ellington's translation of *The Metaphysical Principles of Virtue* and John Hadd's translation of the *Metaphysical Elements of Justice* (all three : Indianapolis—New York, The Bobbs Merrill Company. Inc.) include the Academy pagination, it is not necessary to cite the pages in these editions. Quotations may be modified.

[8] Hegel, 7, 38, § 1.

law inasmuch as the "Idea of duty arising from the law is at the same time the incentive of the action," [9] the distinction between morality and legality, or between ethical and juridical legislation,[10] carries with it the idea that everything that is not part of the motive and does not rest on the internal legislation belongs to the external part of the action and as such merely to the sphere of right. Ethics according to Kant is the doctrine of virtue (*Tugendlehre*) and is thereby distinguished from what was called the "*doctrine of morals*" (*philosophia moralis*) in "ancient times" when the doctrine of morals was equated with ethics. What Kant calls ethics is only a part of the doctrine of morals, namely "the doctrine of those duties which are not subject to external laws." [11] Ethics or practical philosophy of internal legislation deals only with "the moral relations of man to man." [12]

With this idea Kant turned the development of ethics in a radically new direction which cannot be reversed. In the context of the traditional *philosophia moralis* as it originated in Aristotle, ethics was the doctrine of *ethos* as the disposition of individual life in house and polis; *ethos* was developed in ethical life, custom, and heritage. Here freedom was seen as only one problem among many, and it was not until Kant that the problem of freedom was moved to the center; and it was he who recognized that it is the genuine nerve of life in ethics.

The impossibility of justifying freedom philosophically within Aristotle's conception of philosophy is the reason for dissatisfaction with his ethical system, and it is also the basis for Kant's attempt to elevate freedom to the fundamental principle of ethics. Yet if one holds that freedom is self-determining in accordance with the moral law then one reduces all Aristotle's ontological goods—namely the talents of the mind such as intelligence, wit and judgment; the qualities of temper such as courage, resoluteness, perseverance; and the gifts of fortune such as power, riches, honor, and health—to the level of the merely conditionally good. As such their employment "without the principles of a good will....can become extremely bad." [13] What Kant says about the virtues is also valid for those juridical relations of a society the origin and formation of which lie outside of the individual's immediate sphere of influence.

Hegel subscribes to the Kantian turn [14] by emphasizing "The will's

[9] Kant, VI, 219.
[10] Cf. *idem*.
[11] Kant, VI, 378.
[12] Kant, VI, 491.
[13] Kant, IV, 394.
[14] Cf. : R. Kroner, *Von Kant bis Hegel* (Tübingen, J.C.B. Mohr, 1961), 166 ff.

right ... to recognize as its action, and to accept responsibility for only those presuppositions of the deed of which it was conscious in its aim and those aspects of the deed which were contained in its purpose." [15] The moral will knows itself to be too much interwoven into a society the growing and becoming of which is independent of its own volitions and intentions to be held fully responsible for the consequences of its deed.

At the stage of ethical reflection which Kant represents, freedom and necessity are still thought to be separate from one another. Although the moral will is known as a subject confronted with a society, the extent to which society at the same time conditions the will within this confrontation is not recognized. It is Hegel who has to be credited with the discovery that man does actualize his freedom not merely morally but *ethico-socially* as well. This insight permitted him to distinguish not only between abstract right and morality but also between both of them and ethical life. Within the ethical life freedom appears neither as mere *thing* [16] nor as mere *intention* (*Gesinnung*) but as concrete human relation and condition of man's social interaction.

Because right is characterized by the necessary use of force, Hegel sees it as contingent; therefore he concludes that it is not possible to leave necessity as an externality; rather he insisted that the external be taken into the internal. To take legality into morality is to recognize the limit of legality but also that of morality. Family, civil society, and state thereby still remain as the subject of the doctrine of right, but at the same time they are ethically viewed as modes in which the freedom of subjectivity is included. Whereas Kant relegated these institutions to the sphere of right, Hegel interpreted them as ethical realizations of the subjective will. The basis for his interpretation is the superseding (*Aufhebung*) of morality.

Hegel, as we saw, distinguishes among right, morality, and ethical life, for unlike Kant he does not use the two latter concepts as synonymous.[17] This further distinction is of fundamental importance for Hegel because he attempts to renew the Aristotelian concept of the ethical which had become questionable with the discovery of subjectivity and individuality by Christianity and Kant's conceptualization of it. Hegel does not demand a return to an Aristotelian concept of ethical life as a sum of customs. What he demands is an ethical life which has gone through morality and he defines it as follows :

---

[15] Hegel, 7, 174, § 117.
[16] Cf. Hegel, 7, 95, § 41 ad. : "My freedom is realized first of all in an external thing...."
[17] Hegel, 7, 86 f., § 33.

Ethical life is the Idea of freedom in that on the one hand it is the good become alive—the good endowed in self-consciousness with knowing and willing and actualized by self-conscious action—while on the other hand self-consciousness has in the ethical realm its absolute foundation and the end which actuates its effort. Thus ethical life is the concept of freedom developed into the existing world and the nature of self-consciousness.[18]

III

From the short review above, two questions emerge which, in turn, will guide the ensuing reflections.

1. Why does Hegel attempt to accomplish the transition from morality to ethical life?
2. Is he actually able, with the means he is using, to vitiate the Kantian concept of an ethics restricted to the internal determination of the will which in consequence dissolved the ethical life?

Hegel's intentions are very clear, namely to synthesize the Kantian principle of morality with the Aristotelian conception of ethical life. It is less obvious whether the *Philosophy of Right* actually succeeded in renewing the Aristotelian tradition in such a way that the system of human interrelations is animated by the principle of subjectivity through the affirmation of the subject character of morality without having to reduce ethical life to morality.

Hegel repeatedly affirmed that he is not willing to give up the Kantian discovery that the "being-for-itself" of subjectivity belongs to the will as free will and that this relation can never be predicated through the category of right or through the category of the sociological situation since these, "upheld in face of the single will merely being for itself," are "recognized as actual on the score of its [the category's] necessity."[19] For Hegel as for Kant freedom can only be found where man in his intentions, in his internality, and in his conscience can will what he is doing. It makes the difference between the free man and the slave that the latter "allows himself to be constrained in everything by brute force and natural factors;" whereas the free man "develops an inner life and wills that he himself shall be in everything he does."[20] The achievement of the Kantian philosophy, according to Hegel, was that it realized "that freedom is the ultimate pivot on which man turns; it is the highest point, which cannot be impressed

---

[18] Hegel, 7, 226, § 142.
[19] Hegel, 7, 161, § 104.
[20] Hegel, 7, 166, § 107 ad.

by anything at all, so that man can accept nothing as an authority insofar as it is directed against his freedom." [21]

At the end of the section on morality Hegel explains his concept of the ethical life. Ethical life is

> the unity of the subjective and objective good being in itself and for itself....In it we find the reconciliation which accords with the concept. Morality is the form of the will in general on its subjective side. Ethical life is more than the subjective form and the self-determination of the will; in addition it has as its content the concept of the will, namely freedom.[22]

The main difference between Kant and Hegel can be found in Hegel's distinction between objective and subjective good. Kant discarded this distinction on the ground that only an ethical life reduced to morality (self-determination) can guarantee man's responsibility and freedom. In consequence Kant had to answer negatively the question as to whether conscience may err. Where the distinction between objective and subjective good is not considered to be a valid one there is also no need of reconciliation between them. This reconciliation is the program of Hegel's ethics, and he hopes that it will come into being on the level of ethical life. To Kant on the other hand the reconciliation between truth and truthfulness—these are the terms in which this problem occurs to him—is of no extraordinary ethical importance.

Hegel's foundation for the transition from morality to ethical life and the dialectical mediation of it is the critique of Kant's "formal principle of legislation" which "does not, in its self-occupying isolation, arrive at any content." [23] If Hegel is not only to be correct in his critique of Kant but also to be able to fulfill his own program he must prove false the following statement Kant made in *Über das Mißlingen aller philosophischen Versuche in der Theodicee* :

> (Because he may err) he cannot always affirm that what he tells himself or someone else is true but he can and must adhere to the *truthfulness* of his confession and statement, because he is immediately conscious of it. In the first case [when he may err], he is comparing his proposition with the object in a logical judgment (by the means of understanding); in the second case, where someone confesses that he believes something to be true, he is comparing his proposition with the subject (before conscience)." [24]

[21] Hegel, 19, 591.
[22] Hegel, 7, 225, § 141 ad.
[23] Hegel, 19, 591.
[24] Kant, VIII, 267. This statement found its most controversial and radical formulation in the article : "On a supposed Right to Lie from Altruistic Motives." Cf. H. Hofmeister, "The Ethical Problem of the Lie in Kant," *Kant-Studien* 63/3, 1972; and "Truth and Truthfulness," *Ethics* 82/3, 1972.

The possibility of a reconciliation between the objective and subjective good is questioned here in the particular case of the lie. The denial of this possibility is based on the fact that the moral judgment originates merely from the subject, whereas the cognitive judgment has its origin in both the subject and the object. The consequence of this denial is the absolutizing of the moral standpoint. This standpoint is worked out and reaches its culmination in the formal character of the moral law as it is formulated in the *Fundamental Principles of the Metaphysics of Morals* and the *Critique of Practical Reason*.

Hegel's critique concentrates on the insufficiency of an ethical law which is only a formal one. In so far as one agrees with Hegel's critique and accepts his arguments for the necessity of a transition from morality to ethical life, one is confronted with the question as to whether he succeeded, knowing the weakness of Kant's principle, in actually eliminating it. If Hegel did not in fact eliminate it, we have to go on and ask if this limit of human knowledge about the good—as it becomes obvious in the way in which Kant confronts truth with truthfulness — is a characteristic and absolute one. In this case it would be to Hegel's credit to have made visible the limit as limit.[25]

The problem emerging from the foregoing analysis is precisely the question as to the validity of transcendental philosophy in general and transcendental ethics in particular. If on the one side the being of the good cannot be exhaustively exhibited in particular facts and on the other side the undifferentiated good is merely the negation of all good, then for the transcendental philosopher the question remains open : is it possible for the good to be differentiated in so far as it is actual as the good, or is it sufficient just to have a negative concept of it? Kant's and Hegel's answers are diametrically opposed to one another.

To Kant the good remains undetermined with respect to its content and therefore the subject "in its singleness" has to decide what the good is.

---

[25] By studying the works of Kant we meet again and again passages where he finds himself confronted with this problem; but quite a few of them indicate that Kant supposes that by the transcendental philosophy which he has initiated all those problems are finally solvable. He writes, and I quote the last sentence in the *Critique of Pure Reason*, a sentence which certainly also refers to the realm of ethics : "If the reader has had the courtesy and patience to accompany me along this path, he may now judge for himself whether, if he cares to lend his aid in making this path into a high-road, it may not be possible to achieve before the end of the present century what many centuries have not been able to accomplish; namely, to secure for human reason complete satisfaction in regard to that with which it has all along so eagerly occupied itself, though hitherto in vain." III, 552, (B 884).

To give this decision over to abstract singleness is, according to Hegel, nothing but "the evil":

> the evil is the knowledge that the decision-maker has of his singleness, in as far as the singleness does not stay in this abstraction, but gives to itself in its relation to the good, the content of a subjective interest.[26]

What Hegel is declaiming against here is a consequence which Kant did not intend but which Hegel sees implied within the categorical imperative. Kant's self-given law is supposed to be the criterion to distinguish between good and evil. Because of its indeterminateness, it seems to be suitable for this task. Yet as a side effect, Hegel claims, this law is also quite suitable to justify "all wrong and immoral line of conduct." [27] This implication, of course, is against Kant's intentions and happens by the isolation of the subject from the universal since the law's universalizability does not contain "for itself any further principle" other than "the absence of contradiction, and formal identity with itself." [28] As Kant, because of this isolation, restricts the lie to untruthfulness, he also reduced—at least in Hegel's eyes—the problem of ethical truth to truthfulness, to moral certainty. If this reduction, he argues against Kant's position, is a valid one, then "to know the good and to be aware of its distinction from evil" [29] can no longer be called a duty. Where the knowledge of the truth is thought to be impossible and where there is only truthfulness, the truth of an ethical action being thereby surrendered to subjectivity, there evil does not remain evil but becomes error.

If conscience, as Hegel writes in the *Phenomenology of Mind*, "finds for its own part (*für sich selbst*) its truth to lie in the immediate certainty of itself," [30] then one has no ground to claim that this truth in fact represents the full substance of the idea of the good. Kant found himself confronted with this issue in the chapter: "Of the Typic of Pure Practical Judgment." [31] It may have been an act of philosophical modesty in face of the recognition of the finite character of man when Kant willingly accepted the discrepancy between truth and truthfulness as inevitable and contented himself with the fact that the being-for-itself of conscience is supposed to guarantee at the same time the actualization of the good in itself. Whether or not Kant was modest, Hegel's objections possess their own kind of validity. Modesty is

---

[26] Hegel, 10, 396, § 511.
[27] Hegel, 7, 194, § 135.
[28] *Idem.*
[29] Hegel, 7, 213, § 140e.
[30] Hegel, 2, 488.
[31] Kant, *Critique of Practical Reason*, V, 67 ff.

very often closely related to resignation. For Hegel, therefore, the acceptance of the discrepancy cannot substitute for reconciliation between the reason of the world spirit (the idea of the good) and the truth of conscience in its moral self-determination. Attention should be paid to Hegel's argument that the gap between them will only be increased where conscience "holds its incomplete knowledge to be sufficient and complete, because it is its *own* knowledge." [32] To conscience, consequently,

> it is not universal knowledge in general that has a value, but what *it* [conscience] knows of the circumstances. It puts into duty, which is the universal being-in-itself (*Ansichsein*), the content which it derives from its natural individuality : for the content is one that is present in its own being.[33]

The grounds on which Hegel argues for a transition from morality to ethical life have now been sufficiently shown for the purposes of this paper. We may now concentrate on our second question, namely whether Hegel was able to achieve this transition and succeeded in establishing a theory of ethical life that does not leave out the principle of autonomy. The possibilities of bridging the gap between subjective and objective good are very slim. The Hegel of the *Philosophy of Right* gives the impression that the only possible solution is to prove that the finite knowledge of conscience shows itself to be infinite knowledge, for it is only the absolute knowledge that may claim to possess an ultimate criterion as to what is good. The predicate "good" can only be applied to the finite conscience to the extent that it suspends its freedom and individuality in favor of a heteronomous obedience to higher or even absolute power. This power would then, as Hegel remarks in the introduction to the *Philosophy of History* with a critical undertone, "concede to man all his particular passions and interests," but that "which comes into being by them is the execution of its [the heteronomous power's] own purpose which is something other than that which these men [with merely finite knowledge] had in mind; they served merely as an instrument." [34] As Hegel interprets this assumption, individuality is "sacrificed and surrendered to the cunning of reason." [35]

In appreciation and critique of Kant, Hegel affirms the absoluteness of conscience and confronts it with the finitude of its insight :

---

[32] Hegel, 2, 492 (653). See : E. Heintel, *Die beiden Labyrinthe der Philosophie* (Wien und München, Verlag R. Oldenbourg, 1968), 1, 190.
[33] Hegel, 2, 496 (657/58).
[34] Hegel, 8, 420.
[35] Hegel, 11, 63.

Whether the assurance, to act from conviction of duty, is true, whether it really is duty which is done—these questions or doubts have no meaning as directed against conscience. In the case of the question, whether the assurance is true, it would be assumed that the inner attention is different from the one put forward, i.e. that the willing of the individual self can be separated from duty, from the will of the universal and pure consciousness: the latter will would in that case be a matter of words, while the former would be strictly the real moving principle of the act. But such a distinction between the universal consciousness and the individual self is precisely what has been cancelled, and the superceding of it constitutes conscience.[36]

These words should not be read without reference to yet another aspect of which Hegel reminds us in the *Phenomenology* :

When conscience is considered in relation to the single features of the opposition which appears in action, and when we consider its consciousness regarding the nature of those features, its attitude towards the reality of the situation where action has to take place is, in the first instance, that of knowledge. So far as the aspect of universality is present in such knowledge, it is the business of conscientious action *qua* knowledge, to compass the reality before it in an unrestricted exhaustive manner, and thus to know exactly the circumstances of the case, and give them due consideration. This knowledge, however, since it is aware of universality as a moment, is in consequence a kind of knowledge of these circumstances which is conscious all the while of not embracing them, is conscious of not being conscientious in its procedure. The genuinely universal and pure relation of knowledge would be one towards something not opposed, a relation to itself. But action through the opposition essentially implied in action is related to what negates consciousness, to a reality existing *per se*. This reality—being, as contrasted with the simple nature of pure consciousness, the absolute other, multiplicity *per se*—is a sheer plurality of circumstances which breaks up indefinitely and spreads in all directions—backwards into their conditions, sidewards in their associations, forwards in their consequences.

The conscientious mind is aware of this nature of "the fact" and of its relation thereto, and knows it is not acquainted to the full and complete extent required with the situation in which its action takes place, and knows that its pretence of conscientiously weighing and considering *all* the circumstances is futile. This acquaintance with and consideration of all the circumstances, however, are not entirely absent : but they are merely present as a moment, as something which is only for others : and the conscientious mind holds its *incomplete* knowledge to be sufficient and complete, *because* it is its *own* knowledge.[37]

If the finite conscience can overcome the incompleteness of its knowledge or, in Kant's terminology, if the discrepancy between truth and truthfulness can only be resolved by the resignation in favor of an absolute spirit, and if conscience therefore can only actualize itself by the means of the cunning

---

[36] Hegel, 2, 500 (662).
[37] Hegel, 2, 491 (652/53).

of reason, which is not even its own, then it is impossible to think of ethical self-determination.

The "whole of ethical life" Hegel defines as the "objective filled with subjectivity." [38] One readily concurs with this definition. One agrees far less readily that the state and the ethical life which is appropriate to it represents the above mentioned "whole," the "unity of the objective and subjective good, being in itself and for itself." [39]

In contrast to his main writings, the *Philosophy of Right* allows the absolute ethical life to exhaust itself within the positivity of the states. As a consequence Hegel speaks here of a state—the question if such a state ever existed or will ever exist may here be neglected—within which virtue has become habit and that what ought to be is the actual custom. In this case the state as an ethical one would actually be the "interpenetration of the substantial with the particular." [40] It is not difficult to agree that within such a state the individual, by taking up the duties placed upon him, "acquires his substantive freedom" [41] and that "duty is not a restriction on freedom, but only on freedom in the abstract, i.e. on unfreedom." [42] Right and morality are thought here as constitutive moments of ethical life each of them to the degree appropriate for it. Hegel may have had in mind a state like this one but he speaks in a more Kantian way than Kant himself when he transfers the inflexible structure of Kantian morality on to an ethical life which is thought to be actualized in its purity within the state.

Hegel shows some reservations with respect to the "states of classical antiquity" [43] since at that time there was no universal embracing the full freedom of particularity and the welfare of individuals, but he does not show these reservations with respect to the modern state, since here the idea of the state is not veiled any more but actualized "in accordance with its universality and divinity." [44]

---

[38] Hegel, 7, 227, § 144 ad.
[39] Hegel, 7, 225, § 141 ad. See also 7, 328, § 257 : "The state is the actuality of the ethical Idea. It is ethical mind *qua* the substantial will manifest and revealed to itself, knowing and thinking itself, accomplishing what it knows and in so far as it knows it. The state exists immediately in custom, mediately in individual self-consciousness, knowledge, and activity, while self-consciousness in virtue of its sentiment towards the state finds in the state, as its essence and the end and product of its activity, its substantive freedom."
[40] Hegel, 7, 339, § 261.
[41] Hegel, 7, 930, § 149.
[42] Hegel, 7, 230, § 149 ad.
[43] Hegel, 7, 338, § 260 ad.
[44] *Idem.*

Granted that Hegel is right in what he says about the finitude of the moral insight of conscience, granted that his warnings about a subjective and a self-glorifying conscience are justified, we still cannot subscribe to his conclusion that conscience is futile. Although it is essential to the ethical state that in it virtue become a habit, Hegel himself knows very well that "man may be killed by habit, e.g. when he has once come to feel completely at home in life, when he has become mentally and physically dull, and when the clash between a subjective consciousness and mental activity has disappeared; for man is active only in so far as he has not attained his end and wills to develop his potentialities and vindicate himself in struggling to attain it. When this has been fully achieved, activity and vitality are at an end, and the result—loss of interest in life—is mental or physical death." [45]

Without any doubt "steadiness of its character" [46] belongs to the essence of the state; nevertheless stability must not be absolutized. Such absolutization can only be prevented by the operation of conscience working with awareness of its finitude, and not denying it, giving "activity" and "vitality" to the ethical habit. It is not merely a right, Hegel argued in the *Phenomenology*, but even a duty of conscience to "have done with all this calculating and weighing of duties and to decide directly from itself without any such [absolutely true] reasons." [47] Only "in the strength of certainty of itself, does it have the majesty of absolute self-sufficiency, or absolute *Autarkie*, to bind or to loose." [48]

IV

To Hegel Kant is one-sided because of the unreconciled distinction between morality and legality by which he restricts the right to perform those actions that are based on external arbitrariness, for the result of this unreconciled distinction is that Kant knows an internalized morality as the only form of ethical life, and it is not open to any kind of description. Hegel attempted to correct Kant's abstractness. Freedom, according to Hegel, can only be found where we presuppose relations formed by right. It is not the case that he always views these relations as actualized freedom; rather he considers them as the conditions necessary to actualize freedom. Hegel is attempting to supersede the Kantian ethics, which is restricted

---

[45] Hegel, 7, 234, § 151 ad.
[46] Hegel, 7, 233, § 150 ad.
[47] Hegel, 2, 496 (657).
[48] *Idem* (658).

to the internal will. He attempts to introduce morality into ethical life by undertaking to unite individuals and their own will with the universal idea of good and right. This unification happens by moving from the standpoint of morality towards the level of customs, conventions, and political and social institutions which have been conceived as the ethical actuality.[49] Hegel thinks he has found within the state the *topos* where the fundamental relation between the universal and the particular finds its highest fulfillment. Here his argument reads :

the universal does not prevail or achieve completion except along with the particular interest and through the cooperation of particular knowing and willing: and individuals likewise do not live as private persons...but in the very act of willing...they will at the same time within and for the universal, and show an activity which is consciously aimed towards this purpose [i.e. the universal].[50]

By raising morality up into the objective being of ethical life, Hegel can identify the individual's assimilation of the duties of his situation as "rectitude." [51] Hegel considered rectitude to be the universal determination of the ethical : the righteous individual has "nothing to do but to follow the well-known explicit rules of his own situation." [52]

Hegel's critique of Kant is—as repeatedly stated—justified, but he himself failed to see that customs, convention, and traditional orders may be as *hypocritical* as the individual and his moral conscience. His charge of hypocrisy is directed only against morality.

The statement, "the state is the actuality of the ethical idea," [53] with which Hegel opens his analysis of the state, should read, "the state is that actuality of the ethical idea which is attained for the time being."[54] As dialectical actuality of the idea, the actuality of the state may be a moral one as well as an immoral one. A dialectical concept by its very nature contains not merely what ought to be, but simultaneously the opposite of what ought to be. The individual therefore has to insist on his right even with respect to the state, and has to follow the path he has already started :

---

[49] A modern philosophical encounter of man's relation to nature, to himself and his society can be found in K. Ulmer's *Philosophie der modernen Lebenswelt*. (Tübingen, J.C.B. Mohr, 1972). Especially part II : "Die Weltorientierung und die Grundordnung von Gesellschaft und politischer Welt."

[50] Hegel, 7, 330, § 260.

[51] Hegel, 7, 230, § 150.

[52] Hegel, 7, 231, § 150.

[53] Hegel, 7, 328, § 257.

[54] Cf. B. Liebrucks, *Sprache und Bewußtsein* (Frankfurt am Main, Akademische Verlagsgesellschaft, 1966), 3, 605 ff.

In the unfolding of the concept of freedom the individual passed the sphere of right; as moral subject the individual learned not to take the right to be absolute, but rather to conceive it as moment. The individual has his experience in the realm of morality : in reflecting on conscience he becomes aware that conscience is capable of making its own not merely the good but also the evil. This insight made the individual realize that morality also has only the character of a moment, and enables him to enter the stage of ethical life. But with the arrival at this stage the individual must not assume that he has reached the destination of his journey, since

> whether the individual exists or not is all one to the objective ethical life. It alone is permanent and is the power regulating the life of the individuals.[55]

If the individual accepts the actuality of the state as the full actualization of the ethical idea and not merely as that actuality of the ethical idea which is attained for the time being, then he becomes guilty of his own extinction. In this case the individual is guilty of neglecting the fact that "ethical life is the completion of objective spirit" and not of the absolute spirit.[56]

Despite the ethical relevance of the state to the individual, the particular state of a certain time, while it is being objective spirit, cannot be viewed as the objectification of the absolute spirit. If it is so viewed—as I believe it is in the *Philosophy of Right* —individual ethical life, because of the finitude of its knowledge, can only be actualized where it relinquishes its individual freedom. Since at this stage the "laws and institutions of ethical order make up the concept of freedom, they are the substance or universal essence of individuals, who are thus related to them as accidents only :" [57]

> Hence the ethical order is freedom or the absolute will as what is objective, a circle of necessity whose moments are the ethical powers which regulate the life of the individuals. To these powers individuals are related as accidents to substance, and it is in individuals that these powers are represented, have the shape of appearance, and become actualized.[58]

In saying this Hegel is not doing justice to the finite individual and his demand for self-determination, since he views individuality merely as particularity, as accident which in respect to ethics has its truth *outside* of itself, outside not in the sense of hope or faith, but rather in the sense of an actuality which is regarded as reasonable only because of the cunning of reason. The state, according to Hegel, possesses the fulness of this actuality. Since the state is

[55] Hegel, 7, 227, § 145.
[56] Hegel, 10, 397, § 513.
[57] Hegel, 7, 227, § 145.
[58] Hegel, 7, 227, § 145 ad.

the spirit on earth consciously realizing itself there... the march of God in the world, that is what the state is.[59]

Man on the other side is faint and blind. For whether

he knows it or not, this essence [the essence of freedom, which is only fully actualized within the state] is externally realized as a self-subsistent power in which single individuals are only moments.[60]

Ethical life is not the truth of the absolute spirit despite Hegel's reproving argument against the abstractness of conscience to the effect that because of the abstractness, "the state cannot give recognition to conscience in its private form as subjective knowing, any more than science can grant validity to subjective opinion, dogmatism, and the appeal to a subjective opinion."[61]

The question thrown into the philosophical discussion by Kant, namely whether conscience may err, was affirmed by Hegel. A variety of arguments which support the Hegelian position have been presented. The strongest one is that human knowledge is finite. Kant's own answer to this question is opposite to Hegel's. He writes in *The Metaphysical Principles of Virtue* : "There is no such thing as an erring conscience," [62] and justifies his assertion in a similar way to the way he justified the relevance of the distinction between truth and truthfulness. "In the objective judgment as to whether or not something is a duty, one can indeed sometimes be mistaken; but I cannot be mistaken in any subjective judgment as to whether I have compared something with my practical [here judicially acting] reason for the sake of such a judgment." It cannot be assumed as a duty, Kant argues, to act in accordance or in discordance with conscience, "since otherwise it would be necessary to have a second conscience to be aware of the act of the first." [63]

At the end of the attempt to give content to conscience and to move beyond the contentlessness of Kant's *ought to,* Hegel encounters the dilemma

---

[59] Hegel, 7, 334/35, § 258 ad.

[60] Hegel, 7, 336, § 258 ad.

[61] Hegel, 7, 197, § 137. Obviously, Hegel is correct in so far as such formulations only attempt to refute the opinion that it is possible to establish and maintain freedom and the ethical orders of life on a basis of morality alone. And he is just as correct where he wants to show that only the right grounded in freedom and a state being rooted in this right can guarantee the ethical and moral freedom of the individual as concrete freedom. "It is only," he writes, "in times when the world of actuality is hollow, spiritless, and unstable, that an individual may be allowed to take refuge from actuality in his inner life." (7, 199-200, § 138). However, situations like this Hegel can only see as exceptions and not as a rule.

[62] Kant, VI, 401.

[63] *Idem.*

of the *cunning of reason*. Despite this and some other intimations of totalitarianism which we find e.g. in the *Philosophy of Right*, undue weight must not be given to them.[64] For the most part they are not in line with the main train of his thought. Hegel and his idea of dialectical philosophy are misunderstood if on the basis of that intimation he is accused generally of disrespect for the individual and deification of the state.

"According to the stages in the development of the Idea of the will, free in itself and for itself," [65] all shapes are taken up in it as "moments in the development of the Idea." [66] Consequently the "original abstract concept is never abandoned, it merely becomes continually richer in itself,"[67] thereby it has to be noticed that "the moments, whose result is a further determined form of the concept, precede it in the philosophical development, but they do not go in advance of it in the temporal development of shapes."[68] Right and morality are both abstractions, that is, moments "whose truth is ethical life alone." [69] As constitutive moments they are not something that is left behind, but rather they are taken up into the whole (ethical life) to which they belong. As Hegel explains in his *Logic* : "What supersedes itself does not thereby become nothing....It therefore retains the determinateness whence it started.... Thus, what is superseded is also preserved; it only lost its immediacy and is not on that account annihilated." [70] Since the reception of the Kantian morality has a constitutive function for Hegel's concept of ethical life it cannot have been his *intention* to forsake the individual and to affirm that political power and force are of higher importance than moral self-determination, thereby letting them triumph over the powerless individual. The ethical life—and these are

---

[64] Cf. : J.N. Findlay, *Hegel, A Re-Examination*, (London, George Allen & Unwin, 1958), 322. I am in agreement with Findlay's analysis of Hegel's concept of the state, but cannot agree with K. Popper on this issue. Cf. : K. Popper, *The Open Society and its Enemies.* (London, 1965). To see in Hegel merely the necessary link between Plato and the modern form of totalitarianism certainly would do injustice to Hegel. Even if I am convinced that W.H. Walsh plays down the ambiguity of the individual in Hegel, just to state that "Individuals exist for Hegel exactly as they do for the rest of us" does not eliminate the objection generally raised against Hegel's concept of the individual. W.H. Walsh, *Hegelian Ethics* (New York, St. Martin's Press, 1969), 40.

[65] Hegel, 7, 84, § 33.
[66] Hegel, 7, 85, § 33.
[67] Hegel, 7, 83, § 32 ad.
[68] Hegel, 7, 82, § 32.
[69] Hegel, 7, 87, § 33 ad.
[70] Hegel, 4, 120.

Hegel's own words—"is subjective disposition but of the right as it is in itself." [71]

The reason for the dilemma in the *Philosophy of Right* can be seen in the failure to distinguish between the objective spirit as actual in the state, and the absolute spirit. Hegel himself seems to have felt deep dissatisfaction with his result and suggested another, more human solution, a solution which brings him closer to Kant than he himself may have imagined and which the critical remarks on Kant in the *History of Philosophy* would allow us to suppose. In the *Philosophy of History* Hegel points out that it is *faith* that speaks the ultimate word of reason, since

> the appearance of the thought that reason governs the world is connected with one further application which is quite well known to us in the form of *religious truth*, namely that the world is not surrendered to contingency and external contingent causes but rather that a providence governs the world.[72]

Is not ethical life as well as the state seen here as a moment and not as the whole in the process of the unfolding of freedom? Is that assertion not a rehabilitation, even an upgrading of the individual and his conscience in relation to the attained actuality of the state? If it is, then the comparison the *Philosophy of Right* makes with respect to the state also applies to the individual conscience. Conscience would be still conscience just as the "ugliest man, or a criminal, or an invalid, or a cripple, is still always a living man. The affirmative, life, subsists despite his defects, and it is this affirmative factor which" [73] is also the theme of conscience. Of course the suggestion of this paragraph goes beyond what the *Philosophy of Religion* and the *History of Philosophy* actually do say.

In the *History of Philosophy* Hegel accused Kant of being content with merely "talking about morality." [74] Hegel himself undoubtedly attempted to get away from the talk about morality that "has to remain a beyond" [75] because of the "disparity between the particular and the universal will." [76] The correction aimed toward a "perfect ethical life." [77] But, it has to be asked, is not *this* attempt at a reconciliation between the particular and

---

[71] Hegel, 7, 224, § 141.
[72] Hegel, 11, 39.
[73] Hegel, 7, 336, § 257 ad.
[74] Hegel, 19, 593.
[75] *Idem.*
[76] *Idem.*
[77] *Idem.*

the universal will as the basis of perfect ethical life bound to fail because it carries with it from the very beginning the burden of the cunning of reason? Its result is not "perfect" ethical life, rather the mere talking about it. Hegel's perfect ethical life therefore has to remain in a beyond as does Kant's "perfect morality."

HEGEL AND SOLOVYOV

GEORGE L. KLINE

Bryn Mawr College

I

Vladimir Sergeyevich Solovyov (1853-1900) was not only the most impressive speculative thinker produced by Russia in the nineteenth century; he was also the most systematic and original of the Russian neo-Hegelians. Both his philosophical system and his metaphilosophical system were profoundly influenced by Hegel.

Solovyov was distinctive in a number of ways, when compared to both Russian and West European thinkers. I begin by mentioning five of them:

1) Solovyov was unusually *precocious*. He died at age forty-seven, younger than any major thinker except Spinoza (who died at forty-five) and Pascal (who died at thirty-nine). His first article was published when he was twenty and his first book—the master's thesis, *Krizis zapadnoi filosofii* (The Crisis of Western Philosophy)—when he was twenty-one. Solovyov completed three other major systematic works between the ages of twenty-four and twenty-eight. In contrast, at age twenty-one neither Spinoza nor Kant nor Hegel had given any clear evidence of future philosophical greatness. It is probably Schelling, that philosophical *Wunderkind*, who would be Solovyov's closest rival for the prize of precocity. Schelling wrote his master's thesis when he was eighteen, and had published two more books by the time he was twenty![1]

This paper focuses on Solovyov's "first" philosophical system, following a preliminary survey of his "first" metaphilosophical system. It draws mainly from the unfinished, but architectonically complex and detailed *Filosofskie nachala tsel'nogo znaniia* (Philosophical Principles of Integral Knowledge), 1877; also from the master's thesis, and the doctoral disser-

---

[1] As Hegel once remarked, with some venom, Schelling "carried on his philosophical education in public"—that is, he rejected his earlier positions one after the other. In contrast, Solovyov arrived early at his central philosophical conception and held it virtually unchanged throughout his life.

tation, *Kritika otvlechënnykh nachal* (A Critique of Abstract Principles), 1877-80; and it makes some reference to the *Chteniia o Bogochelovechestve* (Lectures on Godmanhood), 1877-1881. Of these early works, only the *Lectures* have thus far been translated into English.

There is, in all of these works, more than a trace of the dogmatism and one-sidedness, as well as the intensity, of youth. For example, Solovyov permits himself such premature generalizations as the claim that English minds are philosophically shallow and incapable of Russo-German speculative profundity, citing as evidence the "coarsely realistic" English terms 'some*thing*', 'no*thing*', 'some*body*', 'no*body*', to which correspond the Russian terms *nechto* (literally, 'somewhat'), *nichto* ('no-what'), *nekto* ('some-who'), and *nikto* ('no-who').[2] Happily, in his later works Solovyov avoided such facile generalizations.

2) Solovyov was markedly *erudite*. He knew at least eight languages—three ancient and five modern—in addition to his native Russian. His early works exhibit a mastery of the history of religious and philosophic doctrines that is truly staggering. As an example of his linguistic erudition, Solovyov ended his master's thesis with a Greek quotation:

... *ek pantōn hen kai ex henos panta*,

not deigning to translate it into Russian or to inform his readers that it is a fragment from Heraclitus (which may be rendered as "From all things [comes] the one, and from the one all things.")

3) He was remarkably *versatile*. Solovyov wrote sensitive literary criticism and penetrating essays on current social, political, and ecclesiastical questions, as well as impressive lyric poetry and delightful light verse. I can think of no other systematic thinker who has been so richly and variously gifted.

4) He commanded an elegant, lucid, generally concise *style*. His use of technical terms was more consistent than Kant's, perhaps more consistent even than Hegel's. With one striking exception—the use of the term *material'ny*, 'material'—he scrupulously avoided ambiguity. (See below, Sec. IV.) He introduced a number of philosophical coinages, e.g., the neologistic distinction between *sub'ektny* ('subject-y') and *sub'ektivny* ('subjective'). Solovyov used the term *normal'ny* in a rather special sense, equivalent not to 'normal' but to 'normative', 'norm-bound', or 'ideal'.

5) He had a vivid *sense of history*, a perception or intuition of the world as process, becoming, dialectical development, that calls to mind the "theurgical restlessness" of Peter Chaadayev (1794-1856), the first Russian philo-

---

[2] *Filosofskie nachala tsel'nogo znaniia, Sochinenia* (2nd ed., St. Petersburg, 1911) [reprint Brussels, 1966], I, 406. Solovyov failed to mention (and perhaps was unaware) that 'someone' and 'no one' are standard English synonyms for 'somebody' and 'nobody'.

sopher of history. According to Solovyov, men are, or should be, doing "God's work — or rather a collaborative divine-human work — in history." But Solovyov had almost no interest in the scholarly or "scientific" study of history—perhaps because his father, Sergei M. Solovyov, the distinguished historian of Russia, was massively concerned with precisely that kind of study.

II

The Crisis of Western Philosophy, subtitled *Against the Positivists*, is Solovyov's principal presentation of his early metaphilosophical system — a Hegelian taxonomy of historical philosophies in their dialectical interconnection and development. Like Hegel, Solovyov sometimes squeezes and trims a little in order to fit individual thinkers into his triadic schemata.

Solovyov takes it as self-evident that (1) in contrast to language, myth, and art, which are products of the creativity of the entire species (cf. Vico, Schelling), philosophy is a matter of "personal or individual world-views" which have emerged with the disintegration of primitive religious unity; and (2) philosophy as abstract, exclusively theoretical knowledge, has reached—in both the speculative, rationalist tradition and the positivist, empiricist tradition—the end of its development.

Philosophy began in the West, according to Solovyov, when Christian (i.e., Roman Catholic) doctrine ceased to be an inner conviction and became an external authority. Scholastic philosophy passed through three dialectical stages:

1) Christian doctrine, as divine revelation, is absolute truth; reason, as fallible, should submit to its authority.

2) Reason cannot contradict (revealed) authoritative truth; the two should be reconciled.

3) Reason does not contradict *true* authority.[3] Thus if (revealed) authority agrees with reason it is unnecessary, and if it contradicts reason, it is false. This involves a reversal of stage (1).[4]

Solovyov sees the development of post-Renaissance thought in Western Europe as exhibiting two dominant historical "syllogisms"—the empiricist and the rationalist.

The empiricist "syllogism" runs as follows:

---

[3] Solovyov quotes in Latin the principle: *Vera auctoritas rectae rationi non obsistit* (*Krizis zapadnoi filosofii, Sochinenia*, I, 30).

[4] *Ibid.*, pp. 29 f.

Major premise (Bacon) : That which truly is
is known only through experience.
Minor premise (Locke) : But in experience
we know only our own states of consciousness.
Conclusion (J.S. Mill) : Therefore, that
which truly is is only our own states of consciousness.

The rationalist "syllogism" runs as follows :

Major premise (Leibniz, Wolff) : That which
truly is is known only through reason.
Minor premise (Kant) : But reason knows only
the forms of thought.
Conclusion (Hegel) : Therefore, that which
truly is is only the forms of thought.[5]

This would seem to push Hegel toward subjective idealism. In fact, Solovyov's understanding of Hegel, even at age twenty-one, was more accurate and more subtle than this would suggest. He saw that, for Hegel, being, or "that which is," is the "self-development of the concept (*poniatie* = *Begriff*)," and went on to note that the Hegelian concept "eternally differentiates itself within itself, has a negative relationship to itself, posits itself as other, changes, and passes into its other in a plurality of dialectical phases." [6]

But his general metaphilosophical conclusion is that Hegel was to philosophy what Louis XIV was to the nation-state : both led to the decline of what they stood for—rationalist philosophy and absolute monarchy. Indeed, Solovyov sees both as threatened with total displacement—by the special sciences (positivism) and the third estate (socialism), respectively.[7]

At the present time (1874), according to Solovyov, the task of synthesizing and transcending both rationalism and empiricism is being carried on by at least one thinker—Eduard von Hartmann, who seeks to reach "speculative conclusions" by means of an empirical, inductive method. Solovyov's choice of Hartmann is, of course, unfortunate, based mainly on the historical contingency that, as of 1874, Hartmann was the most prominent of German philosophers. Solovyov had no respect for Spencer or John Stuart Mill, both of whom he regarded as shallow empiricists and positivists.

---

[5] *Ibid.*, pp. 133-35.
[6] *Ibid.*, p. 57.
[7] *Filosofskie nachala* ..., p. 278.

He apparently knew nothing of Renouvier or Boutroux. In 1874 Peirce and Nietzsche had published only their earliest works.[8]

As one commentator has pointed out, Solovyov's interpretation of Hartmann is arbitary : it pictures him as advocating, and perhaps even prophesying, an ultimate "realm of the spirit" which will be a "complete manifestation of total-unity," a restoration of the lost unity and wholeness of man. In fact Hartmann—like Schopenhauer—advocated a kind of nirvana. His "Philosophy of the Unconscious" rests on a Buddhist metaphysics; but Solovyov twists it to fit what he calls the "Christian philosophy of the East."[9]

Solovyov's *Crisis of Western Philosophy* falls into two parts which are of unequal value : a first, primarily critical part culminates in the plausible claim that Western philosophic thought has foundered on "abstract formalism"; a second, constructive part implausibly claims that the longed-for "universal synthesis" of Eastern and Western thought is being realized in the work of Eduard von Hartmann.[10] Both claims betray the influence of Slavophile ideas, especially those of Dostoyevsky and of Ivan Kireyevsky (1806-1856), whose writings of the 1840s and 1850s had suggested the general plan of the *Crisis* and many of its central notions.[11] Foremost among Slavophile beliefs was the conviction that the Byzantine tradition of Russian Orthodoxy had preserved Christian truth and spirituality, but had neglected secular culture, whereas Western Europe had developed a flourishing secular culture, but had neglected the divine and spiritual.[12]

In his early period, Solovyov preached a moderate Russian messianism : Russia, he maintained, would provide the required synthesis of Eastern and Western values. In time, however, he became disillusioned with Hartmann, abandoned Slavophile "messianism," and became a "good European," defending a universalistic and ecumenical position in matters of culture and religion, and sharply criticizing such defenders of Byzantine spiritual and cultural superiority as Konstantin Leontiev (1831-1891).

---

[8] However, even after Nietzsche was "discovered" by Russian intellectuals, in the early 1890s, Solovyov continued to ignore him. (Peirce was not discovered in Russia until after Solovyov's death.)

[9] Konstantin Mochulski, *Vladimir Solov'ev : Zhizn' i uchenie* (Vladimir Solovyov : Life and Teaching), (2nd ed., Paris, 1951), p. 52.

[10] *Ibid.*, pp. 52 f.

[11] Among them : the idea of a synthesis of philosophy and religion; Western philosophy as a hypertrophied rationalism; the "wholeness" of life; and the need to combine Western thought with Eastern speculation. (Cf. Mochulski, *op. cit.*, p. 54).

[12] Alexander Koschewnikoff [Alexandre Kojève], "Die Geschichtsphilosophie Wladimir Solowjews," *Der russische Gedanke*, I (1929-1930), p. 320.

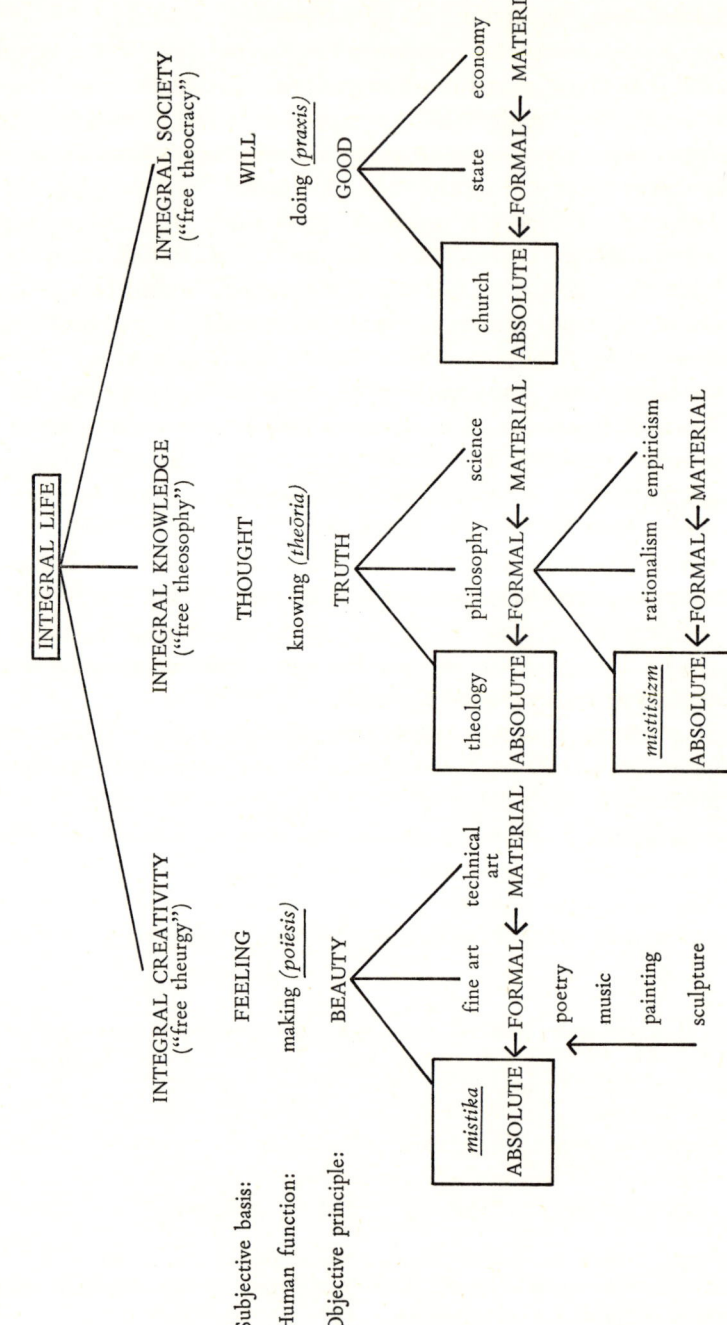

III

Solovyov's philosophical system is a neo-Hegelian and, as compared to Hegel's own philosophy, a moderately de-Aristotelianized and heavily re-Platonized position. It attempts a universal synthesis—not a Hegelian *Aufhebung* in which speculative philosophy or "absolute knowledge" is dominant — of religion, philosophy, and science. Solovyov takes with complete seriousness the Platonic triad of beauty, truth, and goodness.[13] "What the absolute wills as good," he writes, "is the same as what it represents as truth and feels as beauty."[14] To the Platonic form of beauty corresponds the Aristotelian function of making, to the form of truth the function of knowing, and to the form of the good the function of doing.

According to Solovyov, human *making* becomes, when purged and unified, "integral creativity"; *knowing* becomes "integral knowledge"; and *doing* becomes "integral society." Each of these three, in turn, is an integrating synthesis of three subordinate elements : "integral creativity" of mystical experience (*mistika*), fine art, and applied art; "integral knowledge" of theology, abstract philosophy, and positive science; "integral society" of ecclesiastical, political, and economic institutions. The synthesis, in turn, of integral creativity with integral knowledge and integral society is what Solovyov calls "integral life".

In Hegel there is a development which is both historical and dialectical in the order of *knowing*, from art through religion and theology to philosophy. But there seems to be no parallel development to philosophy through the forms of *doing* (social-moral and political institutions). Rather, as in Aristotle, the socio-political and economic order serves as a means or precondition to the end of acquiring philosophical knowledge. For Hegel, *making* is, in a sense, a defective or inadequate form of knowing. But *doing* is surely a condition for, not a form of, adequate knowing.

Solovyov generalizes the structural and dialectical development which Hegel had applied primarily to human institutions (cf. the *Philosophy of Right*), extending it to the entire system. In a subordinate sense, I suppose, the development of one-sided principles—principles which are "abstract" in Hegel's sense of the term, i.e., "one-sided, inadequately related, relatively unmediated"—into integral principles—principles which are "concrete" in Hegel's sense, i.e., "many-sided, adequately related, complexly mediated"

---

[13] In connection with the following discussion, see the diagram on p. 164.
[14] *Lectures on Godmanhood* (trans. by George L. Kline) in James M. Edie, et al., eds., *Russian Philosophy*. (2nd ed., Chicago, 1969), III, 69.

—may be considered a historical, as well as a structural and dialectical, development. Such, presumably, on Solovyov's view is the development from ancient, *unfree* theocracy and theurgy to modern, or rather future, *free* theocracy and theurgy.

Partly as a result of what might be called the "horizontal" character of Solovyov's system, as compared to Hegel's "vertical" system—which exhibits a development through historical time in a sequential, though also dialectical, fashion—Solovyov is able to introduce religious elements at four distinct junctures [15] as compared to only two in Hegel, viz. (1) the *vorgestellter Begriff* of religion and theology as an *Aufhebung* of art's pure *Vorstellung*, and (2) ecclesiastical institutions as one of the many forms of "civil society." Of course, in the *Phenomenology of the Spirit* several proto-religious dialectical phases appear, e.g., in the unhappy consciousness and the Antigone stage (at the beginning of *Geist*). The development of the literary and plastic arts and of music is at the same time a development of religion, which means that religious elements appear in Greek epic, tragedy, and comedy, and in hymns and temple architecture and sculpture.

Perhaps Solovyov's clearest difference from Hegel—as well as from Plato, Aristotle, and Spinoza—lies in his refusal to subordinate either doing or making to knowing. He places all three on the same ontological and axiological level as essential components of "integral life." This is perhaps the point on which Solovyov is most "Russian," most "existential" (in *one* of the senses of that much-abused term), and most original.

IV

The following comments are intended as clarification, criticism, and, to a limited extent, theoretical development of Solovyov's system (schematized in the diagram on p. 164).

1) Solovyov's terms *tsel'nost'* ('wholeness') and *tsel'ny* ('integral') are stronger synonyms for Hegel's 'concreteness' and 'concrete'. We have seen above that in Hegel's usage 'concrete' means 'many-sided, adequately related, complexly mediated'; Solovyov's *tsel'ny* seems, in addition, to connote 'harmoniously unified'. The expressions 'integral creativity', 'integral knowledge', and 'integral society' bring out Solovyov's point less misleadingly, I think, than the Greek terms 'theurgy', 'theosophy', and 'theocracy', which he also uses. The second is particularly unfortunate, since

---

[15] The four "absolute" or religious junctures are enclosed in square outlines on the diagram.

Solovyov's doctrine has nothing to do with the mystical popular religion—an amalgam of Buddhism and Brahmanism—associated with Mme. Blavatsky's "Theosophical Society," founded in New York in 1875.

Solovyov uses the three terms prefixed by the Greek *theo-* ('God') to stress that the "absolute" or "religious" element in each of the integrated spheres of integral life is central. There is, however, a misleading connotation in the term 'theocracy'; since Solovyov is concerned with social institutions in general rather than forms of political authority, he should perhaps have used some such term as 'theo*praxis*'.

I take the term 'free' in the expressions 'free theurgy', etc., to mean 'perfected' or 'integrated', as opposed to earlier forms of theocracy and theosophy in which the "absolute" order one-sidedly and (in Hegel's sense) abstractly dominates the two subordinate spheres — i.e., the ecclesiastical order dominates the political and economic orders; and theology dominates philosophy and science. The term 'free' also suggests that the integrated elements enjoy a relative autonomy.

Solovyov claims that the contradiction between the religious and secular principles in human society—neither being able to eliminate the other, nor to coexist as independent spheres—is removed when we recognize that the secular or natural order provides necessary *means* which serve the absolute *end* of a religious or mystical order which is realizable only by these means. The secular order has *real* independence; but the religious order has *ideal* priority, since it provides the content and end for the secular order. But since it needs both formal and material means (i.e., both political and economic institutions) for its realization, the religious order in turn is dependent on the secular order.[16] According to Solovyov, the guiding principle of the economic order is *utility*, of the political order *justice*, and of the ecclesiastical order *love*. These principles he calls respectively, "material," "formal," and "absolute."

3) Solovyov's use of the term 'material' (*material'ny*) involves a serious equivocation. In one, generally Aristotelian, sense 'material' is the contrary of 'formal' and means 'content-ly' (a concept more gracefully expressible by the German term *inhaltlich* and the Russian term *soderzhatel'ny*). There is no obvious sense in which economic institutions have more or better content and less or worse form that political and ecclesiastical institutions; or the special sciences more or better content and less or worse form than philosophy and theology; or the technical arts more or better content and less or worse form that the fine arts or mystical experience. Furthermore,

---

[16] *Kritika otvlechënnych nachal*, Soch., I, 174 f.

in the case of *doing* there is a conceptual slide from the *inhaltlich* sense of 'material' to the quite distinct economic sense—according to which economic needs, interests, relations, etc. are termed "material" needs, interests, relations, etc. Without such a slide the sequence 'material-formal-absolute' makes no sense. (It makes a certain dialectical sense only if the "absolute" level is understood as an *Aufhebung* — a transcendence, preservation, and cancelling—of the matter-form distinction.)[17]

In the case of *knowing* Solovyov uses the term 'material' in the sense of 'empirical', following the Kantian usage according to which the sense-manifold provides the "matter" or "material" which the understanding "forms" by the application of concepts and categories. Such special sciences as mathematics, mathematical physics, and astrophysics are surely just as "formal" as philosophy; and philosophy surely has an empirical "content" —although Solovyov's Kantian classification suggests that it is exclusively formal. Ethics, aesthetics, ontology, and philosophy of history—though admittedly not formal logic—would seem to have just as much "content" as physics, chemistry, geology or biology, though a quite different one.

It the case of *making*, moreover, Solovyov's use of the form-content distinction to characterize the difference between the fine arts and the technical arts is especially problematic; the line marking off architecture as the highest and most perfect of the technical arts from sculpture as the lowest and least perfect of the fine arts seems to be quite arbitrarily drawn. It is not clear why Solovyov did not follow Hegel's lead and include architecture as one (to be sure, the lowest and least perfect) of the fine arts.

4) In his view of law and the state, Solovyov appears to have been unduly influenced by Schopenhauer. He sees law or right (the Russian term *pravo* has the same fruitful but sometimes troublesome ambiguity as the German *Recht*) as a negative phenomenon—a barrier limiting infringement of the rights of others. For Hegel, of course, such a negative conception applies only at the level of abstract right and law in the *Philosophy of Right* and at the level of Roman formalistic legality—the *Rechtszustand*—in the *Phenomenology*. In his early works Solovyov accepted the pessimistic view that all systems of positive *Recht* and all historical polities are a kind of

---

[17] In at least one place Solovyov offers a rather more convincing account than that based on the "formal-material" distinction of the relation of the economic order to the political and ecclesiastical orders : the first — he says — is the external basis, the second the means, and the third the end of social life. In a cruder, but more vivid, analogy he spoke of the economy, state, and church as, respectively, the "belly, head, and heart" of the body politic! (Cf. *Filosofskie nachala* ..., p. 261.)

"hereditary disease" which must be judged "abnormal" in the light of the absolute ideal of "normal" society.[18]

5) *Prima facie*, it would seem that *mistika* (mystical experience) belongs with neither fine nor technical art. But Solovyov's reasons for putting it where he does make a certain sense. The three orders grouped under creativity have three features in common : (a) they are all *based* or grounded in feeling; (b) they all use imagination as their *means*; (c) they all involve ecstatic inspiration—Platonic *mania*—(presumably as their *end*). This last feature seems doubtfully present in technical art, although Solovyov is a good Greek when he denies any fundamental distinction between the making of a shoe or a ship and the making of a statue or a poem. Still, one might object — to both Solovyov and the Greeks — that the realm which has beauty as its "objective principle" is a hybrid made up of two distinct elements : a certain kind of experience or feeling (*aisthēsis*) and a certain kind of skilled shaping or making (*poiēsis*). The element of feeling in the technical arts would seem to be minimal and the element of skilled shaping would seem to be absent from *mistika* — unless Solovyov means to include mystical *discipline* as well as mystical *experience* (a point which he fails to clarify). In general — *pace* both Aristotle and Solovyov — the combination of *aisthēsis* and *poiēsis* would appear to be limited to the fine arts.

6) Solovyov makes the further, and equally controversial, claim that *mistika* has the same relation to *mistitsizm* (the philosophy which stresses mystical experience) that *empiria* has to *empirizm* (the philosophy which stresses sense experience).[19] But perhaps he is right in regarding *mistika* as in some sense a cognitive, even though nondiscursive, form of experience, which thus falls within the domain of integral *knowledge*, in the (absolute) position corresponding, respectively, to theology and to *mistitsizm*. Since *mistika* has an obvious religious dimension, it also occupies a position which plausibly corresponds to that of the church within "integral society."

V

To sum up : In his early works Solovyov was, as I have suggested, systematically Hegelian in metaphilosophy and systematically neo-Hegelian in philosophy, even though he assigned Hegel a rather reduced role in the history of speculative thought. Later he came to confess his debt to Hegel more honestly and more openly. One of his last published works, a long

---

[18] *Ibid.*, p. 258.
[19] *Ibid.*, p. 263 n.

encyclopedia article on Hegel, is both fair and sympathetic; in fact it is a small model of Hegel scholarship.

In his last years Solovyov changed his mind on a number of key issues: he became less optimistic about the prospects for a "free theocracy" and even gloomily apocalyptic in his final major work, *Three Conversations: on War, Progress, and the End of History* (1900). But his conviction that there is a central and primary place for *mistika* within the fabric of human experience; for theology among the ways of seeking truth; for *mistitsizm* among the forms of philosophy; and for ecclesiastical institutions within the fabric of human society—was as strong at the end of his intellectual life as it had been at the beginning.

HEGEL AND PEIRCE [1]

Max H. Fisch

The University of Illinois

An essay on Hegel and Peirce might compare their philosophies without raising the question of influence; or it might inquire what influence, if any, Hegel exerted on Peirce, without carrying comparison beyond the points of discernible influence; or it might assess Peirce's accuracy, fairness and penetration as an interpreter and critic of Hegel; or it might simply assemble some of the biographical information that one would wish to have in hand before attempting any of those more philosophical tasks. That is, it might report what Peirce had to say of Hegel from time to time in the course of his own philosophical development — what Hegelian enterprises he thought of himself as resuming and continuing, what elements or features of Hegel's philosophy he esteemed or disesteemed as he understood them, and what elements or features of his own philosophy he viewed as roughly equivalent to or corrective of them. It is an essay of this last and most modest kind that I offer here, because that is as far as I have got.

Since in a short essay only a small part of the evidence can be presented, a plan of selection is needed. My plan is to focus (A) on the two principal occasions on which Peirce developed his philosophy at length in relation

---

In the following notes and in the text, references of the form "Ms 943" are to the Charles S. Peirce Papers in The Houghton Library of Harvard University, as numbered and described by Richard S. Robin in his *Annotated Catalogue* (University of Massachusetts Press, 1967). There is a microfilm edition of these Papers. All quotations from them are by permission of the Department of Philosophy of Harvard University.

References of the form "1.622" (as in note 3) are to Peirce's *Collected Papers*, edited by Hartshorne, Weiss and Burks in eight volumes (Harvard University Press, 1931-1958), by volume and paragraph number; in this case, volume 1, paragraph 622.

[1] Though I shall not refer to them, three previous essays deserve mention. H.G. Townsend, "The Pragmatism of Peirce and Hegel," *Philosophical Review* 37 : 297-303, 1928. Matthew J. Fairbanks, "A Note Concerning Peirce's Debt to Hegel," *New Scholasticism* 36 : 219-224, 1962. Antonio Santucci, "Peirce, Hegel e la dottrina delle categorie," in : *Incidenza di Hegel*, ed. Fulvio Tessitore (Naples : Morano, 1970), 965-984.

to Hegel's and (B) on what he took to be his own two principal contributions to philosophy, considered here in relation to Hegel. The two occasions were : (A1) his five contributions to the *Journal of Speculative Philosophy* in 1868-9, and (A2), thirty years later, his eight Cambridge Conferences of 1898. The two contributions were : (B1) his "New List of Categories" in 1867, and (B2), forty years later, the proof of pragmaticism that he was working out from 1903 to 1911. The four parts of my essay will come to these focuses in the order A2, B1, B2, A1. This plan will involve touching incidentally on his relations to the two men who, in his eyes, were the leading American Hegelians of his time : Josiah Royce in Parts I and III and W.T. Harris in Parts III and IV.

I

In Peirce's Cambridge Conferences of 1898 there was a notification implicit in his title, "On Reasoning and the Logic of Things," and explicit in his advance correspondence, that he was inviting comparison with Hegel. To William James, who had made the arrangements for the series, he wrote at first : "I think I will call the course On the Logic of Events. Thus it will be my tychism & synechism, but regarded from the point of view of Objective Logic." [2] Here, from his next letter to James, are brief descriptions of lectures 4, 6, 7 and 8 as he first conceived them.

4. *The Categories* : Quality, Reaction, Representation or Mediation. This is the main thing I have been harping on from the beginning and shows wherein my objective logic differs from that of Hegel.
6. *Objective Deduction.* Shows how deduction works in the world, both in its simplest and more intricate forms.
7. *Objective Induction and Hypothesis.* Same for these modes of inference.
8. *Creation.* Shows how I would conceive the earliest steps of evolution, beginning with the Germinal Nothing and continuing to the point where the special sciences attack the problem, took place. I am writing this last lecture first.[3]

In his notes for the Conferences, Peirce wrote : "It is not my intention at all to attempt a criticism of Hegel. I have not studied him deeply enough

---

[2] Peirce to William James, December 13, 1897, James Papers, The Houghton Library, Harvard University.

[3] Peirce to James, about December 19 or 20, 1897, James Papers. (The first two pages are missing.) For further details, see Ralph Barton Perry, *The Thought and Character of William James* (Boston, 1935), Vol. II, pp. 418-421. See also 1.622. For the "prime difference" between Peirce's objective logic and Hegel's in the Conferences as delivered, see 6.218.

to do so. But certain remarks about him strike me, from time to time; and those I insert" (Ms 943).

That was in Peirce's fifty-ninth year, and there is no evidence that in the remaining sixteen years of his life he made any deeper study.

With that disclaimer before us, our expectation will be that what Peirce says about Hegel will tell us, at least on first consideration, rather more about Peirce than it does about Hegel.

One reason for the disclaimer, however, was that Peirce's audience was to include a philosopher who *had* studied Hegel deeply. That was Josiah Royce. Royce wrote James more than three years later : "As for thoughts, of late, I seem to myself to be on the track of a great number of interesting topics in Logic. Those lectures of poor C.S. Peirce that you devised will always remain quite epoch marking for me. They started me on such new tracks." [4] Nearly a year after that, late in May of 1902, Peirce wrote Royce that if he would come to Arisbe, Peirce's country place on the Delaware, and spend the summer there, "you and I could pitch into the logical problems and I am sure I could make it well spent time for you, while with all you should teach me of Hegel etc. I am equally sure it would tremendously benefit my own work." [5] But Royce replied that, attractive as the proposal was, he had engaged to teach that summer at Berkeley.[6] So the one occasion when Peirce *might* have made a deeper study of Hegel did not come off.

We shall briefly return to the Cambridge Conferences in Part II, paragraph (19). And we shall find reason in Parts II-IV to think that Peirce's study of Hegel had not been altogether lacking in depth, and that when the Cambridge Conferences are eventually published and examined in the light of all the drafts and notes, they will afford a basis for a detailed and fruitful comparison.

II

In 1905, in his sixty-sixth year, Peirce said that the one contribution he had made to philosophy was the "New List of Categories" he had published in 1867, in his twenty-eighth year (8.213); and that the one contribution he had still to make was a proof of his pragmaticism, since that "would

---

[4] *The Letters of Josiah Royce*, ed. John Clendenning (University of Chicago Press, 1970)), p. 422.

[5] Peirce to Royce, May 28, 1902, in *Royce on the Human Self*, by James Harry Cotton (Harvard University Press, 1954), p. 301.

[6] Royce to Peirce, June 20, 1902, *ibid.*, p. 302.

essentially involve the establishment of the truth of synechism" (5.415). That second contribution never reached print, and its reconstruction from the numerous surviving manuscripts is perhaps the chief remaining task of Peirce scholarship. But though for his first attempts at a definition of continuity he turned to Aristotle and Kant (6.120-126), Peirce the synechist thought of Leibniz and Hegel as his leading forerunners among philosophers, because it was they who, in their different ways, and Hegel more than Leibniz, had made continuity a central principle of philosophy (1.40-42).[7] I shall return to that point in Part III. Meanwhile I trace the Hegelian bearings of the one contribution to philosophy that Peirce had already made.

Peirce in his twenties was an avid system-builder. A system of philosophy began, of course, with a system of logic, and the prime business of logic was establishing a table of categories.

Though Peirce in his published 1867 paper "On a New List of Categories" (1.545-559) made no reference to older lists, we know from drafts of it that he had those of Aristotle, Kant and Hegel chiefly in mind.[8] With the further assistance of later accounts we gather that the order of development was about as follows:

(1) He at first accepted Kant's list, as if from Sinai (4.2).

(2) He began finding among the categories in Kant's list relations other than those that Kant himself pointed out.

(3) About the same time, he detected a fallacy in Kant's logic that emancipated him from his previous idolatry (4.2).

(4) It appeared to him that these other relations, if they belonged to a system of conceptions at all, belonged to a larger one than that of Kant's list (1.563; 4.2).

(5) He devoted two years—"the two most passionately laborious years" of his life (1.288)—to the endeavor to make out what that larger system might be. Before trying various constructions of his own, he examined other systems. Preëminent among these was Hegel's.

(6) In order not to overlook any conception that might belong to that larger system, he began compiling a philosophical vocabulary, using a large bound Universal Index notebook, which his father had previously used for mathematical terms, and which he himself had previously used for chemical terms (Ms 1156).

---

[7] See "Peirce and Leibniz," by Max H. Fisch, *Journal of the History of Ideas* 33 : 485-496, 1972, esp. p. 494.

[8] Murray Murphey, *The Development of Peirce's Philosophy* (Harvard University Press, 1961), pp. 411-422, at 412. See also Donald E. Buzzelli, "The Argument of Peirce's 'New List of Categories' ", *Transactions of the Charles S. Peirce Society* 8 : 63-89, 1972.

(7) In conjunction with the notebook, he worked up a card file, with at least one card for each conception, definition, problem, controversial issue, and position, and for each author and work, giving the abbreviation under which it was referred to on other cards. For Hegel his primary sources were his own copy of the second edition of the *Encyclopädie* and his own set of the posthumous edition of Hegel's *Werke*, in eighteen volumes.[9]

(8) He also began a Logic Notebook to record the day-to-day explorations that should issue in the system of logic that should be built upon his own deduction of the categories. On an early page of the Notebook he wrote in 1865 :

> Hegel makes a great boast of the fact that his Logic developes its own method. Mine pursues a rational method of which the logic itself is but the deduction & proof. Moreover I am not forced to make my book unintelligible in order to follow mine, but on the contrary it is the very proceedure which perspicuity demands. Another thing; Hegel never deduces the necessity of considering what he considers before considering it; but I never introduce a distinction without having deduced the necessity for it.[10]

(9) After two years of intense pursuit of a larger system like Hegel's, he found himself with no satisfactory result.

(10) It occurred to him that there might be two sets of categories. Besides the long list, as long or longer than Hegel's, there might be a short list, shorter than Kant's twelve or Aristotle's ten. And the short list might be the shortest, if not the only, way to the long one.

(11) By a method which seemed to him to combine the opposite strengths of Kant's and Hegel's, and to avoid their opposite weaknesses, Peirce came out in 1867 with a list of three categories. He called them Quality, Relation, and Representation (1.555).

(12) The deduction of the three categories in the "New List" of 1867 was backed up (if not superseded) in 1870 by a much simpler deduction in his "Logic of Relatives" (3.63, 144).

(13) Years later, it dawned upon him that, though his three categories were quite disparate from those that Hegel called by that name, they did correspond nearly to Hegel's three stages of thought (8.267-268, 329).

(14) He then began calling his three categories Quality, Reaction and

---

[9] Ms 1596, box 5 (to be renumbered Ms 1156a).

[10] Ms 339 p. 5, Dec. 14, [1865]. In the spring of that year, in his Harvard University Lectures on "The Logic of Science," Peirce intended to include a lecture on Hegel, which seems not to have been written or delivered. But there were important brief passages on Hegel in the third and eighth lectures. See Part IV below, under 1865 Spring.

Mediation (after Hegel's *Vermittlung*); or Firstness, Secondness, and Thirdness (6.32; 4.3; 1.530).

(15) To distinguish the categories of the short list from those of the long list, he called the former universal or formal, quantitative or valential, and the latter particular, qualitative or material (1.284; 8.213; Ms 1338 p. 39). He could then say : "In Hegel his long list which gives the divisions of his Encyclopaedia are his Particular Categories. His three stages of thought, although he does not apply the word Category to them, are what I should call Hegel's Universal Categories" (5.43). "In regard to these, it appears to me that Hegel is so nearly right that my own doctrine might very well be taken for a variety of Hegelianism...." (5.38).

(16) In sum, "My three categories...resulted from two years incessant study in the direction of trying to do what Hegel tried to do. It became apparent that there were such categories as his. But bad as his are, I could substitute nothing radically better." [11] That is, his short list resulted from the attempt to improve on Hegel's long list. And "I should not have attempted [that] had I thought Hegel's system satisfactory as a whole" (Ms 1338 p. 39).

(17) Though his two-year quest of a larger system to take the place of Hegel's had failed, he never gave it up. He continued work on his Philosophical Vocabulary. He ransacked the sciences. He studied the scholastics and labored over Bonitz's monumental index to Aristotle. He wrote definitions for the Century Dictionary. He examined languages as remote as possible from the Indo-European, because it seemed to him that Hegel's Logic was in a sense a treatise on the German language.[12]

(18) On one occasion, Peirce ventured to commit himself to producing a longer list comparable with Hegel's *Encyclopedia*. At the end of 1893 he projected a twelve-volume work, *The Principles of Philosophy; or, Logic, Physics, and Psychics, considered as a unity, in the Light of the Nineteenth Century*. In the prospectus inviting subscriptions he said :

> The principles supported by Mr. Peirce bear a close affinity with those of Hegel; perhaps are what Hegel's might have been had he been educated in a physical laboratory instead of in a theological seminary. Thus, Mr. Peirce acknowledges an objective logic (though its movement differs from the Hegelian dialectic), and like Hegel endeavors to assimilate truth got from many a looted system.

And he described the eleventh volume as follows :

---

[11] Ms L 463, draft letter to Lady Welby, July 1905.
[12] *Nation* 75 : 390, 1902 (Peirce's review of Baillie's *Origin and Significance of Hegel's Logic*).

Vol. XI. *A Philosophical Encyclopaedia.* The philosophy of continuity leads to an objective logic, similar to that of Hegel, and to triadic categories. But the movement seems not to accord with Hegel's dialectic, and consequently the form of the scheme of categories is essentially different. Systematic perfection seems to be for the present neither requisite nor attainable; but something like Hegel's Encyclopaedia is proposed.[13]

There were not enough subscribers, the project was abandoned, and Peirce was not obliged to deliver on that commitment. The next occasion was that of the Cambridge Conferences of 1898, with which we began, and to which we now return.

(19) Ideally, Peirce thought, the categories of the longer list should stand in some determinable relation to those of the shorter list. He tried various ways of generating the longer out of the shorter. Here is a passage from his notes for the Cambridge Conferences :

Were I to take the categories of First, Second, and Third, and to classify in their order all the forms of secondness, and then all those of thirdness, connecting each with the preceding by a process of transition, — a work which, by the way I have performed, — I should be developing my doctrine as it seems to me very much in the spirit and method in which Hegel developes his Encyclopädie.

But having gone through with that work and studied its result as thoroughly as I have been able to do, I am convinced that whatever utility it may have,—it does not proceed according to the true logic. The second does not spring out of the first directly; but firstness looked at from a second point of view gives birth to a thirdness and the secondness comes out of the thirdness. This is the true logic of events (Ms 943).

(20) In the end, Peirce concluded that the longer list was incompletable. It was not derivable from the shorter in any *a priori* fashion. One had to wait on experience and on the progress of the sciences. Advance derivations, like that of his sixty-six classes of signs, were only heuristic devices, to guide the search. The best we could hope for was that as new categories were added to the long list, or took the place of old ones, they would yield to analysis in terms of the short list.[14]

(21) Nevertheless, in presenting successive reformulations of his short list, Peirce served notice from time to time that he did *not* hold it to be "the sole true set of logico-metaphysical categories." For example, in 1906 he wrote of himself in the third person : "It is merely the only set the study of which he has sufficiently matured for publication. He has had another

---

[13] *Collected Papers*, vol. 8, pp. 283, 285.
[14] Ms L 75, Carnegie Application, "Statement," pp. 2-6 of longer draft with that heading.

list under active advisement for more than forty years"; that is, from 1865 or earlier until 1906.[15]

With respect, then, to the "one contribution to philosophy" that Peirce had made early in life (8.213), I conclude that he associated with Hegel the original two-year quest of the longer list that had led to the short one, the short list itself, the more than forty years of further searching for the longer list, and the successive reformulations of the short one to which he was thereby led.

III

Turning now to "the one contribution of value" that in 1905 he had still to make, the proof of pragmaticism, I repeat that the value of the proof was to lie in its essentially involving the establishment of the truth of synechism (5.415) and that Leibniz and Hegel were the chief precursors of the synechism. Leibniz had had a mathematical grasp of the principle of continuity which Hegel had lacked, but Hegel had done more to make it a central principle of philosophy; and Peirce hoped to take up and unite the two roles, that of Leibniz and that of Hegel, at a later stage.

In a draft of his review of Royce's *The World and the Individual* Peirce wrote that Hegel's "presentations of half a dozen of most fundamental conceptions of philosophy...were of the utmost service to thought."

The first of these was the conception of mediation, culminating in that of continuity, which had, it is true, been far more distinctly apprehended by the mathematicians since Leibniz and Newton than he ever apprehended it, but which had been totally ignored by philosophers generally.[16]

One of Leibniz's successors was Boole, and Boole's algebra of logic was the point at which Peirce had come in (3.1-19). He saw relations between it and Hegel that were not obvious to others. Reviewing in 1894 the translation of Spinoza's *Ethic* by White and Stirling, he wrote :

Mathematical reasoning consists in thinking how things already remarked may be conceived as making a part of a hitherto unremarked system, especially by means of the introduction of the hypothesis of continuity where no continuity had hitherto been thought of....Boole discovered that if he simply assumed 1 to signify what is, and O what is not...he could without any further assumption

---

[15] Ms 283, p. 34 of a draft sequence.

[16] Ms 1461, which continues : "Then his conception of thought as something independent of the individual man who apprehends it was almost as good as reinstating the Aristotelian final cause." See again Part IV below, under 1865 Spring.

express the premises of a syllogism as two equations from which, by ordinary algebraical rules, the conclusion could be deduced. This was a genuine, living thought, and as such is quite beyond the appreciation of seminary logicians. Its value consisted in its bringing the conceptions of being and nothing into relation with the system of numbers, and especially exhibiting them as the mere punctual terminations of the continuous quantity between them. This last part of the idea coincides with that of Hegel's Becoming, though this latter, besides its inconvenient lugging in of Time, is less useful as being less diagrammatic. However, Hegel's reasoning and Boole's were essentially the same, and this was nothing but an example of the ordinary mathematical proceeding.[17]

A book will sometime be written on Peirce's synechism in relation to Hegel's, after the much needed book on Peirce's synechism itself. But what about the pragmaticism, and what about the proof of it, both in relation to Hegel?

The first thing to say about the pragmaticism is that James saw its Hegelian affinity from the beginning. In lecture notes for his 1876-77 course in physiological psychology, he wrote:

...the logical idealists...Hegel, Green and C.S. Peirce...point to the fact that as a rule our sensations are merely contributory to our *opinions* about *things*... There is an inevitable drift in thought, a logical destiny precipitated out of all experience, which takes up every sensation and makes it contributory to its ends.... This conclusion to which all sensations, all men, all opinions converge is inevitable, if time and experience enough are given, and is "the Truth."[18]

The second thing to say is that the pragmaticism to be proved had undergone extensive revisions. It had been purged of its "principal positive error... its nominalism" (8.216). The requisite antecedent step had been taken in 1897, when Peirce (at 3.527 ff.) repudiated "the nominalistic view of possibility" which he had held until 1896 and "explicitly" returned to "the Aristotelian doctrine of a *real possibility*. This was the great step that was needed to render pragmaticism an intelligible doctrine." [19] Having admitted the reality of *can be*'s and *would be*'s, he had been led to put restrictions upon the principles of contradiction and of excluded middle (8.216)—restrictions that he associated with Hegel's.[20] The third grade of clarity was no longer the highest (5.3). And in numerous other respects his pragmatism

---

[17] *Nation* 59 : 344, 1894 (November 8).

[18] Perry, *op. cit.* (see n. 3 above), I, 477; cf. 541 f. Max H. Fisch, "A Chronicle of Pragmaticism, 1865-1879," *Monist* 48 : 441-466, 1964, at 458 f., 462 f.

[19] Ms 288 pp. 128-129 (draft of 5.527, c. 1905). Max H. Fisch, "Peirce's Progress from Nominalism toward Realism," *Monist* 51 : 159-178, 1967, at 172 f.

[20] E.g., in Ms 137 p. 13 of a draft sequence (1904), and in *Charles S. Peirce's Letters to Lady Welby*, ed. Irwin C. Lieb (New Haven, 1953), p. 30 (1908).

had become so different from James's, Schiller's, or Dewey's, that he could say that it was "closely allied to the Hegelian absolute idealism" (5.436) and that "Royce's conception in *The World and the Individual*...comes nearer to the genuine upshot of pragmaticism than any exposition that a pragmatist has given,—that any *other* pragmatist has given" (Ms 284 p. 4). So that it was not without Peirce's encouragement that Royce—"the greatest of living metaphysicians" (Ms 284 p. 91) though still in Peirce's eyes an Hegelian—began about 1906 to call himself an "absolute pragmatist." [21]

The third thing to say — and this will bring us to the proof — is that Peirce did not finish revising his pragmaticism and then proceed to prove it. His every attempt to construct the proof led him into further revisions of the pragmaticism. It was no longer—if it had ever been—a simple take-it-or-leave-it maxim for attaining the grade of clearness of ideas that characterizes the scientific method. It was a doctrine, connected with other doctrines in a system, and therefore susceptible of proof (8.191). And the proof was not a simple demonstration. The doctrine was not true by arbitrary definition; it was not tautologically or trivially true. To prove it was to bring it to the test of indubitable experience,[22] and only the system to which it belonged could do that, just as only the system could locate and explicate the doctrine in the first place.

So the question of the Hegelian bearings of what Peirce variously called his proof (5.415; 8.209) or defence (4.534) of, his apology (4.530) or argument (5.470, 474; 8.209, 210, 211) for, pragmaticism, becomes the question of the Hegelian bearings of the revisions of the system during the period (1900-1913) in which it was being focused on the construction of the proof. That is a question for a book. Only a few brief indications can be offered here. And since major revisions of the system are reflected in revisions of Peirce's classification of the sciences, I first present in tabular form his two principal classifications (see table, p. 181).

Imagine being asked, with these tables as reminders, to single out the most conspicuous constant feature of Peirce's philosophy over the sixty years that he devoted to it, and then to put beside that the most conspicuous change. One could scarcely make better reply than this. The constant was

---

[21] *Royce's Logical Essays*, ed. D.S. Robinson (Dubuque, Iowa, 1951), pp. 96, 350-351, 364, 369; *Lectures on Modern Idealism* (Yale University Press, 1919), p. 258; *The Problem of Christianity* (New York, Macmillan, 1913), II, 123. In a draft letter to Lady Welby late in 1904, Peirce had written : "*my* pragmatism is very different from Schiller's & I believe reconciles the truth in Hegel with the truth in scientific ideas" (Ms L 463).

[22] Draft letter to J.S. Engle, February 14, 1905 (Ms L 133). Cf. 3.432 (1896).

PEIRCE'S TWO PRINCIPAL CLASSIFICATIONS OF THE SCIENCES

(Ignoring nearly all the variants of each, and omitting the subdivisions of
mathematics, metaphysics, psychics, physics, science of review, and practical science) [23]

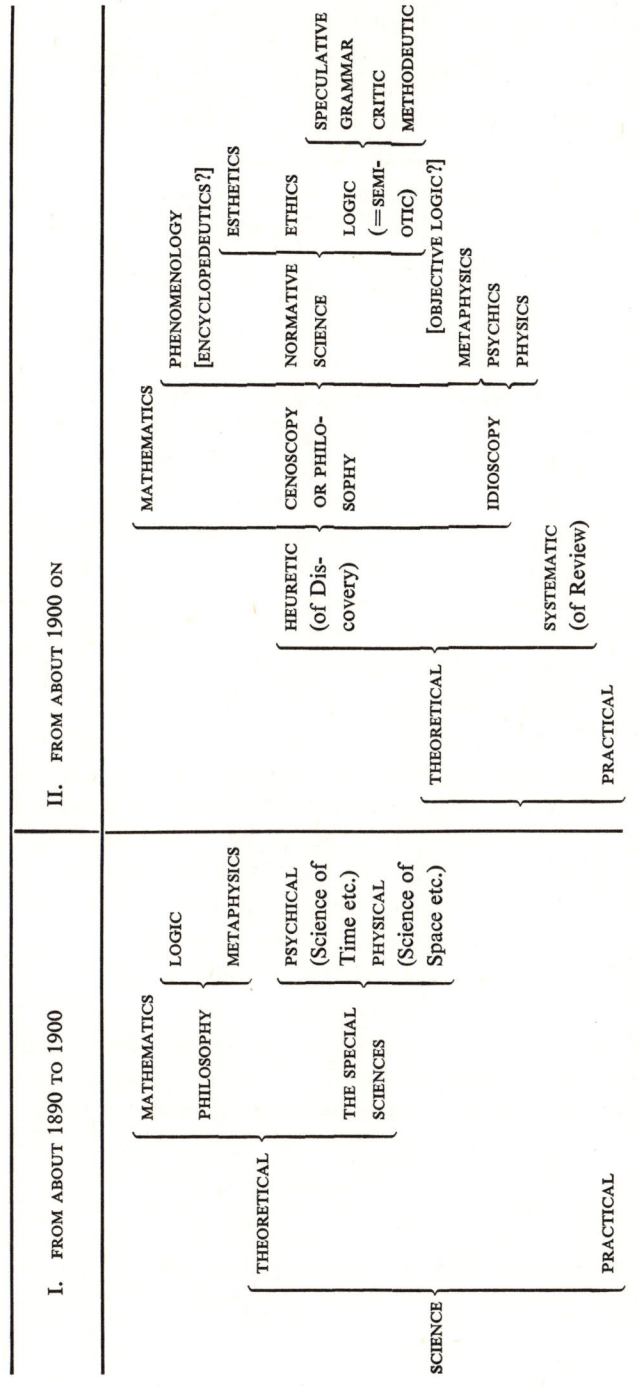

[23] For classification I, see 3.427 (1896); for details, Ms 15, pp. 14-17 (1896). For II, 1.180-202 (1903); in tabular form, Thomas A. Goudge, *The Thought of C.S. Peirce* (University of Toronto Press, 1950), facing p. 48. With the subdivisions of logic in II, compare the trivium of 1.559 (1867); see also 3.430 (1896).

his conception of philosophy as research science, intermediate between mathematics and the special sciences, in an "ontological line" [24] in which each science borrows principles from the sciences above it and data from those below it. And the change was that, whereas until the turn of the century he recognized only logic and metaphysics as having the research character, and did not conceive logic as normative, from around the turn of the century onward logic was for him a normative science, with two others, ethics and esthetics, above it, and above all three of them a new science which for a time he called phenomenology. Until then, ethics had been down among the practical sciences (or more recently in part under the special science of sociology), and esthetics had been nowhere.

Just *how* logic became for Peirce a normative science is a story still to be told. But once that change had taken place, the theory of the categories could no longer be the work of logic itself, but must be presupposed by it, and indeed by the prior normative sciences of esthetics and ethics also. But why assign it to a new science which should have that for its sole business, and why call that science phenomenology?

A decade before the change, Peirce had assigned to mathematics the proposition that first, second and third—something, other, and medium or middle—are irreducible categories, and that there is no fourth. "In this mathematical proposition (for such it is shown to be,) you have all logic and all metaphysics in a nut-shell." He gave Sylvester credit for importing into mathematics from chemistry "the method of graphs" that made its truth more evident, but for the proposition itself, and the argument for it, he rightly claimed priority. "Of course, Hegel preceded us both; but he was not exact enough" (Ms 915; cf. 3.63, 144, 469 f.).

The need remained, however, for a science that should observe the phenomena found in every experience and draw the simplest generalizations from them (7.538). Just before the change Peirce was calling this new science "High Philosophy" (7.526); just after it, in 1902, Phenomenology (1.280; 2.197).[25] "This is the science which Hegel made his starting-point," said Peirce in the first of his Harvard Lectures of 1903 (5.37), and it was from this science that the proof of pragmaticism, to which those eight lectures

---

[24] Manley Thompson, *The Pragmatic Philosophy of C.S. Peirce* (University of Chicago Press, 1953), pp. 168-172, 178, 193.

[25] Yet as late as July 22, 1902, while struggling in his Logic Notebook with the theory of collections in relation to that doctrine of real or objective or substantial possibility that was required to make pragmatism an intelligible doctrine, Peirce entertained the idea of calling his new science Categoric and putting it *above* mathematics (Ms 339 p. 222r)! But that was a momentary aberration.

were devoted, took its start. In Peirce's system, as in Hegel's, phenomenology did not depend upon any other positive science; but in Peirce's, though not in Hegel's, it did depend, to its great advantage, upon the conditional or hypothetical science of pure mathematics (5.40).

Thirty-five years earlier, in 1868-9, in the same three numbers of the *Journal of Speculative Philosophy* in which Peirce's own system was first presented, there was an analysis of Hegel's *Phenomenology* by the editor, W.T. Harris, and a partial translation, in three instalments, by Harris and Brockmeyer. Though Peirce thanked Harris at the time,[26] until the 1890s he almost never referred to any work of Hegel's but the *Encyclopedia*, the larger *Logic*, and the *Propaedeutic*.

In 1890, however, Harris published his major work, *Hegel's Logic : A Book on the Genesis of the Categories of the Mind*, in which he devoted four chapters to the *Phenomenology*, under the title of "Hegel's 'Voyage of Discovery'." [27] After that, Peirce began associating the *Phenomenology* with the *Logic* as "rich mines of philosophic thought." [28] By 1900, he is ready to call the *Phenomenology* Hegel's "greater masterpiece" (8.112) — greater, that is, than the *Logic*. And by 1903 it is "a work...perhaps the most profound ever written" (Ms 478 p. 27), and Hegel is "in some respects the greatest philosopher that ever lived" (1.524). It pleased Peirce that his new science should bear the name of a work that had risen so high in his esteem.

For several years Peirce had been half playfully calling his three categories Kaino- or Ceno-Pythagorean (7.528; 2.87). In the same vein he sometimes called his new science Cenopythagorean Phenomenology.[29] And at least once he called his revised pragmatism Cenopythagorean Pragmaticism (5.555*). It begins to appear, therefore, that the contribution he had still to make, the proof of pragmaticism, was a further development of the one he had already made in his "New List of Categories." And the Hegelian bearings of the first contribution are a chief part of the Hegelian bearings of the second.

In drafting a syllabus to accompany his Lowell Lectures in the fall of 1903, Peirce went so far as to insert another Hegelian science between Phenomenology and the Normative Sciences.

[26] Wallace Nethery, "C.S. Peirce to W.T. Harris," *The Personalist* 43 : 35-45, 1962, at p. 40. Quoted in Part IV below, under 1868 June 11.
[27] See William Elton, "Peirce's Marginalia in W.T. Harris' *Hegel's Logic*," *Journal of the History of Philosophy* 2 : 82-84, 1964.
[28] *Nation* 57 : 393, 1893.
[29] See his definitions of "cenopythagorean" (p. 217) and of "cenopythagorean phenomenology" (p. 981) in *The Century Dictionary Supplement*, 2 vols., 1909. For the playfulness see Ms 298 p. 16.

Phenomenology studies the Categories in their forms of Firstness. It ought to be followed by a science which should study them in a general way as they present themselves throughout common experience. This seems to be approximately, though not exactly, what Hegel intended in his *Encyclopädie*. This study may be termed, in advance of any serious undertaking of it, *Encyclopedeutics*. Then, and only then, should succeed the *Normative Sciences* (Ms 478 p. 40).

In drafting his lecture on the normative sciences as a further part of his argument for pragmaticism in the Harvard Lectures in the spring of 1903, Peirce had begun by remarking that the three categories of his previous lectures on phenomenology were of course no discovery of his.

If they were, that circumstance would be an almost conclusive proof of the falsity of the list.... No, all that I have done is to give an exposition of them which, I hope, puts them in a clearer light than that of Hegel.

The first year of my own serious study of philosophy, in 1856, forty-seven years ago, was devoted to esthetics. My good angel must have prompted me to take up first that branch of philosophy which ought immediately to follow the study of the categories, and to study it in a German book which though it was too old to be sensibly influenced by Hegel [30] was nevertheless one of those books in which the three categories, in an almost unrecognizable disguise, played a great part. It was Schiller's *ästhetische Briefe*, — a very good book for an infant philosopher (Ms 310 pp. 3-4).

In another draft, he had said that Schiller's book had been his introduction to phenomenology as well as to esthetics (Ms S 80).

Passing over ethics, for which Peirce does not look to Hegel (Ms 893), and coming again to logic, I remark first that, besides conceiving it now as a normative science, dependent on ethics, as ethics is on esthetics, he explicitly identifies it with semiotic, the general theory of signs, and therefore as including two disciplines from which he had usually, though not always, distinguished it. In an essay of about 1896 called "The Logic of Mathematics : An Attempt to develop my categories from within," he had written (1.444) :

The term "logic" is unscientifically by me employed in two distinct senses. In its narrower sense, it is the science of the necessary conditions of the attainment of truth. In its broader sense, it is the science of the necessary laws of thought, or, still better (thought always taking place by means of signs), it is general semeiotic, treating not merely of truth, but also of the general conditions of signs being signs (which Duns Scotus called *grammatica speculativa*), also of the laws of the evolution of thought, which since it coincides with the study of the necessary conditions of the transmission of meaning by signs from mind to mind, and from

---

[30] If there was any influence, it was of course the other way around. H.S. Harris, *Hegel's Development : Toward the Sunlight, 1770-1801* (Oxford University Press, 1972), pp. 253, 411 n.

one state of mind to another, ought, for the sake of taking advantage of an old association of terms, be called *rhetorica speculativa*, but which I content myself with inaccurately calling *objective logic*, because that conveys the correct idea that it is like Hegel's logic.

But when logic became a normative science, logic in the broader sense became normative semiotic, consisting of normative speculative grammar, normative critic, and normative speculative rhetoric or methodeutic. Not only, therefore, was it necessary to move category-theory up into a higher discipline, but, since objective logic, whether Hegel's or Peirce's, is not normative, it was necessary to move it down into a lower one—either into metaphysics or into a new discipline placed tentatively between logic and metaphysics, as encyclopedeutics was between phenomenology and normative science. Here is how Peirce approached the problem is his *Minute Logic* of 1902 (2.111):

> With Speculative Rhetoric, Logic, in the sense of Normative Semeotic, is brought to a close. But now we have to examine whether there be a doctrine of signs corresponding to Hegel's objective logic; that is to say, whether there be a life in Signs, so that—the requisite vehicle being present—they will go through a certain order of development, and if so, whether this development be merely of such a nature that the same round of changes of form is described over and over again whatever be the matter of the thought or whether, in addition to such a repetitive order, there be also a greater life-history that every symbol furnished with a vehicle of life goes through, and what is the nature of it.

"...a doctrine of signs corresponding to Hegel's objective logic...a life in signs..." That there is such a doctrine and such a life, Peirce doubts not; and much of his own life is devoted to giving an account of them. But the pragmaticism itself, in the strict sense, is not *that* doctrine but a prior doctrine of normative semiotic which it presupposes and of which it is a further development. To say what that prior doctrine is, even roughly, we should have to pass in review the phenomenology, the normative sciences with their *summum bonum*, and then the semiotic in detail, with attention first to the triadic structure of sign-action, of signs *in actu*, of semiosis, as distinguished from dyadic or dynamical action (5.472, 484). Then more particularly to symbols, and within symbols to arguments, and within arguments to abductions, since "the question of Pragmatism is the question of Abduction" (5.197). So much under Speculative Grammar. Then, under Critic, to "the bottom question of logical Critic" (6.475; cf. 5.196)—that of the *validity* of abduction. Then, under Methodeutic, to the strategy of abduction, deduction, and induction as successive stages in a repeating but advancing cycle—stages corresponding very roughly to Hegel's three.

Along the way, we should have to come to grips with the semiotic of modalities, and especially with that of the several degrees of possibility, since the acknowledgment of real or objective possibility "was the great step that was needed to render pragmaticism an intelligible doctrine." [31] In that connection, we should have to make out just *how* the proof of pragmaticism "would essentially involve the establishment of synechism" (5.415). All this for a rough account of what pragmaticism is. For a more precise account, in which alone the full cogency of the proof would emerge, we should have to follow Peirce's system of existential graphs—"my *chef d'œuvre*" [32]—in its first discovery and gradual development, and more particularly those parts of it that he designed to deal with the modalities.

This would take a volume or two.[33] We must content ourselves here with the most essential point, the triadic (object-sign-interpretant) structure of thought as sign-interpretation, sign-action or semiosis. "A *Sign* is anything which is related to a Second thing, its *Object*, in respect to a Quality, in such a way as to bring a Third thing, its *Interpretant*, into relation to the same Object, and that in such a way as to bring a Fourth into relation to that Object in the same form, *ad infinitum* (2.92; cf. 2.203). It was with reference primarily to this triadicity of thought—the open sesame to all that followed, including the synechism—that Peirce began about 1890 to say that he was working on a doctrine, a formula, a method, a system more general than Hegel's, of which Hegel's dialectic was a special case; and that the general doctrine led more securely and clearly than the special one to the true conception of continuity.[34] But alas! the general doctrine was never finished, because

I am, as far as I know, a pioneer, or rather a backwoodsman, in the work of clearing and opening up what I call *semiotic*, that is, the doctrine of the essential nature and fundamental varieties of possible semiosis; and I find the field too vast, the labor too great, for a first-comer (5.488).

---

[31] See note 19 above.

[32] Draft letter to P.E.B. Jourdain, December 5, 1908 (Ms L 230a), quoted by the editors of the *Collected Papers*, vol. 4, p. 291. For the context see Don D. Roberts, *The Existential Graphs of Charles S. Peirce* (The Hague : Mouton & Co., 1973), p. 110.

[33] The nearest approach so far to an adequate statement of the proof is a book by John J. Fitzgerald, *Peirce's Theory of Signs as Foundation for Pragmatism* (The Hague : Mouton & Co., 1966). It falls short in three respects. It makes no use of the unpublished papers in which Peirce's latest efforts are recorded. It omits the existential graphs. And it does not show how the proof involves the establishment of synechism. But its author plans to make good these deficiencies in a second edition.

[34] 1.368 (c. 1890); 6.31 (1891); 6.305 (1893); Mss 397-398 (c. 1893); Peirce to Francis C. Russell, September 8, 1894 (Ms L 387); 1.453, 491 (c. 1896); 2.32-35 (1902); 5.37 (1903).

Nevertheless, with his intent and aim in mind, we may put a more charitable construction on his many overemphatic criticisms of Hegel, which might otherwise strike us as hostile and arrogant. They are all in the family, and full of the affectionate and humorous hyperbole of free expression of family differences. And they assume no infallibility on the critic's part. "Hegel, of course, blunders monstrously, as we shall all be seen to do" (8.268).

We are prepared also for the discovery that Peirce was best understood, in this crucial respect, not by other pragmatists at home or abroad, but by Josiah Royce, the philosopher of his acquaintance who, after W.T. Harris, had studied Hegel most deeply. In 1913, in a series of four lectures in the second volume of *The Problem of Christianity*, Royce developed Peirce's "doctrine of signs" at length, applied it to metaphysics, and stated its relation to Hegel in the most important paragraph so far written on "Hegel and Peirce." It is noteworthy, however, that he drew his understanding of the doctrine not from Peirce's later writings on the subject, most of them unpublished, nor from the pragmatism papers of 1877-78, which made almost nothing of it, but from the "New List" of 1867 and the three articles of 1868-9 on the sign-theory of cognition in Harris's *Journal of Speculative Philosophy* (5.213-357)—four papers whose significance Royce had not until recently appreciated.[35] In the latter half of the paragraph just mentioned he says that

Peirce's concept of interpretation defines an extremely general process, of which the Hegelian dialectical triadic process is a very special case. Hegel's elementary illustrations of his own processes are ethical and historical. Peirce's theory of comparison is quite as well illustrated by purely mathematical as by explicitly social instances. There is no essential inconsistency between the logical and psychological motives which lie at the basis of Peirce's theory of the triad of interpretation, and the Hegelian interest in the play of thesis, antithesis, and higher synthesis. But Peirce's theory, with its explicitly empirical origin and its very exact logical working out, promises new light upon matters which Hegel left profoundly problematic.

Royce sent Peirce a copy of *The Problem of Christianity*, and Peirce replied in a letter which Royce received in time to read it to his seminar on October 28, 1913, and in which, as he later wrote, what few interpreters

---

[35] *The Problem of Christianity* (New York : The Macmillan Co., 1913), Volume II, Lectures XI-XIV, "Perception, Conception, and Interpretation," "The Will to Interpret," "The World of Interpretation," and "The Doctrine of Signs." Peirce's early papers are listed in the note on p. 114. The only later item listed is his brief article "Sign" in Baldwin's *Dictionary*. The paragraph from which I quote is on pp. 184-186. See also Vol. I, p. xi.

of Peirce were ever able to write, "my interpretation of him gained on the whole, his approval." [36]

IV

At this point a reader may well ask, if Royce found it profitable to go back to those early papers, would it not be still better to go back to the very beginning and pick up in chronological order *all* the evidences of Peirce's awareness of Hegel? I assure such a reader that I could not have written the present essay without first attempting just that. And further, that I have used but a small fraction of the evidence collected—less than a tenth of it—and that many of the most important and revealing things about "Hegel and Peirce" remain to be said. They can best be said in a book-length monograph on chronological lines.[37] To convey some idea of what the bare bones of such a chronological monograph would look like, I conclude with a few of the entries for a six-year period near the beginning. This will take us through the year of his contributions to the *Journal of Speculative Philosophy* and the two of his correspondence with its editor, W.T. Harris.

1863

Nov. 12. Peirce presents to a reunion of the Cambridge High School Association "The Place of Our Age in the History of Civilization." Extensive extracts are published in the *Cambridge Chronicle* for Nov. 21. There is a key sentence on Hegel.[38] [Thirty years later, Peirce writes: "On lines laid down by [Kant], I began to think for myself, setting out, as he did, from Formal Logic. That path inevitably led to an objective logic; and the first thing I printed was a Hegel-like paper on the philosophy of history, with predictions as to the subsequent course of events. I did not recognize the affinity of my thought to Hegel's, because in all details it was entirely different, and because his weak logic and pretentiousness repelled me then more than now." [39]]

[36] J.H. Cotton, *op. cit.* (n. 5 above), p. 218. *Josiah Royce's Seminar, 1913-1914*, ed. Grover Smith (New Brunswick, N.J.: Rutgers University Press, 1963), pp. 37-39, 41-42.

[37] Since writing this paper I have seen the abstract, dated December 1972, of a Pennsylvania State University thesis answering to this description: *Peirce on Hegel*, by Joseph A. Petrick. He informs me that he is revising it for publication.

[38] *Values in a Universe of Chance: Selected Writings of Charles S. Peirce*, ed. Philip P. Wiener (Doubleday Anchor Books, 1958), pp. 4-14, at p. 8.

[39] Ms 958, in a draft of 6.605.

1865

Spring. In his Harvard University Lectures "On the Logic of Science" Peirce seems to have planned one on Hegel's logic (Ms 340 p. 6) but not to have given it. In Lecture III he illustrates boundary problems by a sheet of paper of which part is red and part green. "It seems to me...that the boundary is both red and green; — the distinction between them vanishing at this point. And this is the answer which was made by Hegel and which mathematicians give to similar questions" (Ms 342 p. [33]). In Lecture VIII he objects to the contamination of logic with anthropology and psychology. "Kant's definition, which is the best yet given, is nearly freed from all such admixture. And perhaps the strongest point of Hegelianism is the purely impersonal character which it attributes to the unity of apperception. In this respect I follow Hegel; but I do so without budging from the critical standpoint" (Ms 346 p. 1).[40]

Dec. 11. Peirce writes to Charles Eliot Norton, editor of the *North American Review*, to ask if a reviewer has been engaged for Stirling's *The Secret of Hegel*. "If not, I would like to write about two pages of fine print on the subject if you will admit it." [41] But Norton has already engaged Henry James the elder, and James's review appears in the January 1866 issue. [Three years later, James publishes *The Secret of Swedenborg*, and Norton has Peirce review that.]

Dec. 14. Peirce writes in his Logic Notebook the paragraph quoted above in Part II, paragraph (8).

1866

Nov. 21. In his Lowell Institute Lectures on "The Logic of Science; or, Induction and Hypothesis," Lecture IX contains what may be regarded as a draft of the "New List of Categories." In this draft Peirce argues that "Hegel is wrong in making Negation enter so early as he does into Logic" (Ms 357 p. 11).

Not long before or after this, Peirce writes the draft numbered 2 by Murray Murphey. This contains a crucial paragraph on Hegel.[42]

---

[40] See n. 16 above; also n. 10.
[41] Norton Papers (bMS Am 1088) 5425, The Houghton Library, Harvard University. Quoted by permission.
[42] Murphey, *op. cit.* (n. 8 above), p. 412.

1866-1867?

In still another draft of the "New List," intended as Chapter I of a treatise on *The Logic of Science* (Ms 769), Peirce begins by arguing for a return to the earlier and more general conception of *Vorstellung* or representation as against the restricted senses in which these terms have been used by Kant, the Hegelians, and Hamilton. [This is the most important single clue to the derivations of (1) the third of the three categories of the "New List," (2) the conception of logic as semiotic, and (3) the conception of semiosis as a more general process of which Hegel's dialectic is a special case.]

1867

The *Journal of Speculative Philosophy*, the first philosophical journal in English, begins publication in St.Louis. Peirce subscribes. The first volume includes translations from Leibniz, Fichte, Schelling, and Schopenhauer; an essay on Hegel's aesthetics; the first four instalments of an Hegelian "Introduction to Philosophy" by the editor, W.T. Harris; and an article by Harris on "Paul Janet and Hegel."

March 29. Peirce acquires a copy of the second edition of Hegel's *Encyclopädie* and inscribes on the flyleaf the Greek of Parmenides's saying about those who are persuaded that to-be and not-to-be are the same, yet not the same.[43]

November. Peirce draws up a "Specimen of a Dictionary of the Terms of Logic and the Allied Sciences, A-ABS" based on the notebook and card file described above in Part II, paragraphs (6) and (7). He quotes Hegel on abstract freedom, and suspects him of confusing abstraction and generalization with denial "when he says that *being* and *nothing* are the same because they are equally the absence of all determination" (Ms 1174 pp. 23, 28-29).

Dec. 10. In acknowledging receipt of Peirce's *Three Papers on Logic*, the third of which is "On a New List of Categories," Harris calls attention to passages on the categories in his own 'Introduction to Philosophy" (Ms L 183).

1868

Jan. 1. Peirce replies to Harris that he has read the "Introduction" as far as published (i.e. the first three instalments) and thinks it very good yet totally disagrees, since he acts wholly in the interest of the "understanding"

---

[43] Widener Library, Harvard University, call number Phil 3425.44.

and does not believe in the "reason" of the Hegelian school. "I admit there is music in the logic of Hegel, but that is all I discover there." He has written Harris "a long letter relative to Hegel" but decided not to trouble him with it.[44]

Jan. 24. Peirce writes Harris criticizing a paragraph in his article on "Paul Janet and Hegel." [45] Harris publishes the criticisms and his replies under the title "Nominalism *versus* Realism"—the nominalism of Peirce *versus* the realism of Hegel as interpreted by Harris (6.619-624).

April. The *North American Review* has a long article on Hegel by J.E. Cabot, concluding that "all philosophy at present must take this road, and the first question to be put to any new attempt is, whether it has got as far as this or not so far." [Peirce says later that among his elders it was Cabot from whom he had got most encouragement.[46]]

April 9. Having been invited by Harris to consider how on his nominalistic principles the validity of the laws of logic could be other than inexplicable (5.318), Peirce sends the first of three articles, which appear in the second, third and fourth issues of the second volumes of the *Journal*. In the third issue there is also a continuation of the controversy with Harris in which Peirce defends his definition of Pure Being as seeming to be "in accord with the explanations of almost all, if not all, the commentators and expositors of Hegel" (6.628).

The same three issues of the *Journal* contain an analysis of Hegel's *Phenomenology* by Harris in two instalments and a partial translation by Harris and Brockmeyer in three instalments.

Though in his three principal articles Hegel is named only three times (5.310, 330, 332), Peirce's letters to Harris show that Hegel is on his mind throughout. The thesis of the articles is that all thought is dialogic, or in signs, or representational, and therefore triadic; that none of it is dyadic in the way that a non-representational intuition, sensation, perception, conception—*Anschauung, Empfindung, Wahrnehmung, Begriff*—might be supposed to be. There are no first or last cognitions—no "first impressions of sense," no intuited first principles, no final comprehensions. Every thought interprets another, and is interpreted by still another. We are in thought, not thoughts in us. Moreover, sign-interpretation is *irreducibly* triadic; it is no synthesis, say, of a dyadic perception and a dyadic conception; nor

---

[44] Nethery, *op. cit.* (n. 26 above), p. 37. This and subsequent passages from Peirce's letters to Harris are quoted by permission of Harris's daughter, Edith Davidson Harris.

[45] *Ibid.*, pp. 37 f.

[46] *John Jay Chapman and His Letters*, ed. M.A. DeWolfe Howe (Boston : Houghton Mifflin Co., 1937), p. 97.

can it be analyzed into dyadic relations of any kind. [It is this irreducible sociality, triadicity and continuity of the process of interpretation that Royce later seizes as the key to Peirce's early papers and thereby to the whole of his philosophy.[47] And as we have seen (1865 Spring), Peirce associates it, and the nonpsychological logic that results, with "the strongest point of Hegelianism."]

May 13. Peirce objects to Harris's assumption that his argument is anti-Hegelian. If thinkers had to be divided between Hegelians and non-Hegelians, "I should come on the same side as Hegel, because I am idealistic."[48]

June 11. Peirce to Harris : "I am most pleased at your giving us the Phänomenologie." [49]

Nov. 30. Peirce to Harris : In proof-sheets of the second article, "I struck out the paragraph referring to Hegelians. I intended no *slur* on them, or any appeal to the ignorant against them. What I meant was to protest respectfully but energetically *to* them against a certain tendency in their philosophy" (8.246).

1869

Dec. 8. Peirce ends his last letter to Harris : "I should like to write a systematic series of essays on logic—objective & subjective—and take say just two sheets [32 pages] in every number of the Journal, and enter into an arrangement with a publisher here to purchase a certain number of copies of each one on such terms as would at once be advantageous to the Journal & yet render it easy for me to find a publisher. The whole to be bound as a book when it was finished. But this is only a passing dream."[50]

[In respect of publication in Harris's Journal it *was* a passing dream; but in other respects it remained with him throughout his life, and he never ceased working toward its fulfilment.]

Epilogue

In postponing all questions of influence, of critical comparison, and of accuracy of interpretation, and confining myself to the Hegelian "bearings" of two focal occasions and two focal contributions, I have taken my metaphor from the first year of Peirce's professional life — the year 1859-1860,

[47] *Op. cit.* (n. 35 above), Lecture XI.
[48] *Op. cit.* (n. 26 and n. 44 above), p. 40.
[49] *Loc. cit.*
[50] *Ibid.*, pp. 44 f.

just after his graduation from Harvard College. He spent that year with two field parties of the Coast Survey, the first on the Maine coast near Machias, the second on the Gulf coast around the delta of the Mississippi; the first on land, the second in large part at sea. With that experience of triangulation behind him, it was natural for him to locate his own changing positions in relation to the nearest eminent landmarks. And the most eminent of the nearest was Hegel.

BIBLIOGRAPHY

Joseph C. Flay

The Pennsylvania State University

The following bibliography is the result of a search of the secondary literature on Hegel and his relationship to the history of philosophy. It is part of a larger bibliographical survey of the literature on Hegel from his own time to the present which I hope to publish in the near future. In this present essay I have restricted myself to the literature in English, French, German and Italian. While I make no claim to completeness, I have made an effort to notice all of the articles and books which have appeared in the major journals and presses. If there are any glaring omissions, I invite the reader to call my attention to them. I have, however, intentionally omitted general histories of philosophy and scholarly essays which do not give a prominent place to Hegel or are not written from a specific Hegelian point of view. In short, I have tried to include those articles and books which focus on Hegel and his relationship to the history of philosophy, a period or school, or some individual thinker.

A word of caution is necessary for some of the entries. In some cases I have found the entry in other bibliographies on Hegel. I have not yet concluded the process of verifying all of these entries and consequently some inaccuracies in date of publication or pagination may be present. But the editors and publisher considered the inclusion of the bibliography in this volume valuable enough to warrant the risk of some of these errors.

I should like to thank the Central Fund for Research, the College of the Liberal Arts, and the Department of Philosophy of the Pennsylvania State University for the released time and the monies which made my work on the general bibliography possible. I should also especially like to acknowledge the work of Mr. Michael DeArmey who contributed a sizable number of entries and who will be co-editor of the general bibliography. Finally, I must express my gratitude to those graduate research assistants who over the years have aided me in surveying the literature.

I. HEGEL AND THE HISTORY OF PHILOSOPHY : GENERAL

1. Apelt, O. *Die Behandlung der Geschichte der Philosophie bei Fries und bei Hegel*. Göttingen, Vandenhoeck und Ruprecht, 1912.
2. Beaussire, E. *Antécédents de l'hégélianisme dans la philosophie française*. Paris, Germer-Baillière, 1865.

3. Chalybäus, H. "Philosophie der Geschichte und Geschichte der Philosophie in Bezug auf Hegels Vorlesungen über die Philosophie der Geschichte," *Zeitschrift für Philosophie und spekulative Theologie*, hrsg. J.H. Fichte, 1837-1844.

4. Croce, B. *Saggi filosofici*, Vol. III : Studio sullo Hegel e altri scritti di storia della filosofia. Bari, Giuseppi Laterza, 1913.

5. ———. "La place de Hegel dans l'histoire de la philosophie," *Revue de Métaphysique et de Morale*, 1939 (46), 211-24.

6. ———. "Il posto di Hegel nella storia della filosofia," *Critica*, 1939 (37), 190-200.

7. Doz, André. "La nécessité interne de l'histoire de la philosophie chez Hegel," *Hegel-Jahrbuch*, 1968/1969, 202-07.

8. Drechsler, Adolph. *Charakteristik der philosophischen Systeme seit Kant*. Dresden, 1863.

9. Drews, A. *Die deutsche Spekulation seit Kant*. Leipzig, 1895.

10. Dreyer, H. *Der Begriff "Geist" in der deutschen Philosophie von Kant bis Hegel*. Berlin, 1908.

11. Erdmann, Johann Eduard. *Die Entwicklung der deutschen Speculation seit Kant*. (*Versuch einer wissenschaftliche Darstellung der Geschichte der neueren Philosophie* : Teil III, 1, 2.) Leipzig, 1848-53.

12. Feuerbach, Ludwig. "Hegels Geschichte der Philosophie," in *Sämtliche Werke*, Bd. II, 1-18. Leipzig, 1846.

13. Fiorentino, F. "Sul concetto della storia della filosofia di Hegel," *Giornale napoletano di filosofia e lettere*, March, 1872. Reprinted in *Scritti varii di letteratura, filosofia e critica*, 331-47. Naples, 1876.

14. Flöter, Hans H.F. *Die Begründung der Geschichtlichkeit der Geschichte in der Philosophie des deutschen Idealismus*. Halle, Akademie Verlag, 1936.

15. Gropp, Rugard Otto. "Ueber Hegels *Geschichte der Philosophie*," *Deutsche Zeitschrift für Philosophie*, 1957 (5), 457-75.

16. Joja, Crizantema. "La science et l'histoire de la philosophie chez Hegel." Ithaca (26, VIII, 1962-2 IX 1962), (Proceedings of the Tenth International Congress of the History of Science.) Paris, Hermann, 1962.

17. Laratschiwijew, Weliko. "Hegel und die Historizität der Philosophie," *Hegel-Jahrbuch*, 1971, 347-51.

18. Kimmerle, Heinz. "Notwendige geschichtliche und philosophische Bemerkungen zum Verhältnis von Geschichte und Philosophie bei Hegel," *Hegel-Jahrbuch*, 1968-1969, 135-46.

19. ———. "Histoire et philosophie selon Hegel," *Archives de Philosophie*, 1970 (33), 787-99.

20. Kym, A.L. *Hegels Dialektik in ihrer Anwendung auf die Geschichte der Philosophie*. Zürich, 1849.

21. Lakebrink, Bernhard. *Die europäische Idee der Freiheit*, Bd. I : *Hegels Logik und die Tradition der Selbstbestimmung*. (Studien zur Problemgeschichte der antiken und mittelalterlichen Philosophie, 4). Leiden, E.J. Brill, 1968.

22. Lauer, Joseph Quentin. *Hegel's Idea of Philosophy*. Bronx, New York, Fordham University Press, 1971.

23. Lombardi, Franco. "Hegel et nous : À propos du problème de l'histoire de la philosophie," *Revue Internationale de Philosophie*, 1970 (24), 31-52.

24. Malorny, Heinz. "Philosophie und Philosophiegeschichte bei Hegel," in

Hegel und wir, hrsg. Erhard Lange, 133-73. Berlin, Deutscher Verlag der Wissenschaften VEB, 1970.

25. Michelet, K.L. *Hegel und der Empirismus*. Berlin, Verey, 1873.
26. Náder, György. "Hegel on Empiricism," *Ratio*, 1964 (6), 154-60.
27. Noiray, André. *Historique*. L'idée de philosophie depuis Hegel. Paris, Culture, Art, Loisirs, 1969.
28. Ott, A. *Hegel et la philosophie allemande, ou exposé et examen critique des principaux systèmes de la philosophie allemande depuis Kant, et spécialement de celui de Hegel*. Paris, Joubert, 1844.
29. Paci, E. "Hegel e il problema della storia della filosofia," in *Verità e storia*. Un dibattito sul metodo della storia della filosofia (Saggi di Abbagnano, Antoni, Calogero, Cantoni, Frondizi, Geymonat, Garin, Lombardi, Mondolfo, Paci e Spirito, presentati dal Prof. Lombardi). Asti, Arethusa, 1956.
30. Pokorny, Ignaz. *Zur Geschichte der Lehre von Gefühlen, von Wolff bis Hegel*. Iglau, 1863.
31. Robinet, André. "Les fantaisies de l'histoire de la philosophie de Hegel : Malbranche," *Hegel-Jahrbuch*, 1968/1969, 372-95.
32. Sabetti, Alfredo. *Hegel e il problema della filosofia come storia*. Napoli, Ed. Glaux (Tip. *Aurora* di R. Contessa), 1957.
33. Schultz, Werner. "Begegnungen Hegels mit der deutschen Mystik," in *Sammlung und Sendung* (Festgabe für H. Rendtorff), 339-43. Berlin, Christlicher Zeitschriftenverlag, 1958.
34. Volkmuth, P. *Der dreieinige Pantheismus von Thales bis Hegel*. Köln, 1837.
35. Walsh, W.H. "Hegel on the History of Philosophy," *History and Theory*, 1964/1965 (4), 67-82.
36. Willms, Bernard. *Revolution und Protest oder Glanz und Elend des bürgerlichen Subjekts*. Stuttgart, Kohlhammer, 1969.

See also 632.

II. PERIODS AND MOVEMENTS

Ancient philosophy

37. Buchner, Hartmut. "Zur Bedeutung des Skeptizismus beim jungen Hegel," *Hegel-Studien*, Beiheft 4 (1969), 49-56.
38. Carbonara Naddei, Mirella. "Un antico e un moderno di fronte a un problema attuale," *Logos*, 1971 (3), 109-36.
39. De Magalhaes-Vilhena, V. "Hegel, Aristote et Anaxagore. Une source méconnue de la pensée Hégélienne," *Pensée*, 1968, n. 139, 89-113.
40. Düsing, Klaus. "Die Bedeutung des antiken Skeptizismus für Hegels Kritik der sinnlichen Gewissheit," *Hegel-Studien*, 1973 (8), 119-30.
41. Flay, Joseph C. "Hegel, Hesiod and Xenophanes," in *Essays in Metaphysics*, ed. Carl Vaught, 39-49. University Park, Pa., The Pennsylvania State University Press, 1970.
42. Gadamer, H.-G. "Hegel und die antike Dialektik," *Hegel-Studien*, 1961 (1), 173-99.
43. Gray, J. Glenn. *Hegel's Hellenic Ideal*. New York, 1941. Reprinted as *Hegel and Greek Thought*, New York, Harper Torchbooks, 1969.

44. Heidegger, Martin. "Hegel und die Griechen," in *Die Gegenwart der Griechen im neueren Denken* (Festschrift für Hans-Georg Gadamer zum 60. Geburtstag) 43-57. Tübingen, Mohr, 1960.

45. ——. "Hegel et les Grecs," *Cahiers du Sud*, 1958 (45), n. 349, 355-68.

46. Merker, Nicolao. "Hegel et lo scetticismo," *Società* (Milano), 1960 (16), 545-83.

47. Prauss, G. "Hegels Parmenidesdeutung," *Kant-Studien*, 1966 (57), 276-85.

48. Sandvoss, Ernst. "Hegels Antisokratismus," *Antike und Abendland*, 1966 (12), 156-79.

49. Sichirollo, Livio. "Hegel e i Greci. Note sulla genesi e sull'evoluzione della *Philosophie der Weltgeschichte*," *Studi Urbinati di Storia, Filosofia e Letteratura*, 1961 (35), 57-71.

50. ——. "Hegel und die griechische Welt. Nachleben der Antike und Entstehung der *Philosophie der Weltgeschichte*," *Hegel-Studien*, Beiheft 1 (1964), 263-83.

51. ——. "Hegel und die Antike," in *Dialegesthai-Dialektik*. Von Homer bis Aristotles, 171-204. Hildesheim, 1966.

52. ——. "Hegel e il pensiero antico," in *Incidenza di Hegel*, a cura di Fulvio Tessitore, 411-36. Napoli, Morano Ed., 1970.

53. ——. "Il seminario su 'Hegel e il pensiero greco' a Poitiers," *Pensiero*, 1970 (15), 99-105.

54. Spranger, Eduard. "Hegel über Sokrates," in *Sitzungsberichte der Preussischen Akademie der Wissenschaften* (Philosophisch-historische Klasse, 27), 284-96. Berlin, de Gruyter, 1938.

55. Stenzl, J. "Hegels Auffassung der Griechischen Philosophie," in *Verhandlungen des zweiten Hegelkongresses*, hrsg. Wigersma, 168-83. Tübingen/Haarlem, 1932.

56. ——. "Hegel e la filosofia greca," in Livio Sichirollo, *Antropologia e dialettica nella filosofia di Platone*. Milano, Ed. Veronelli (Tip. Elzeviriana), 1957. Reprinted in *Hegeliana*. Studi di J. Stenzel e A. Kojève, Urbino, Argalia, 1965 and in *Differenze*, 1965, n. 5, 7-26.

57. Taminiaux, Jacques. "Le jeune Hegel et l'hellénisme Schillerien," in *La nostalgie de la Grèce à l'aube de l'idéalisme allemand*, 1-32. La Haye, Martinus Nijhoff, 1967.

58. ——. "L'itinéraire de Hegel," in *Ibid.*, 206-66.

59. Tedeschi, F.A. "Ragione e fede in Socrate, Cartesio ed Hegel," *Educare*, 1961 (12), 50-61.

60. Verneaux, Roger. "L'essence du scepticisme selon Hegel," in *Histoire de la philosophie et métaphysique*. Paris, Desclée De Brouwer, 1955.

61. Wolff, E. "Hegel und die griechische Welt," *Anitike und Abendland*, 1945 (1), 163-81.

Medieval Philosophy

62. Coreth, Emerich. *Dialektik und Analogie des Seins*. Zum Seinsproblem bei Hegel und in der Scholastik. Freiburg-im-Breisgau, Herder, 1951.

63. Sichirollo, Livio. "Hegel e il medioevo. Spirito oggettivo e unità della storia" in *Per una storiografia filosofica* (Pubblicazioni dell'università di Urbino. Serie de lettere e filosofia, 27, 1), 294-322. Urbino, 1970.

64. ———. "Le moyen-âge selon Hegel," in *Hegel. L'esprit objectif. L'unité de l'histoire* (Actes du IIIème congrès international de l'Association internationale pour l'étude de la philosophie de Hegel), 311-23. Lille, 1970.

65. Swiezawski, Stefan. "Hegel und die mittelalterliche Philosophie," *Archiv für Philosophie*, 1960 (10), 24-78.

The Enlightenment

66. Bahner, W. "Geschichtsbewusstsein in der Aufklärung und bei Hegel," *Hegel-Jahrbuch*, 1968/1969, 194-201.

67. Chitas, Eduardo. "Hegel et l'Aufklärung," *Hegel-Jahrbuch*, 1971, 112-16.

Hegel and his Contemporaries

68. *Hegel in Berichten seiner Zeitgenossen*, hrsg. Günther Nicolin (Philosophissche Bibliothek, 245). Hamburg, Meiner, 1970.

69. Kroner, Richard. "The Year 1800 in the Development of German Idealism," *Review of Metaphysics*, 1948, 1-32.

70. Pöggeler, Otto. *Hegels Kritik der Romantik*. Bonn, Bouvier, 1956.

71. Rosenkranz, J.F.K. "Hegel's Relation to his Philosophical Contemporaries," *Journal of Speculative Philosophy*, 1877 (11). 399-410.

Post-Hegelian Philosophy : General

72. Aliotta, A. "La dialettica in Hegel e nei nuovi Hegeliani," *Logos*, 1922, n. 1.

73. Bernstein, Richard J. "From Hegel to Darwin," in *John Dewey*, 9-21. New York, Washington Square Press, 1966.

74. Brazill, William J. *The Young Hegelians*. New Haven and London, Yale University Press, 1970.

75. Burkle, Howard R. *The Non-existence of God*. Antitheism from Hegel to Duméry. New York, Herder & Herder, 1969.

76. Cesa, Claudio. "Enrico de Negri interprete di Hegel," *Giornale Critico della Filosofia Italiana* (Firenze), 1970 (49), 559-65.

77. Chlebik, Franz. *Die Philosophie des Bewusstseins und die Wahrheit des Unbewussten in den dialektischen Grundlinien der Freiheit und Rechtsbegriffs nach Hegel und Michelet*. Berlin, 1870.

78. Cornelius, Alfred. *Die Geschichtslehre Victor Cousins*. Unter besonderer Berücksichtigung des Hegelschen Einflusses. Genève, Droz, Paris, Minard, 1958.

79. Croce, B. "I 'neo' in filosofia," *La Critica* (Napoli), 1941 (39) n. 5, 289-95.

80. de Guibert, B. "Hegelianism in France," *Modern Schoolman*, 1949 (26), 173-77.

81. Dod, A.B. *Two Articles from the Princeton Review Concerning the Transcendental Philosophy of the Germans and of Cousin*. Cambridge, John Owen, 1840.

82. Duhrssen, Alfred. "Some French Hegelians," *Review of Metaphysics*, 1953/1954 (7), 323-37.

83. Dumas, Jean-Louis. "Renouvier critique de Hegel," *Revue de Métaphysique et de Morale*, 1971 (76), 32-52.

84. Easton, L.D. *Hegel's First American Followers*. Athens, Ohio, Ohio University Press, 1967.

85. Ehrenberg, Hans. *Die Parteiung der Philosophie*. Studien wider Hegel und die Kantianer. Leipzig, Felix Meiner, 1911.

86. Erdmann, J.E. *Die deutsche Philosophie seit Hegels Tode*. (Faksimile-Neudruck der Berliner Ausgabe 1896. Mit einer Einleitung von Hermann Lübbe) Stuttgart-Bad Cannstatt, Frommann, 1964.

87. Fortlage, K. *Genetische Geschichte der Philosophie seit Kant*. Leipzig, 1852.

88. Glockner, H. "Hegelrenaissance und Neuhegelianismus," *Logos*, 1931 (20).

89. Harris, Henry. "Hegelianism of the 'Right' and 'Left'," *Review of Metaphysics*, 1958 (11), 603-09.

90. Harris, William Torey. "Trendelenburg and Hegel," *Journal of Speculative Philosophy*, 1875 (9), 70-81.

91. Hartmann, A. *Der Spätidealismus und die Hegelsche Dialektik*. Darmstadt, Wissenschaftliche Buchgesellschaft, 1969.

92. Hess, M.W. "Hegelianism and the Making of the Modern Mind," *Thomist*, 1951 (14), 335-50.

93. Höhne, Horst. "Hegel und England," *Kant-Studien*, 1931 (36), 301-26.

94. ——. *Der Hegelianismus in der englischen Philosophie*. Eine problemgeschichtliche Studie (Junge Forschungen, 2). Halle, Akademie Verlag, 1936.

95. Iakovenko, B. *Geschichte des Hegelianismus in Russland*. Prag, 1939.

96. Kohler, J. "Neuhegelianismus," *Archiv für Rechts- und Wirtschaftsphilosophie*, 1907 (1).

97. ——. "Vom Positivismus zum Neuhegelianismus," *Archiv für Rechts- und Wirtschaftsphilosophie*, 1909 (3).

98. Knoop, B. *Victor Cousin, Hegel und die französische Romantik*. München, 1932.

99. ——. *Hegel und die Franzosen*. Stuttgart, Kohlhammer, 1941.

100. Kroner, Richard. "Mure and Other English Hegelians," *Review of Metaphysics*, 1953 (7), 64-73.

101. Kühne, W. "Hegels Schule, ein Menschenalter nach seinem Tod. Unveröffentlichte Briefe der Hegelianer aus den Jahren 1868-1871," *Mitteilungen der deutschen Akademie*, 1935 (4), 596-618.

102. ——. "Hegels Philosophie und ihre Metamorphose im Polen," *Geisteskultur* (Berlin), Jahrgang 34, 304-17.

103. Levy, A. *Die Hegelrenaissance in der deutschen Philosophie mit besonderer Berücksichtigung des NeuKantianismus*. Charlottenburg, 1927.

104. Löwith, Karl. *Von Hegel zu Nietzsche*. Der revolutionäre Bruch im Denken des neunzehnten Jahrhunderts. Zürich, Wien, Europa, 1941.

105. ——. *Da Hegel a Nietzsche*. La frattura rivoluzionaria nel pensiero del secolo XIX. Torino, G. Einaudi, 1949.

106. ——. *From Hegel to Nietzsche*. The Revolution in Nineteenth Century Thought. New York, Holt, 1964, Doubleday, 1967; London, Constable & Company, 1965.

107. ——. *De Hegel à Nietzsche*. Paris, Gallimard, 1969.

108. Lindsay, T.M. "Recent Hegelian Contributions to English Philosophy," *Mind*, 1877 (2), 476-93.

109. Lunteren, S. A. van. "Der niederländische Hegelianismus," *Logos : Internationale Zeitschrift für Philosophie der Kultur*, 1925 (14), 240-57.

110. Mackintosh, R. *Hegel and Hegelianism*. Edinburgh, 1913.

111. Maclennan, S.F. "Trans-Subjective Realism and 'Hegelianism'," *Philosophical Review*, 1901.

112. Marcuse, Herbert. *Vernunft und Revolution*. Hegel und die Entstehung der Gesellschaftstheorie. Neuwied am Rhein, Luchterhand, 1962.

113. ——. *Reason and Revolution*. Hegel and the Rise of Social Theory. Oxford, Oxford University Press, 1941; New York, Beacon Press, 1960; London, Routledge, 1955.

114. ——. *Ragione e rivoluzione*. Hegel e il sorgere della "teoria sociale". Bologna, Il Mulino, 1966.

115. Marx, Werner. *Reason and World*. Between Tradition and Another Beginning. The Hague, Martinus Nijhoff, 1971.

116. Metzke, Erwin. *Karl Rosenkranz und Hegel*. Ein Beitrag zur Geschichte der Philosophie des sogenannten Hegelianismus im 19. Jahrhundert. Leipzig, W. Heim, 1929.

117. Michelet, K.L. "L'hégélianisme en 1867," *Théologie et Philosophie*. 1867, 130-43.

118. Monrad, M.J. "Ueber die gegenwärtige Stellung und Aufgabe der Hegelschen Philosophie," *Der Gedanke* (Berlin), 1860 (1), Heft 1.

119. Moog, Willy. *Hegel und die hegelsche Schule*. München, Reinhardt, 1930.

120. Muirhead, John Henry. "How Hegel Came to England," *Mind*, 1927 (36). 423-47. Reprinted in *The Platonic Tradition in Anglo-Saxon Philosophy*. New York, Humanities Press, 1965, 147-73.

121. ——. "Hesitations and Arrest," in *The Platonic Tradition in Anglo-Saxon Philosophy*, 204-18. New York, Humanities Press, 1965.

122. ——. "How Hegel Came to America," *Philosophical Review*, 1928 (37).

123. Navickas, Joseph L. "Hegel and the Doctrine of Historicity in Vladimir Solovyov," in *The Quest for the Absolute* (Boston College Studies in Philosophy, 1), 135-54. Boston College and Martinus Nijhoff, 1966.

124. Salomaa, J.E. "Die Anfänge des Hegelianismus in Finnland," *Kant-Studien*, 1934 (39), 301-15.

125. Sandor, P. "Der Einfluss Hegels auf die Ungarische Philosophie," *Hegel-Jahrbuch*, 1961.

126. Scherer, Edmund. "Hegel et l'hégélianisme," *Revue des deux mondes*, 1861 (31), 812-56. Reprinted in *Mélanges d'histoire religieuse*, Paris, 1864.

127. Serra, T. "Hegel e la filosofia del diritto in Italia," *Rivista internazionale di Filosofia del Diritto* (Milano), 1970 (47), 268-74.

128. Smith, W.R. "Dr. Stirling, Hegel, and the Mathematician," *Fortnightly Review* (London), 1873 (13), 495-510.

129. Simon, T. Collins. "Hegel and his Connexion with British Thought," *Contemporary Review* (London), 1870 (13), 47-79, 399-421.

130. Steininger, Wilhelm. "Systematische Betrachtungen über den Begriff der Persönlichkeit Gottes in der Philosophie Hegels und seiner Schule," *Philosophisches Jahrbuch* (München), 1956/1957 (65), 182-231.

131. Valensin, A. *L'histoire de la philosophie d'après Hegel*. Paris, 1923.

132. Vasa, Andrea. "De Ruggiero a l'interpretazione neoidealistica italiana della dialettica di Hegel," *Rivista di storia della filosofia* (Milano), 1948 (3), 275-89.

133. Villoro Toranzo, Miguel. "Influencia del pensamiento hegeliano," *Hegel-Studien*, Beiheft 4 (1969), 280-99.

134. Volhard, E. *Zwischen Hegel und Nietzsche : der Ästhetiker Friedrich Theodor Vischer*. Frankfurt am Main, Klostermann, 1932.

135. von Rintelen, F.J. "Entwicklung des Idealismus in Deutschland nach Hegel," *Journal of the History of Philosophy*, 1967, 237-243.

136. Zoltowski, Adam. "Hegel et la conception de l'histoire en Pologne,"in *La Pologne au 7e Congrès international des Sciences historiques*, Vol. I, 171-76. Varsovie, 1933.

137. Walicki, Andrej. "Hegel, Feuerbach and the Russian 'philosophical left' 1836-1848," *Annali dell' Istituto Giangiacomo Feltrinelli*, 1963 (6), 105-36.

138. Walker, L.J. "Hegelianism in Great Britain," *Rivista di filosofia neo-scholastica*, Vol. 23, Supplement.

Positivism

139. Engel, Otto. *Der Einfluss Hegels auf die Bildung der Gedankenwelt Hippolyte Taines*. Stuttgart, 1920.

140. Radermacher, Hans. "Hegel und der Positivismus," in *Aktualität und Folgen der Philosophie Hegels*, hrsg. Oskar Negt, 94-122. Frankfurt am Main, Suhrkamp, 1970.

141. Rensi, G. "Hegel e il positivismo," in *Realismo*, Milano, Unitas, 1925.

Contemporary Philosophy

142. Badi, Amir Mehdi. *Hegel et les origines de la pensée contemporaine*. Lausanne, Payot, 1964.

143. Betti, Emilio. *Recenti reazioni liberali contro il pensiero di Hegel*. Padova, CEDAM, 1950.

144. Colletti, Lucio. "Da Hegel a Marcuse," *De Homine*, 1968 (26), 91-118.

145. Earle, William. "Hegel and Some Contemporary Philosophies," *Philosophy and Phenomenological Research*, 1959/1960 (20), 352-64.

146. Findlay, J.N. "The Contemporary Relevance of Hegel," in *Language, Mind and Value*, 217-31. London, 1963.

147. Hook, Sidney. "The Contemporary Significance of Hegel's Philosophy," *Philosophical Review*, 1932 (41), 237-60.

148. Hyppolite, Jean. "Hegel et Kierkegaard dans la pensée française contemporaine," in *Figures de la pensée philosophique. Écrits (1931-1968)*, T. I., 196-208. Paris, Presses Universitaires de France, 1971.

149. ——. "La *Phénoménologie* de Hegel et la pensée française contemporaine," in *Ibid.*, T. I, 231-41.

150. Kline, George L. "Some Recent Reinterpretations of Hegel's Philosophy," *The Monist*, 1964 (48), 34-76.

151. Knox, T.M. "Hegel in English-speaking Countries Since 1919," *Hegel-Studien*, 1961 (1), 315-18.

152. Kroner, Richard. "Hegel heute," *Hegel-Studien*, 1961 (1), 135-53.

153. Lasson, G. "Hegel und die Gegenwart," *Kant-Studien*, 1931 (36).

154. Lombardi, Franco. "La 'morte della filosofia' dopo Hegel e la situazione presente della filosofia," *Rivista di Filosofia*, 1958 (49), 486-508.

155. Metzger, W. "Hegel und die Gegenwart," *Zeitschrift für Philosophie und philosophische Kritik*, 1913.

156. Mueller, Ferdinand-Lucien. *La pensée contemporaine en Italie et l'influence de Hegel*. Genève, Kundig, 1941.
157. Ogiermann, Helmut. "Hegelianische Dialektik heute," *Scholastik*, 1960 (35), 1-26.
158. Rosenthal, J. "Hegel and Contemporary Thought," *Symposium*, April, 1932.
159. Schmidt, Friedrich W. "Hegel in der kritischen Theorie der Frankfurter Schule," in *Aktualität und Folgen der Philosophie Hegels*, hrsg. Oskar Negt, 17-57. Frankfurt am Main, Suhrkamp, 1970.
160. Scholz, H.D. "Die Bedeutung der Hegelschen Philosophie für das philosophische Denken der Gegenwart," in *Philosophische Vorträge der Kantgesellschaft*, 1921. Berlin, Reuther & Reichard, 1921.
161. Schütz, P. "Hegel und unsere Zeit," *Der Türmer* (Stuttgart), Juli, 1920, 319-28.
162. Smith, John E. "Professor Weiss, 'Existenz' and Hegel," *Philosophy and Phenomenological Research*, 1948 (9), 322-25.
163. Wahl, Jean. "Le rôle de A. Koyré dans le développement des études Hégéliennes en France," *Archives de Philosophie*, 1965 (28), 323-36.
164. Weil, Eric. "Hegel et nous," *Hegel-Studien*, Beiheft 4 (1969), 7-15.

Pragmatism

165. Ackerman, Phyllis. "Some Aspects of Pragmatism and Hegel," *Journal of Philosophy*, 1918 (15), 337-56.

Phenomenology

166. Schrader, George A. "Hegel's Contribution to Phenomenology," *The Monist*, 1964 (48), 18-33.

The St. Louis Hegelians

167. Hoffmann, Fr. "Die Hegelsche Philosophie in St. Louis in den Vereinigten Staaten Nordamerikas," *Philosophische Monatshefte*, 1871 (7), Heft 2, 58-63.
168. Leidecker, Kurt F. "William Torrey Harris and the St. Louis Movement in Philosophy," *The Personalist*, 1951 (32), 235-50.

Existentialism

169. Croce, Benedetto. "L'odierno 'Rinascimento esistenzialistico' di Hegel," *Quaderni della Critica*, 1949, n. 15, 14-20.
170. Kline, George L. "The Existentialist Rediscovery of Hegel and Marx," in *Phenomenology and Existentialism*, ed. E.N. Lee and M. Mandelbaum, 113-38. Baltimore, The Johns Hopkins University Press, 1967.
171. Lessing, Arthur. "Hegel and Existentialism : On Unhappiness," *The Personalist*, 1968 (49), 61-77.
172. Merleau-Ponty, Maurice. "L'existentialisme chez Hegel," *Temps modernes*, 1945/1946 (1), n. 7, 1311-19.
173. Vogeler, Johan Jürgen. "Das Problem des sozialen Determinismus in der Philosophie Hegels, des Marxismus und des Existentialismus," in *Akten des XIV*.

Internationalen Kongresses für Philosophie, Wien, 2-9. September, 1968, VI, 546-52.

174. Christensen, Darrel E. "Nelson and Hegel on the Philosophy of History," *Journal of the History of Ideas*, 1964 (25), 439-44.

III. INDIVIDUAL PHILOSOPHERS

Plato

175. Baron, R. "Dialectique et humanisme chez Platon et Hegel," *Giornale di Metafisica*, 1965 (20), 142-49.

176. Bratuschek, E. "Wie Hegel Plato auffasst," *Philosophische Monatshefte* (Berlin), 1871/1872 (7).

177. Despotopoulos, C.J. "La guerre chez Platon et chez Hegel," *Entretiens Philosophiques d'Athènes*, April, 1955, 57-62.

178. Duerr, K. "Die Entwicklung der Dialektik von Platon bis Hegel," *Dialectica* (Neuchâtel), I, 1, 45-62.

179. Duso, G. "L'interpretazione hegeliana della contraddizione nel 'Parmenide', 'Sofista' e 'Filebo'," *Il Pensiero*, 1967 (12), 206-20.

180. ——. "Bildung, Politik und Philosophie in der Hegelschen Interpretation Platos," in *Akten des XIV. Internationalen Kongresses für Philosophie*, Wien, 1969, Bd. 4, 478-85.

181. ——. *Hegel interprete di Platone.* (Pubblicazioni della Scuola di Perfezionamento in Filosofia dell'Università di Padova. Quaderni di storia della filosofia, 2). Padova, CEDAM, 1969.

182. Foster, M.B. *The Political Philosophies of Plato and Hegel.* Oxford, Clarendon Press, 1935; New York, Russell and Russell, 1965.

183. Gauss, Hermann. "Von Kant über Hegel zu Plato," *Studia Philosophica* (Basel), 1947 (7), 114-76.

184. Janet, Paul. *Études sur la dialectique dans Platon et dans Hegel.* Paris, Ladrange, 1861.

185. Keidel, H. "Friedrich Hebbel, Hegel und Plato," *Journal of English and German Philology*, 1918 (17), 175-97.

186. Kojève, Alexandre. "Filosofia e sagezza," *Differenze*, 1965 (5), 27-55.

187. Kümmel, Friedrich. *Platon und Hegel zur ontologischen Begründung des Zirkels in der Erkenntnis.* Tübingen, Verlag Max Niemeyer, 1968.

188. Lakebrink, Bernhard. "Der Platonismus und die Hegelsche Metaphysik," in *Dialektik und Dynamik der Person*. Festschrift für Robert Heiss zum 60. Geburtstag. Köln und Berlin, 1963, 239-51.

189. Rosen, Stanley. "Sophrosyne und Selbstbewusstsein," *Review of Metaphysics*, 1973 (26), 617-42.

190. Sichirollo, L. *Storicità della dialettica antica. Platone, Aristotele, Hegel.* Padova, Marsilio, 1965.

191. Vera, Auguste. *Platonis, Aristotelis et Hegelii de medio termino doctrina.* Paris, Ladrange, 1845.

192. ——. "Dio secondo Platone, Aristotele ed Hegel," in *Atti di R. Accad. di sc. mor. e pol. di Napoli*, 1886.

193. Vircillo, Domenico. "L'estetica di Platone," *Teoremi*, 1971 (26), 63-150.

194. Wiehl, Reiner. "Platos Ontologie in Hegels Logik des Seins," *Hegel-Studien*, 1965 (3), 157-80.

Aristotle

195. Bartoš, Jaromir. "Ein Beitrag zur Frage des Aristotelischen Erbguts in der Philosophie Hegels," in *Antiquitas Graeco-Romana ac Tempora Nostra*, 223-30. Prague, 1968.

196. Bullinger, A. *Metakritische Gänge, betreffend Aristoteles und Hegel.* München, 1887.

197. Cosenza, Paolo. "Tra Aristotele e Hegel," *Rivista internazionale di Filosofia del Diritto*, 1954 (31), 789-96.

198. Frank, E. "Das Problem des Lebens bei Aristoteles und Hegel," *Deutsche Vierteljahrsschrift für Literaturwissenschaft und Geistesgeschichte*, 1927 (5), 609-43.

199. Hartmann, N. *Aristoteles und Hegel.* Beiträge zur Philosophie des deutschen Idealismus. Bd. I. Erfurt, 1923.

200. Heyder, Carl L.W. *Kritische Darstellung und Vergleichung der Methoden Aristotelischer und Hegelscher Dialektik.* Erlangen, 1845.

201. Hötschl, S. *Das Absolute in Hegels Dialektik.* Sein Wesen und seine Aufgaben, dargestellt im Hinblick auf Wesen und systematische Stellung Gottes als Actus purus der Aristotelischen Akt-Potenz-Metaphysik. Paderborn, Schöningh, 1941.

202. Ilting, Karl-Heinz. "Hegels Auseinandersetzung mit der Aristotelischen Politik," *Philosophisches Jahrbuch*, 1963 (71), 38-58.

203. Kern, Walter. "Aristoteles in Hegels Philosophiegeschichte : eine Antinomie," *Scholastik*, 1957 (32), 321-45.

204. ———. "Die Aristotelesdeutung Hegels. Die Aufhebung des Aristotelischen 'Nous' in Hegels 'Geist'," *Philosophisches Jahrbuch*, 1971 (78), 237-59.

205. Oeser, Erhard. *Begriff und Systematik der Abstraktion.* Die Aristotelesinterpretation bei Thomas von Aquin, Hegel und Schelling als Grundlegung der philosophischen Erkenntnislehre. Wien, München, Oldenbourg, 1969.

206. Paolucci, Henry. "The Poetics of Aristotle and Hegel," *Review of National Literatures*, 1970 (1), 165-213.

207. Pelloux, Luigi. "La struttura del reale in Aristotele ed in Hegel," *Rivista di Filosofia Neo-Scolastica*, 1949 (41), 153-67.

208. Ritter, Joachim. *Metaphysik und Politik.* Studien zu Aristoteles und Hegel. Frankfurt am Main, Suhrkamp, 1969.

209. Roeder von Diersburg, Egenolf. "Hegels Methode gemessen an der Methode des Aristoteles," *Archiv für Philosophie*, 1960 (10), 3-23.

210. Rollwage, Jürgen. *Das Modalproblem und die historische Handlung.* Ein Vergleich zwischen Aristoteles und Hegel. (Epimeleia, 14) München, Salzburg, Pustet, 1969.

211. Vollrath, Ernst. *Die These der Metaphysik.* Zur Gestalt der Metaphysik bei Aristoteles, Kant und Hegel. Wuppertal-Ratingen, Henn, 1969.

212. Weiss, Frederick G. *Hegel's Critique of Aristotle's Philosophy of Mind.* The Hague, Martinus Nijhoff, 1969.

See also 39, 190, 191, 192, 305 and 765.

Plotinus

213. Beierwaltes, W. von. "Hegel und Plotin," *Revue Internationale de Philosophie*, 1970 (92), 348-57.

214. Doering, A. *Plotin und Hegel.* Berlin, 1906.

215. Jong, K.H.E. de. "Hegel und Plotin," *Psychische Studien*, 1916, 184-95.
216. Schiavone, Michele. "Plotino nell' interpretazione dello Hegel," *Rivista di Filosofia Neo-Scolastica*, 1952 (44), 97-108.

Augustine

217. De Negri, Enrico. "L'elaborazione hegeliana di temi agostiniani," *Revue Internationale de Philosophie*, 1952 (6), n. 19, 62-78.
218. Padovani, Umberto. "Storicismo teologico-agostiniano e storicismo filosofico-hegeliano," in *S. Agostino e le grandi correnti della filosofia contemporanea* (Atti del Congresso italiano di filosofia agostiniana, Roma 20-30 ottobre 1954). Edizioni Agostiniane, Deposito di Tolentino (Marcerata), 1956.
219. ——. "Storicismo teleogico-agostiniano e storicismo filosofico-hegeliano," *Humanitas*, 1954 (9), 966-76.
220. Perkins, Robert L. "One Function of the Idea of Providence in Augustine's and Hegel's Historical Thought," *Hegel-Jahrbuch*, 1968/1969, 421-36.

Proclus

221. Beierwaltes, W. "Hegel und Proklos," in *Hermeneutik und Dialektik* (Aufsätze. Hans-Georg Gadamer zum 70. Geburtstag), II, 243-72. Tübingen, Mohr (Siebeck), 1970.

Anselm

222. Lakebrink, Bernhard. "Anselm von Canterbury und die Hegelsche Metaphysik," in *Parusia. Studien zur Philosophie Platons und zur Problemgeschichte des Platonismus* (Festgabe für J. Hirschberger), 455-70. Frankfurt am Main, 1965.

Bonaventura

223. Grégoire, P. "Hegel et saint Bonaventure," *Études franciscaines*, août, 1904.

Aquinas

224. Cappello, G. *La libertà di scelta e la libertà assoluta in Hegel e in S. Tommaso*. Palermo, Travi, 1939.
225. Chaix-Ruy, Jules. "Hegel et saint Thomas : dialectique et logique," in *Sapientia Aquinatis*, I (Communicationes IV Congressus Thomistici Internationalis. Romae, 13-17 Septembris, 1955. Bibliotheca Pontificiae Academiae Romanae S. Thomas Aquinatis, I), 212-20. Romae, Officium Libri Catholici, 1955.
226. Deckers, Hermannus. "La notion d'être chez Hegel et saint Thomas," in *Sapientia Aquinatis*, II (Relationes, Communicationes, et Acta IV Congressus Thomistici Internationalis. Romae, 13-17 Septembris, 1955.) Romae, Officium Libri Catholici, 1956.
227. Fabro, Cornelio. "Nuova interpretazione dell' uomo (Hegel, Feuerbach, S. Tommaso)," *Doctor communis* (Roma), 1964 (17), 144-58,
228. Garrigou-Lagrange, Réginald. "Dialectique hégélienne et métaphysique thomiste," in *Sapientia Aquinatis*, I (Communicationes IV Congressus Thomistici Internationalis. Romae, 13-17 Septembris, 1955. Bibliotheca Pontificiae Academiae

Romanae S. Thomas Aquinatis, I), 271-81. Romae, Officium Libri Catholici, 1955.

229. Grégoire, F. "Doctrina S. Thomas comparata cum dialectica hegeliana et marxista," in *Sapientia Aquinatis*, II (Relationes, Communicationes et Acta IV Congressus Thomistici Internationalis. Romae, 13-17 Septembris, 1955). Romae, Officium Libri Catholici, 1956.

230. ———. "Thèmes hégéliens et dépassements d'inspiration thomiste," in *Sapientia Aquinatis*, I (Communicationes IV Congressus Thomistici Internationalis. Romae, 13-17 Septembris, 1955. Bibliotheca Pontificiae Academiae Romanae S. Thomas Aquinatis, I), 282-91. Romae, Officium Libri Catholici, 1955.

231. Kern, Walter. "Das Verhältnis von Erkenntnis und Liebe als philosophisches Grundproblem bei Hegel und Thomas von Aquin," *Scholastik*, 1959 (34), 394-427.

232. Lakebrink, Bernhard. *Hegels dialektische Ontologie und die thomistische Analektik*. Ratingen, Verlag A. Henn, 1968.

233. Lobkowicz, Nicholas. "Abstraction and Dialectics," *Review of Metaphysics*, 1968 (21), 468-90.

234. Lotz, J.B. "Hegel und Thomas von Aquin. Eine Begegnung," *Gregorianum*, 1967 (3), 449-80.

235. McCoy, Charles N.R. "Hegel, Feuerbach, Marx and the Doctrine of St. Thomas Aquinas," in *Sapientia Aquinatis*, I (Communicationes IV Congressus Thomistici Internationalis. Romae, 13-17 Septembris, 1955. Bibliotheca Pontificiae Academiae Romanae S. Thomas Aquinatis, I), 328-38. Romae, Officium Libri Catholici. 1955,

236. Möller, Joseph. "Thomistische Analogie und Hegelsche Dialektik," *Doctor communis* (Roma), 1958 (11), 159-84.

237. Przywara, E. "Thomas oder Hegel? Zum Sinn der 'Wende zum Objekt'," *Logos*, 1926 (15).

238. Vanni Rovighi, Sophia. "Doctrina S. Thomae comparata cum dialectica hegeliana et marxista," in *Sapientia Aquinatis*, II (Relationes, Communicationes et Acta IV Congressus Thomistici Internationalis. Romae, 13-17 Septembris, 1955). Romae, Officium Libri Catholici, 1956.

See also 769.

Meister Eckhart

239. Lichtenstein, Ernst. "Von Meister Eckhart bis Hegel," in *Kritik und Metaphysik*. Studien (Heinz Heimsoeth zum achtzigsten Geburtstag, hrsg. Friedrich Kaulbach und Joachim Ritter). Berlin, de Gruyter, 1966.

Nicholas of Cusa

240. Gabriel, Leo. "Il pensiero dialettico in Cusano e in Hegel," *Filosofia*, 1970 (21), 537-47.

241. Metzke, Erwin. "Nicolaus von Cues und Hegel. Ein Beitrag zum Problem der philosophischen Theologie," *Kant-Studien*, 1956/1957 (48), 216-34.

242. Stallmach, Josef. "Das Absolute und die Dialektik bei Cusanus im Vergleich zu Hegel," *Scholastik*, 1964 (39), 495-509.

Machiavelli

243. Alderisio, Felice. "La politica del Machiavelli nella rivalutazione dello Hegel e del Fichte," *Nuova rivista di storia*, 1931 (15), 273-98.

Bruno

244. Maturi, S. *Bruno ed Hegel*. A cura di A. Guzzo. Firenze, Vallecchi, 1926.
245. Viellard-Baron, Jean-Louis. "De la connaissance de Giordano Bruno à l'époque de l'idéalisme allemand," *Revue de Métaphysique et de Morale*, 1971 (76), 406-23.

Böhme

246. Haldane, Elizabeth S. "J. Böhme and His Relation to Hegel," *Philosophical Review*, 1897 (6).
247. Schüssler, Ingrid. "Böhme und Hegel," *Jahrbuch der Schlesischen Friedrich-Wilhelms-Universität zu Breslau* (Würzburg), 1965 (10), 46-58.

Descartes

248. Doz, A. "Passage du concept à l'être chez Descartes et Hegel," *Revue de Métaphysique et de Morale*, 1967 (72), 216-30.
249. Schwarz, J. "Die cartesianische Reflexion und die Methode der Denker des deutschen Idealismus," in *Congrès Descartes*, III, 63-69.
See also 59.

Spinoza

250. Bertauld, P. *De la méthode. Méthode spinoziste et méthode hégélienne*. Paris, 1871.
251. Chiereghin, Franco. *L'influenza dello spinozismo nella formazione della filosofia hegeliana*. Padova, CEDAM, 1961.
252. Copleston, F.C. "Pantheism in Spinoza and the German Idealists," *Philosophy*, 1946 (21), 42-56.
253. Delbos, V. *Le problème moral dans Spinoza et dans l'histoire du Spinozisme*. Paris, 1893.
254. Foss, Laurence. "Hegel, Spinoza, and a Theory of Experience as Closed," *The Thomist*, 1971 (35), 435-46.
255. Gancikov, L. "Aporie del panlogismo," in *Spinoza*. Milano, Vita e Pensiero, 1933.
256. Gilbert, K.E. "Hegel's Criticism of Spinoza," in *Philosophical Essays in Honor of James Edwin Creighton*, 26-41. Freeport, New York, Books for Libraries Press, 1967.
257. Grunwald, Max. *Spinoza in Deutschland*. Berlin, Calvary & Co., 1907.
258. Härting, Thomas. "Hegel und die spinozistische Substanz," *Philosophisches Jahrbuch*, 1967/1968 (75), 416-419.
259. Janicaud, D. "Dialectique et substantialité. Sur la réfutation hégélienne du spinozisme," in *Hegel et la pensée moderne*, ed. Jacques d'Hondt, 161-92. Paris, Presses universitaires de France, 1970.

260. Lacharrière, René de. *Études sur la théorie démocratique. Spinoza, Rousseau, Hegel, Marx* (Bibliothèque politique et économique). Paris, Payot, 1963.

261. McMinn, J.B. "A Critique on Hegel's Criticism of Spinoza's God," *Boletín informativo del Seminario de Derecho político* (Universidad de Salamanca), mayo-oct, 1957. Reprinted in *Kant-Studien*, 1959 (51), 294-314.

262. Myers, H.A. "Systematic Pluralism in Spinoza and Hegel," *The Monist*, 1935 (45), 237-63.

263. ——. *The Spinoza-Hegel Paradox*. A Study of the Choice between Traditional Idealism and Systematic Pluralism. Ithaca, Cornell University Press, 1944.

264. Orelli, K. von. *Spinozas Leben und Lehre*. Nebst einem Abrisse der Schelling'schen und Hegel'schen Philosophie. Aarau, 1843, 1850.

265. Shmueli, Efraim. "Hegel's Interpretation of Spinoza's Concept of Substance," *International Journal of the Philosophy of Religion*, 1970 (1), 176-91.

266. ——. "Some Similarities between Spinoza and Hegel on Substance," *The Thomist*, 1972 (36), 645-57.

267. Tarozzi, G. "Di alcuni concetti di Hegel messi in rapporto col determinismo spinoziano e col positivismo," in *Rendiconto delle Sessioni della R. Accad. delle Scienze dell' Istituto di Bologna* (Classe di Scienze Morali), 1934/1935, 1935/1936 (9), 54-65.

Leibniz

268. Basch, Victor. *Les doctrines politiques des philosophes classiques de l'Allemagne : Leibniz, Kant, Fichte, Hegel*. Paris, F. Alcan, 1927.

269. Belaval, Yvon. "La doctrine de l'essence chez Hegel et chez Leibniz," *Archives de Philosophie*, 1970 (33), 547-78.

270. Bruaire, Claude. "Leibniz et la critique hégélienne," in *Akten des Internationalen Leibniz-Kongresses*, Hannover, 14.-19. November, 1966, Bd. V, *Geschichte der Philosophie* (Studia Leibnitiana, Suppl. Vol. V), 116-24. Wiesbaden, F. Steiner, 1971.

271. Holz, Hans Heinz. *Herr und knecht bei Leibniz und Hegel*. Zur Interpretation der Klassengesellschaft. Berlin, 1968.

272. Horn, J.C. *Monade und Begriff. Der Weg von Leibniz zu Hegel*. Wien und München, Oldenbourg, 1965.

273. ——. "Hinweise auf eine Theorie sensibler Erfahrung," *Zeitschrift für Philosophische Forschung*, 1971 (25), 48-59.

274. Moeller, N. *De Leibnitz à Hegel*. Un chapitre de l'histoire de la philosophie en Allemagne. Bruxelles, Bureaux de Durendal, 1910.

275. Saisset, E. "Leibniz et Hegel," *Revue des deux mondes*, 1860 (30), 961-97.

Vico

276. De Negri, E. "Theologen des Historismus : Vico und Hegel," *Romanische Forschungen*, 1950 (42), 277-93.

See also 362 and 728.

Berkeley

277. Fawcett, E.D. "From Berkeley to Hegel," *The Monist*, (7), 41-81.

278. Stäbler, Eugen. *George Berkeley's Auffassung und Wirkung in der deutschen Philosophie bis Hegel.* Dresden, Risse-Verl. in Komm., 1935.

Montesquieu

279. Trescher, H. *Montesquieus Einfluss auf die philosophische Staatslehre Hegels.* Leipzig, 1918.

Rousseau

280. Braun, Hellmut Walter. "Rousseaus Einfluss auf die Hegelsche Staatsphilosophie in ihrer Entwicklung und Vollendung," *Schmollers Jahrbuch für Gesetzgebung, Verwaltung und Volkswirtschaft im Deutschen Reiche*, 1926, Jahrgang 50, Halbband 2, 807-32.

281. Bruno, Antonio. *Illuminismo e romanticismo in Rousseau e in Hegel.* Bari, G. Laterza e. F., 1953.

282. Dubsky, Ivan. "Entfremdung : ein Thema von Rousseau und Hegel," in *Sbornik k 60. narozeniam prof. J. Popelové (Festschrift zum 60. Geburtstag von J. Popelovà),* 127-34. Praha, Acta Universitatis Carolinae, 1964.

283. Duguit, Léon. "Jean-Jacques Rousseau, Kant et Hegel," *Revue du droit ublic et de la science politique en France et à l'étranger,* 1918.

284. Dyke, C. "Collective Decision Making in Rousseau, Kant, Hegel and Mill," *Ethics,* 1969 (80), 21-37.

285. Loreau, Max. "Rousseau et la pensée dialectique : quelques textes (Hegel, Marx, Engels)," *Morale et Enseignement* (Bruxelles), 1961 (10), n. 40, 15-32.

286. Löwith, Karl. "Diritti dell' uomo e diritti del cittadino in Rousseau, Hegel e Marx," *La Cultura,* 1965 (3), 113-28.

287. ———. "Human Rights in Rousseau, Hegel and Marx," in *Le fondement des droits de l'homme,* 58-68. Firenze, La Nuova Italia, 1966.

288. Müller, Friedrich. *Entfremdung. Zur anthropologischen Begründung der Staatstheorie bei Rousseau, Hegel, Marx.* Berlin, 1970.

289. ———. "Der Denkensatz der Staatsphilosophie bei Rousseau und Hegel," *Der Staat* (Berlin), 1971 (10), 215-27.

290. Secrétan, Philibert. "Le thème de la propriété à travers Rousseau, Hegel et Marx," *Revue de théologie et de philosophie* (Lausanne), 1970 (20), 209-29.

See also 260.

Kant

291. Aliotta, A. "Hegel," in *L'estetica di Kant e degli idealisti romantici.* Roma, Perrella, 1942.

292. Apelt, Willibald. *Hegelscher Machtstaat oder Kantsches Weltbürgertum* (Vortrag, gehalten an der Universität München im Nov. 1947). München, Leibniz-Verlag, 1948.

293. Battaglia, F. "Linee di sviluppo del pensiero filosofico-giuridico in Kant e in Hegel," *Rivista internazionale di Filosofia del Diritto,* 1931, n. 6.

294. Berolzheimer, F. "Hegel und Kant in der modernen Rechtsphilosophie," *Deutsche Juristenzeitung* (Berlin), 1911, 1005.

295. Biedermann, Gustav. *Kants Kritik der reinen Vernunft und die Hegelsche Logik in ihrer Bedeutung für die Begriffswissenschaft.* Prag, 1969.
296. Biemel, Walter. "De Kant à Hegel," *Convivium* (Barcelona), 1962 (13/14), 69-146.
297. Bosio, Franco. "Le antinomie kantiane della totalità cosmologica e la loro critica in Hegel," *Il Pensiero*, 1964 (9), 39-104.
298. *Bulletin de la Société Française de Philosophie*, 1969 (62), n. 2. "Hegel. critique de Kant." Séance de 23 Novembre 1968. Exposé : M. Alexis Philonenko. Discussion : MM. Ferdinand Alquié, Jacques D'Hondt, Maurice de Gandillac, le R.P. Marty, Brice Parain, le R.P. Régnier, Jean Wahl, Edgar Wolff, Sylvain Zac. Lettre de MM. Georges Bénézé, Joseph Ohana, Aimé Patri. Paris, Armand Colin, 1969.
299. Chalybeäus, H.M. *Historische Entwicklung der spekulativen Philosophie von Kant bis Hegel.* Dresden, 1837, 1860.
300. ——. *Historical Development of Speculative Philosophy from Kant to Hegel.* Edinburgh, 1854.
301. Czolbe, H. *Die Grenzen und der Ursprung der menschlichen Erkenntnis im Gegensatze zu Kant und Hegel.* Jena und Leipzig, 1865.
302. Delbos, V. "Les facteurs kantiens dans la philosophie allemande à la fin du XVIIIe siècle et au commencement du XIXe," *Revue de Métaphysique et de Morale*, 1921/1922.
303. Denis, Ch. "De l'influence de la philosophie de Kant et de celle de Hegel sur la critique historique appliquée aux origines chrétiennes," *Annales de philosophie chrétienne*, Oct., 1900.
304. D'Ercole, P. "Kant quale immediato antecessore di Hegel nella logica ontologica," *Rivista di Filosofia neoscolastica*, 1911, n. 3-4.
305. ——. "La logica aristotelica, la logica kantiana ed hegeliana e la logica matematica con alcuni accenni alla logica indiana," in *Atti Acc. delle Scienze di Torina*, Torino, Bona, 1912.
306. Ebbinghaus, Julius. *Relativer und absoluter Idealismus.* Historisch-Systematische Untersuchung über den Weg von Kant zu Hegel. Leipzig, Veit, 1910.
307. Flach, Werner. "Kroner und der Weg von Kant bis Hegel. Die systematischen Voraussetzungen der Kronerschen Kantkritik," *Zeitschrift für Philosophische Forschung*, 1958 (12), 554-79.
308. Fleischmann, Eugène J. "Hegels Umgestaltung der Kantischen Logik," *Hegel-Studien*, 1965 (3), 181-207.
309. Frank, E. *Das Prinzip der dialektischen Synthesis und die Kantische Philosophie* (Ergänzungshefte der Kantstudien, Nr. 21), 1911.
310. Griffiss, James E. "The Kantian Background of Hegel's Logic," *The New Scholasticism*, 1969 (43), 509-29.
311. Guéroult, Martial. "Les 'déplacements' (*Verstellungen*) de la conscience morale Kantienne selon Hegel," in *Hommage à J. Hyppolite*, par Suzanne Bachelard et al., 48-80. Paris, Presses universitaires de France, 1971.
312. Harris, William Torrey. "Hegel Compared with Kant," *Journal of Speculative Philosophy*, 1881 (15), 241-52.
313. Hoernle, Reinhold F. "The Idealism of Kant and Hegel," and "The Dialectical Method and the Absolute," in *Idealism as a Philosophical Doctrine*, 137-59. London, Hodder & Stoughton Ltd., 1924.

314. Hoffmeister, J. *Die Problematik des Völkerbundes bei Kant und Hegel* (Recht und Staat in Geschichte und Gegenwart, 111). Tübingen, Mohr, 1934.
315. Holzheimer, Franz. *Der logische Gedanke von Kant bis Hegel.* Paderborn, Schöningh, 1936.
316. Hoor, E. "Das Völkerrecht bei Kant, Fichte und Hegel," *Acta Scandinavica Juris Gentium* (København), 1934 (5), 81-103.
317. Hyppolite, Jean. "La critique hégélienne de la réflexion kantienne," *Kantstudien*, 1953/1954 (45).
318. ———. "La critique hégélienne de la réflexion kantienne," in *Figures de la pensée philosophique.* Écrits (1931-1968), I, 175-95. Paris, Presses universitaires de France, 1971.
319. Kirscher, Gilbert. "Hegel et Jacobi critiques de Kant," *Archives de Philosophie*, 1970 (33), 801-28.
320. Klug, Ulrich. "Abschied von Kant und Hegel," in *Programm für ein neues Strafgesetzbuch*, 36-41. Frankfurt am Main. 1968.
321. ———. "Phänomenologische Aspekte der Strafrechts-philosophie von Kant und Hegel," in *Phänomenologie, Rechtsphilosophie, Jurisprudenz* (Festschrift für Gerhart Husserl zum 75. Geburtstag, hrsg. Thomas Würtenberger), 212-33. Frankfurt am Main, V. Klostermann, 1969.
322. Knox, T.M. "Hegel's Attitude to Kant's Ethics," *Kant-Studien*, 1957/1958 (49), 70-81.
323. Kroner, Richard. *Von Kant bis Hegel.* Tübingen, Mohr, 1921, 1924, and 1961.
324. La Via, V. "La riforma del trascendentalismo kantiano e della dialettica hegeliana," in *L'idealismo attuale di G. Gentile.* Trani, Vecchi, 1925.
325. Liebrucks, Bruno. *Sprache und Bewusstsein*, Bd. III : *Wege zum Bewusstsein. Sprache und Dialektik in den ihnen von Kant und Marx versagten, von Hegel eröffneten Räumen.* Frankfurt am Main, Akademische Verlagsgesellschaft, 1966.
326. Marck, S. *Kant und Hegel.* Eine Gegenüberstellung ihrer Grundbegriffe. Tübingen, 1917.
327. Maier, Josef. *On Hegel's Critique of Kant.* New York, Columbia University Press, 1939.
328. Marini, Giuliano. "Lo stato di diritto Kantiano e la critica di Hegel," *Rivista internazionale di Filosofia del Diritto*, 1964 (41), 227-37.
329. Mayer, Helmut. "Kant, Hegel und das Strafrecht," in *Festschrift für Karl Engisch zum 70. Geburtstag*, 54-79. Frankfurt am Main, 1969.
330. Michelet, Carl Ludwig. *Geschichte der letzten Systeme der Philosophie in Deutschland von Kant bis Hegel.* Berlin, 1837/1838.
331. O'Sullivan, John M. *Vergleich der Methoden Kants und Hegels auf Grund ihrer Behandlung der Kategorie der Quantität.* Berlin, Reuther und Reichard, 1908.
332. Pappalardo, A. "I postulati della morale kantiana nella prospettiva hegeliana della 'Fenomenologia'," *Il Pensiero*, 1966, 208-26.
333. Philonenko, Alexis. "Hegel critique de Kant," in *Hegel critique de Kant* (Bulletin de la Société de Philosophie), 1969 (63), n. 2.
334. Pecilli, D. "Osservazioni sul problema della volontà etica nel Kant e in Hegel," *Rivista internazionale di Filosofia del Diritto*, 1967, 67-79.
335. Rackwitz, Max. *Hegels Ansicht über die Apriorität von Zeit und Raum und*

die kantischen Kategorien. Eine philosophische Kritik nach Hegels *Phänomenologie des Geistes.* Halle, 1891.

336. Ritter, Heinrich. *Versuch zur Verständigung über die neueste deutsche Philosophie.* Braunschweig, 1953.

337. Ritter, Joachim. "Moralität und Sittlichkeit. Zu Hegels Auseinandersetzung mit der kantischen Ethik," in *Kritik und Metaphysik.* Studien (Heinz Heimsoeth zum achtzigsten Geburtstag, hrsg. Friedrich Kaulbach und Joachim Ritter). Berlin, de Gruyter, 1966.

338. ———. "Zum Primat des Rechts bei Kant und Hegel," in *Recht und Ethik.* Zum Problem ihrer Beziehung im 19. Jahrhundert, hrsg. J. Blühdorn und J. Ritter, 77-82. Frankfurt am Main, 1970.

339. Rohrmoser, Günter. "Die theologische Bedeutung von Hegels Auseinandersetzung mit der Philosophie Kants und dem Prinzip der Subjektivität," *Neue Zeitschrift für systematische Theologie und Religionsphilosophie* (Berlin), 1962 (4), 89-111.

340. Rotta, P. "Kant quale immediato antecessore di Hegel nella logica ontologica," *Rivista di Filosofia neoscolastica,* 1911, n. 3-4.

341. Royce, Josiah. *Lectures on Modern Idealism.* New Haven, Conn., 1919, 1964.

342. Sander, Josef. *Die Begründung der Notwehr in der Philosophie von Kant und Hegel.* Bleicherode, Nieft, 1939.

343. Schrimpf, Hans Joachim. "From Kant to Hegel. Some Aspects of Hegel's Concept of Right," in *Festschrift für D.W. Schumann,* 256-66. München, 1970.

344. Simon, Josef. "Reine und sprachliche Anschauung (Kant und Hegel)," in *Das Problem der Sprache* (Achter deutscher Kongress für Philosophie, Heidelberg, 1966, hrsg. Hans-Georg Gadamer), 159-67. München, Wilhem Fink Verlag, 1967.

345. Smith, John E. "Hegel's Critique of Kant," *Review of Metaphysics,* 1973 (26), 438-60.

346. Sodens, G. *Die Staatslehre Kants und Hegels.* Erlangen, 1893.

347. Spaventa, B. "Idealismo o realismo? Nota sulla teoria della conoscenza : Kant, Herbart, Hegel," in *Rendiconti della R. Accad. di sc. mor e polit.,* April-June, 1874, 87-97. Reprinted in *Scritii filosofici,* ed. G. Gentile, 353-66.

348. Specht, Ernst Konrad. *Der Analogiebegriff bei Kant und Hegel* (*Kantstudien.* Ergänzungsheft 66, hrsg. im Auftr. der Kantgesellschaft Landesgruppe Rheinland-Westfalen). Köln, Kölner Universitätsverlag, 1952.

349. Sydow, E. von. *Kritischer Kant-Kommentar.* Zusammengestellt aus den Kritiken Fichtes, Schellings, Hegels. Halle, 1913.

350. ———. *Der Gedanke des Idealreiches in der idealistischen Philosophie von Kant bis Hegel.* Leipzig, Meiner, 1914.

351. Thilo, E.A. "Die Grundirrthümer des Idealismus in ihrer Entwicklung von Kant bis Hegel," *Zeitschrift für exacte Philosophie im Sinne des neueren philosophischen Realismus,* 1860 (1), Heft 1.

352. Vanni Rovighi, Sofia. "Hegel critico di Kant," *Rivista di Filosofia neoscolastica,* 1950 (42), 289-312.

353. Verene, Donald Phillip. "Kant, Hegel, and Cassirer. The Origins of the Philosophy of Symbolic Forms," *Journal of the History of Ideas,* 1969 (30), 33-46.

354. Vogt, Carl. *Darstellung und Beurteilung der Kant'schen und Hegel'schen Christologie.* Marburg, 1878.

355. Wacker, Herbert. *Das Verhältnis des jungen Hegel zu Kant.* Berlin, Junker und Dünnhaupt, 1932.
356. Werkmeister, W.H. "Hegel's *Phenomenology of Mind* as Development of Kant's Basic Ontology," in *Hegel and the Philosophy of Religion*, ed. Darrel Christensen, 93-110. The Hague, Martinus Nijhof, 1970.
357. Wulf, Berthold. *Idee und Denken.* Beiträge zum Verständnis der Philosophie des deutschen Idealismus mit besonderer Berücksichtigung von Kant, Fichte, und Hegel. Stuttgart, Verlag Freies Geistesleben, 1964.
358. Wyncken, A.G. *Hegels Kritik Kants.* Zur Einleitung in die Hegelsche Philosophie. Abel, Greifswald, 1898.

See also 183, 211, 268, 284, 284, 359, 378, 392, 411, 443, 465, 684, 728, 732, 741, 742, 748, 769, 775.

Lessing

359. Oelmüller, Willi. *Die unbefriedigte Aufklärung.* Beitrag zu einer Theorie der Moderne von Lessing, Kant, und Hegel. Frankfurt am Main, Suhrkamp, 1969.

Hamann

360. Nadler, K. "Hamann und Hegel. Zum Verhältnis von Dialektik und Existentialität," in *Logos*, 1931 (20).

Burke

361. Suter, Jean-François. "Burke, Hegel and the French Revolution," in *Hegel's Political Philosophy*, ed. Z.A. Pelczynski, 52-72. Cambridge, 1971.

Condorcet

362. Ciavarini, Doni Ivo. *La legge del progresso umano, considerata in Vico, Herder, Condorcet ed Hegel.* Ancona, t. del Commercio. 1871.

Jacobi

363. Brueggen, M. "La critique de Jacobi par Hegel dans *Foi et Savoir*," *Archives de Philosophie*, 1967, 187-98.
364. Höhn, Gerhard. "F.H. Jacobi et G.W. Hegel ou la naissance du nihilisme et la renaissance du 'Logos'," *Revue de Métaphysique et de Morale*, 1970 (75), 129-50.
365. Kirscher, Gilbert. "Hegel et la philosophie de F.H. Jacobi," *Hegel-Studien*, Beiheft 4 (1969), 181-91.

See also 319.

Herder

366. Franz, Herbert. *Von Herder bis Hegel.* Eine bildungsgeschichtliche Ideenvergleichung. Frankfurt am Main, Diesterweg, 1938.
367. Merkel, R.F. "Herder und Hegel über China," *Sinica*. China-Institut, Frankfurt am Main, 1942 (17), 5-26.

See also 347 and 362.

Reinhold

368. Leopoldsberger, Jürgen. "Anfang und Methode als Grundproblem der systematischen Philosophie : Reinhold, Fichte, Hegel," *Salzburger Jahrbuch für Philosophie*, 1968/1969, (12-13), 7-48.

Fichte

369. Beyer, Wilhelm R. "Hegels ungenügendes Fichte-Bild," in *Wissen und Gewissen* (Beiträge zum 200. Geburtstag Johann Gottlieb Fichtes, hrsg. M. Buhr), 241-77. Berlin, 1962.
370. Buhr, Manfred. *Der Uebergang von Fichte zu Hegel*. Berlin, Akademie-Verlag, 1965.
371. Darmstaedter, Friedrich. "L'esperienza statuale in Fichte e Hegel," *Rivista internazionale di Filosofia del Diritto*, 1936 (16), 157-94.
372. Galluppi, P. "Due Lettere ignorate su Fichte, Schelling e Hegel," *Rivista di Filosofia neoscolastica*, 1932, n. 4.
373. Girndt, Helmut. "La critique de Fichte par Hegel dans la 'Differenzschrift' de 1801," *Archives de Philosophie*, 1965 (28), 37-62.
374. ——. *Die Differenz des Fichteschen und Hegelschen Systems in der Hegelschen "Differenzschrift"*. Bonn, Bouvier, 1965.
375. Haering, Th. "Fichte-Schelling-Hegel : ein Vergleich," in *Das Deutsche in der deutschen Philosophie*. Stuttgart, Kohlhammer, 1941.
376. Hartkopf, Werner. "Die Dialektik Fichtes als Vorstufe zu Hegels Dialektik," *Zeitschrift für Philosophische Forschung*, 1967 (21), 173-207.
377. Heinrichs, Johannes. "Fichte, Hegel und der Dialog. Ein Bericht in systematischer Absicht," *Theologie und Philosophie*, 1972 (47), 90-131.
378. Jaurès, Jean. *De primis socialismi germanici lineamentis apud Luterium, Kant, Fichte, et Hegel*. Paris, 1892.
379. Petruzzellis, Nicola. "Il problema della società da Fichte ed Hegel," *Rassegna di Scienza filosofica* (Napoli), 1955 (8), 201-37.
380. Rütter, Hans. *Ein klassisches Gepräch : Fichte und Hegel*. Zürich, Kommerzdruck und Verlag AG., 1945.
381. Schaub, Edward L. "Hegel's Criticism of Fichte's Subjectivism," *Philosophical Review*, 1912 (21), 566-84.
382. ——. "Hegel's Criticism of Fichte's Subjectivism," *Philosophical Review*, 1913 (22).
383. Siep, Ludwig. *Hegels Fichtekritik und die Wissenschaftslehre von 1840*. Freiburg im Breisgau, München, Alber, 1970.
384. Thilo, C. *Die Religionsphilosophie des absoluten Idealismus. Fichte, Schelling, Hegel und Schopenhauer*. Langensalza, Beyer, 1905.
385. Wagner, Falk. *Der Gedanke der Persönlichkeit Gottes bei Fichte und Hegel*. Gütersloh, Gütersloher Verlagshaus G. Mohn, 1971.
386. Zahn, Manfred. "Fichtes, Schellings und Hegels Auseinandersetzung mit dem 'Logischen Realismus' Christoph Gottfried Bardilis," *Zeitschrift für philosophische Forschung*, 1965 (19), 201-32, 453-79.
387. ——. "Fichte, Schelling et Hegel en face du 'réalisme logique' de C.G. Bardili," *Archives de Philosophie*, 1967 (30), 61-88, 199-230.

See also 243, 249, 268, 316, 336, 341, 349, 357, 368, 392, 395, 405, 414, 465, 684, and 703.

Baader

388. Hoffman, Franz. *Franz Baader im Verhältnisse zu Spinoza, Leibniz, Kant, Jacobi, Fichte, Schelling, Hegel, Herbart.* Leipzig, 1851.
389. ──. *Franz von Baader in seinem Verhältnis zu Hegel und Schelling.* Leipzig, 1850.
390. Lakebrink, Bernhard. "Hegels Einfluss auf die Religionsphilosophie Franz von Baaders," *Philosophisches Jahrbuch*, 1964/1965 (72), 120-33.

Schleiermacher

391. Brandt, Richard B. "Schleiermacher and Hegel," in *The Philosophy of Schleiermacher. The Development of His Theory of Scientific and Religious Knowledge*, 322-26. New York, Greenwood Press, 1968.
392. Fichte, J.H. "Der bisherige Zustand der praktischen Philosophie in seinen Umrissen. Kant, Fichte, Hegel, Schleiermacher," *Zeitschrift für Philosophie und spekulative Theologie*, 1843 (11), Heft 2.
393. George, L. *Prinzip und Methode der Philosophie mit besonderer Rücksicht auf Hegel und Schleiermacher dargestellt.* Berlin, 1842.
394. Glockner, H. "Hegel und Schleiermacher im Kampf um Religionsphilosophie und Glaubenslehre," *Deutsche Vierteljahrsschrift*, 1929 (8).
395. Hirsch, Emanuel. *Fichtes, Schleiermachers und Hegels Verhältnis zur Reformation.* Göttingen, Vandenhoeck und Ruprecht, 1930.
396. Schultz, W. *Die Grundprinzipien der Religionsphilosophie Hegels und die Theologie Schleiermachers. Ein Vergleich.* (Neue deutsche Forschungen, Abteilung Religions- und Kirchen-Geschichte, Bd. V) Berlin, Junker und Dünnhaupt, 1938.
397. Schultz, Werner. "Die Transformierung der theologia crucis bei Hegel und Scheiermacher," *Neue Zeitschrift für systematische Theologie und Religionsphilosophie*, 1964 (6), 290-317.
398. Vowinckel, E. *Religion und Religionen bei Schleiermacher und Hegel.* Eine Verhältniss-bestimmung. Erlangen, 1896.
See also 493.

Schlegel

399. Behler, Ernst. "Friedrich Schlegel und Hegel," *Hegel-Studien*, 1963 (2), 203-50

Schelling

400. Assunto, Rosario. "Le relazioni fra arte e filosofia nella *Philosophie der Kunst* di Schelling e nelle *Vorlesungen über die Ästhetik* di Hegel," *Hegel-Jahrbuch*, 1965, 84-121.
401. Deser, Erhard. *Die antike Dialektik in der Spätphilosophie Schellings.* Ein Beitrag zur Kritik des Hegelschen Systems. Wien und München, Oldenbourg, 1965.
402. Düsing, Klaus. "Spekulation und Reflexion. Zur Zusammenarbeit Schellings und Hegels in Jena," *Hegel-Studien*, 1969 (5), 95-128.
403. Fichte, J.H. "Hegels philosophische Magister-Dissertation und sein Ver-

hältnis zu Schelling," *Zeitschrift für Philosophie und spekulative Theologie*, 1844 (12), Heft 1, 142-86.

404. Fuhrmans, Horst. "Schelling und Hegel : Ihre Entfremdung," in *F.W.J. Schelling, Briefe und Dokumente*, Bd. I : 1775-1809, hrsg. H. Fuhrmans, 451-553. Bonn, 1962.

405. Gilbert, Katharine and Kuhn, Helmut. "Absolute Idealism : Fichte, Schelling, Hegel," in *A History of Esthetics*, 436-55. Bloomington, Indiana University Press, 1953.

406. Glaser, J.K. *Differenz der Schelling'schen und Hegel'schen Philosophie*. Leipzig, 1842.

407. Hayes, Victor C. "Schelling : Persistent Legends, Improving Image," *Southwestern Journal of Philosophy*, 1972 (3), 63-73.

408. Henderson, J.S. "Mr. G.H. Lewes on Schelling and Hegel," *The Contemporary Review* (London), 1872 (20), 529-42.

409. Hinkel, C. *Die spekulative Analysis des Begriffs "Geist," mit Darlegung des Differenzpunkts zwischen dem Hegel'schen und Neu-Schelling'schen Standpunkte Weber's anderseits*. Rinteln, 1840.

410. Klaiber, Julius. *Hölderlin, Hegel und Schelling in ihren schwäbischen Jugendjahren*. Stuttgart, 1877.

411. Kloss, O. *Kepler und Newton und das Problem der Gravitation in der Kantischen, Schellingschen und Hegelschen Naturphilosophie*. Heidelberg, 1908.

412. Krug, W.T. *Schelling und Hegel oder die neueste Philosophie im Vernichtungskriege mit sich selbst begriffen*. Leipzig, 1835.

413. Marbach, G.O. *Schelling, Hegel, Cousin und Krug*. Erörterungen auf dem Gebiete der Philosophie. Leipzig, 1835.

414. Maréchel, Joseph. "L'idéalisme de Fichte, Schelling et Hegel," in *Le point de départ de la métaphysique*, cahier IV, 441-53. L'édition universelle, Bruxelles, Desclée de Brouwer, Paris, 1947.

415. Marquet, J.-F. "Système et Sujet chez Hegel et Schelling," *Revue de Métaphysique et de Morale*, 1968 (73), 167-83.

416. ———. "Le destin de la philosophie chez Hegel et Schelling," in *Hegel. L'esprit objectif. L'unité de l'histoire*. (Actes du IIIème congrès international de l'Association internationale pour l'étude de la philosophie de Hegel), 221-37. Lille, 1970.

417. Rinaldi, Francesco. "Della presenza schellinghiana nella critica di Kierkegaard a Hegel," *Studi Urbinati di Storia, Filosofia et Letteratura*, 1969 (43), 243-62.

418. Rosenkranz, K. *Ueber Schelling und Hegel*. Sendschreiben an Pierre Leroux. Königsberg, 1843.

419. Salat, J. *Schelling und Hegel oder Rückblicke auf die höhere Geistesbildung im deutschen Süden und Norden*. Heidelberg, 1842.

420. Sandkühler, Hans Jörg. "Geschichte und Entfremdung : Zur Differenz des Hegelschen und Schellingschen Systems oder Hegels Kritik der konter-revolutionären Entwirklichung der Geschichte und ihrer Philosophie," *Hegel-Jahrbuch*, 1968/1969, 107-22.

421. Schleiden, Mathias Jakob. *Schellings und Hegels Verhältnis zur Naturwissenschaft*. Leipzig, 1844.

422. Schmidt, Friedrich W. *Zum Begriff der Negativität bei Schelling und Hegel*. Stuttgart, Metzler, 1971.

423. Schneider, Robert. *Schellings und Hegels schwäbischen Geistesahnen*. Würzburg, Triltsch, 1938.

424. Schulz, Walter. "Das Verhältnis des späten Schelling zu Hegel. Schellings Spekulation über den Satz," *Zeitschrift für Philosophische Forschung*, 1954 (8), 336-52.

425. Semerari, Giuseppe. "La critica di Schelling a Hegel," in *Incidenza di Hegel*, a cura di Fulvio Tessitore, 445-96. Napoli, Morano Ed. 1970.

426. Staiger, E. *Der Geist der Liebe und das Schicksal*. Schelling, Hegel und Hölderlin (Wege zur Dichtung, 19). Leipzig, Huber, 1935.

427. Stallo, J.B. *General Principles of the Philosophy of Nature, with an outline of Some of its Recent Developments Among the Germans, Embracing the Philosophical Systems of Schelling and Hegel, and Oken's System of Nature*. Boston, W. Crosby and H.P. Nichols, 1848.

428. Steinkrueger, W.A. *Die Ästhetik der Musik bei Schelling und Hegel*. Ein Beitrag zur Musikästhetik der Romantic. Bonn, 1927.

429. Theunissen, Michael. "Die Dialektik der Offenbarung. Zur Auseinandersetzung Schellings und Kierkegaards mit der Religionsphilosophie Hegels," *Philosophisches Jahrbuch*, 1964/1965 (72), 134-60.

430. Thrandofoff, K. *Schelling und Hegel oder das System Hegels als letztes Resultat des Grundirrtums in allen bisherigen Philosophien*. Berlin, 1842.

431. Tilliette, Xavier. "Schelling critique de Hegel," *Hegel-Studien*, Beiheft 4 (1969), 193-203.

432. ——. "Schelling contre Hegel," *Archives de Philosophie*, 1966 (29), 89-108.

433. ——. "Hegel et Schelling à Iena," *Revue de Métaphysique et de Morale*, 1968 (73), 194-206.

434. Vogel, Emil Ferdinand. *Schelling oder Hegel oder Keiner von Beiden*? Ein Separat-Votum über die Eigenthümlichkeiten der neueren deutschen Philosophie. Leipzig, 1843.

See also 249, 264, 336, 341, 349, 372, 375, 384, 386, 387, 388, 389, 441, 502, and 722.

Fries

435. Dooren, Wilhem van. "Hegel und Fries," *Kantstudien*, 1970 (61), 217-26.
See also 1.

Herbart

436. Ewald, O. *Welche wirklichen Fortschritte hat die Metaphysik seit Hegels und Herbarts Zeiten in Deutschland gemacht*? (*Kantstudien*, Ergänzungshefte, 53). Berlin, 1920.
See also 347.

Schopenhauer

437. Bahnsen, J.F.A. *Zur Philosophie der Geschichte*. Eine kritische Besprechung des hegel-hartmannschen Evolutionismus aus schopenhauerschen Prinzipien. Berlin, C. Duncker, 1872.

438. Deussen, P. "Bericht über Hegel und Schopenhauer," *Archiv für Geschichte der Philosophie*, 1889 (3), 147-68.

439. Foucher de Careil, A. *Hegel et Schopenhauer. Études sur la philosophie allemande moderne depuis Kant jusqu'à nos jours*. Paris, Hachette et Compagnie, 1862.

440. ——. *Hegel und Schopenhauer, ihr Leben und Wirken*. Wien, Konegen, 1888.

441. Hartmann, E. von. *Schellings Positive Philosophie als Einheit von Hegel und Schopenhauer*. Berlin, 1869.

442. Hermann, Conrad. "Hegel und Schopenhauer in französischer Auffassung," *Wissenschaftliche Beilage zur Leipziger Zeitung*, Jahrgang 88, 467.

443. Knox, Israel. *The Aesthetic Theories of Kant, Hegel, and Schopenhauer*. New York, Columbia University Press, 1936; London, Milford, 1936.

444. Royce, Josiah. "Two Philosophers of the Paradoxical : Hegel, Schopenhauer," *Atlantic Monthly*, 1891 (67), 45, 161.

See also 384 and 697.

Comte

445. Dittman, F. "Die Geschichtsphilosophie Comtes und Hegels. Ein Vergleich," *Vierteljahrsschrift für wissenschaftliche Philosophie und Soziologie* (Leipzig, Reisland), Jahrgang 38, Heft 3.

446. Gokberk, Macit. *Die Wissenschaft von der Gesellschaft im System Hegels und Auguste Comtes*. Berlin, Ebering, 1940.

447. Hayek, Friedrich A. "Comte e Hegel," *L'Industria*, 1965 (1), 3-22.

448. ——. "L'influsso comune di Comte e di Hegel sul pensiero delle scienze sociali," *Il Politico*, 1951 (17), 137-56.

449. Mehlis, S. "Die Geschichtsphilosophie Hegels und Comtes," *Jarhbuch für Soziologie*, 1925 (3), 91-100.

450. Negt, Oskar. *Strukturbeziehungen zwischen den Gesellschaftslehren Comtes und Hegels*. Frankfurt am Main, Europ. Verl.-Anst., 1964.

451. Reboul, Olivier. La pensée politique de Comte et de Hegel," *Dialogue*, 1970 (9), 181-202.

452. Salomon-Delatour, G. "Comte ou Hegel," *Revue positiviste* (Paris), 1935, 220-27.

453. Spinner, H.F. "Wege und Irrwege der Wissenschaft. Die Soziologie zwischen Hegel und Comte," *Soziale Welt*, 1969 (20), n. 3, 329-58.

454. Toennies, F. "Neuere Philosophie der Geschichte : Hegel, Marx, Comte," *Archiv für Geschichte der Philosophie*, 1894 (7), 486.

Rosmini

455. Chiesa, M. "Rosmini e Hegel," *Rivista Rominiana di Filosofia e di Cultura*, 1932, n. 3.

456. Cipriani, C. *Conoscenza e moralità nel sistema di filosofia del diritto di Hegel e Rosmini*. Sassari, tip. della Libertà, 1914.

457. Contri, Siro. *Parallelo fra Hegel e Rosmini*. Palermo, Roma, Mori, 1970.

458. Cristaldi, Giuseppe. "La libertà come valore in Hegel e in Rosmini," in *Atti XII Congr. intern. Filos.*, 115-20. Firenze, Sansoni, 1961.

459. Giannini, Giorgio. "La critica di Rosmini a Hegel in un recente studio," *Aquinas*, 1958 (1), 268-74.
460. Mazzantini, C. "Rosmini e Hegel," *Rivista Rosminiana di Filosofia e di Cultura*, 1932, n. 3.
461. Micelli, R. "Rosmini e Hegel," *Rivista Rosminiana di Filosofia e di Cultura*, 1932, n. 3.
462. Muzio, Giuseppe. "L'idea dell' essere in S. Tommaso, in Rosmini, in Hegel," *Rivista Rosminiana di Filosofia e di Cultura*, 1956 (50), 6-12.
463. Piovani, P. "Hegel nella filosofia del diritto di Rosmini," in *Scritti giuridici in onore di Piero Calamandrei*. Padova, CEDAM, 1956.
464. Troilo, E. "La critica di Rosmini alla filosofia tedesca dopo Kant," in *Figure e dottrine di pensatori*. Padova, CEDAM, 1941.

Leopardi

465. Luporini, Cesare. *Filosofi vecchi e nuovi*. M. Scheler, G.F. Hegel, Kant, Fichte, Leopardi. (Studi filosofica) Firenze, Sansoni, 1947.

Newman

466. Brunner, August. "Idee und Entwicklung bei Hegel und Newman," *Scholastik*, 1957 (32), 1-26.
467. Schwarz. Balduin, "Die Zukunft der Kunst : Hegel und Newman," *Hegel-Jahrbuch*, 1965, 122-41.

Feuerbach

468. Ascheri, Carlo. "Aspetti dell' hegelismo del giovane Feuerbach," *Hegel-Studien*, Beiheft 4 (1969), 205-14.
469. Dhanis, R.P.E. "En marge d'un cours sur Hegel et sur Feuerbach," in *Atti della Riunione costitutiva*, Roma, 20-23 settembre. 1949. Napoli, Pironti e Figli, 1950. Also printed in *Gregorianum*, 1949 (30), 574-86.
470. Dicke, Gerd. *Der Identitätsgedanke bei Feuerbach und Marx*. Köln und Opladen, Westdeutscher Verlag, 1960.
471. Engels, Friedrich. *Ludwig Feuerbach und der Ausgang der klassischen deutschen Philosophie*, Stuttgart, 1888; Leipzig, Meiner, 1947.
472. Grégoire, Franz. "Hegel et Feuerbach," in Pierre Ayraud, *Les livres et le problème de l'humanisme*. Témoignages, 1849.
473. Gregor, A.J. "Marx, Feuerbach, and the Reform of the Hegelian Dialectic" *Science and Society*, 1965 (29), 66-80.
474. Löwith, Karl. "Mediation and Immediacy in Hegel, Marx and Feuerbach," in Warren E. Steinkraus, ed., *New Studies in Hegel's Philosophy*, 119-41. New York, Holt, Rinehart and Winston, 1971.
475. Nerrlich, P. "Ueber das Verhältnis L. Feuerbachs zu Hegel," *Preussische Jahrbücher* (Berlin), 1895 (80).
476. Orsini, G.N.G. "Feuerbach's Supposed Objection to Hegel," *Journal of the History of Ideas*, 1969 (30), 85-90.
477. Polizzi, Paolo. "Crisi de fondamento e istanza storico-esistenziale in Feuerbach e Marx," *Giornale di Metafisica*, 1966 (21), 540-54.

478. Vancourt, R. "Feuerbach entre Hegel et Marx, et face aux théologiens," *Mélanges de Science Religieuse* (Lille), 1971 (28), 165-88.
See also 137, 227, 235, 559, 589, 705, and 725.

Mazzini

479. Morandi, R. "La eticità dello stato : Hegel e Mazzini," *Critica sociale*, 1924, n. 8-9.

Mill

See 284.

Stirner

480. Fleischman, Eugène. "The Role of the Individual in Pre-revolutionary Society : Stirner, Marx and Hegel," in *Hegel's Political Philosophy*, ed. Z.A. Pelczynski, 220-29. Cambridge, 1971.
481. Mautz, K.A. *Die Philosophie Max Stirners im Gegensatz zum Hegelschen Idealismus*. Berlin, Junker und Dünnhaupt, 1936.
See also 705.

Bauer

482. Kempski, Jürgen von. "Ueber Bruno Bauer. Eine Studie zum Ausgang des Hegelianismus," *Archiv für Philosophie*, 1963 (11), 223-45.

Kierkegaard

483. Arbaugh, George E. and George B. "Appendix : Reaction to Hegel," in *Kierkegaard's Authorship*. A Guide to the Writings of Kierkegaard, 74-76. Rock Island, Ill., Augustana College Library, 1967.
484. Baeumler, A. "Hegel und Kierkegaard," *Deutsche Vierteljahrsschrift für Literaturwissenschaft und Geistesgeschichte* (Stuttgart), 1924 (2), 116-30. Reprinted in *Studien zur deutschen Geistesgeschichte*, Berlin, Junker und Dünnhaupt, 1937.
485. Bense, M. *Hegel und Kierkegaard*. Eine prinzipielle Untersuchung. Köln, Staufen-Verlag, 1948.
486. Bogen, James. "Remarks on the Kierkegaard-Hegel Controversy," *Synthese*, 1961 (13), 372-89.
487. Collins, J. "Kierkegaard's Critique of Hegel," *Thought*, 1943 (18), n. 68.
488. ——. "Mind of Kierkegaard : the Attack upon Hegelianism," *The Modern Schoolman*, 1949 (26), 219-51.
489. ——. "The Attack Upon Hegelianism," in *The Mind of Kierkegaard*, 98-136. Chicago, Henry Regnery, 1965.
490. Crites, S. *In the Twilight of Christendom*. Hegel Versus Kierkegaard on Faith and History. Chambersburg, Pa., American Academy of Religion, 1972.
491. Fabro, Cornelio. "La dialettica della libertà e l'assoluto. Per un confronto tra Hegel e Kierkegaard," in *Kierkegaard e Nietzsche* (*Archivio di Filosofia*, 1953, n. 2, 45-69). Milano-Roma, Fratelli Bocca, 1953.

492. ———. "Kierkegaard critico di Hegel," in *Incidenza di Hegel*, a cura di Fulvio Tessitore, 499-563. Napoli, Morano Ed., 1970.

493. Gerdes, Hayo. *Das Christusbild Sören Kierkegaards, verglichen mit der Christologie Hegels und Schleiermachers*. Düsseldorf, E. Diederichs, 1960.

494. Gigante, M. "Il messaggio esistenziale di Kierkegaard e la filosofia hegeliana," *Asprenas* (Napoli), 1970 (17), 392-412.

495. Heiss, Robert. *Die grossen Dialektiker des 19. Jahrhunderts. Hegel, Kierkegaard, Marx*. Köln, Berlin, Kiepenheuer und Witsch, 1963.

496. Johansen, Udo. "Kierkegaard und Hegel," *Zeitschrift für Philosophische Forschung*, 1953 (7), 20-53.

497. Joest, Wilfred. "Hegel und Kierkegaard. Bemerkungen zu einer prinzipiellen Untersuchung," in *Sören Kierkegaard*, hrsg. H.-H. Schrey, 81-89. Darmstadt, 1971.

498. Kroner, Richard. "Kierkegaard or Hegel?", *Revue internationale de Philosophie*, 1952 (60), n. 19, 79-96.

499. ———. "Kierkegaards Hegelverständnis," *Kant-Studien*, 1954/1955 (46), 19-27.

500. Leisegang, Hans. *Hegel, Marx, Kierkegaard*. Zum dialektischen Materialismus und zur dialektischen Theologie. Berlin, Wissenschaftlich Editionsgesellschaft, 1948.

501. Löwith, K. "L'achèvement de la philosophie classique par Hegel et sa dissolution chez Marx et Kierkegaard," *Recherches philosophiques*, 1934/1935 (4), 232-67.

502. Majoli, Bruno. "La critica ad Hegel in Schelling e Kierkegaard," *Rivista di Filosofia Neo-Scolastica*, 1954 (46), 232-63.

503. Moore, W.G. "Kierkegaard and His Century," *Hibbert Journal*, 1938 (36), 133-44.

504. Melchiorre, Virgilio. "Kierkegaard ed Hegel. La polemica sul 'punto di partenza'," in *Studi Kierkegaardiani*, a cura di Cornelio Fabro, 243-66. Brescia, Morcelliana Editrice, 1957.

505. Perkins, Robert L. "The Family : Hegel and Kierkegaard's Judge Wilhelm" *Hegel-Jahrbuch*, 1967, 89-100.

506. ———. "Two Nineteenth Century Interpretations of Socrates : Hegel and Kierkegaard," *Kierkegaard-Studies*, 1967 (4), 82-87.

507. ———. "Beginning the System : Kierkegaard and Hegel," in *Akten des XIV. Internationalen Kongresses für Philosophie*, Wien, 2.-9. September, 1967 (VI), 478-85.

508. ———. "Hegel and Kierkegaard : Two Critics of Romantic Irony," *Review of National Literatures*, 1970 (1), 232-54.

509. Radermacher, Hans. *Kierkegaards Hegelverständnis*. Köln. 1958,

510. Ramsey, P. "Existenz and the Existence of God : Kierkegaard and Hegel," *Journal of Religion*, 1948 (28).

511. Reinhardt, K.F. "Cleavage of Minds : Kierkegaard and Hegel," *Commonweal*, 1936 (25), 523-24.

512. Ritschl, D. "Kierkegaards Kritik an Hegels Logik," *Theologische Zeitschrift*, 1955 (11), 437-65.

513. Sciacca, G.M. *L'esperienza religiosa e l'io in Hegel e Kierkegaard*. Palermo, Palumbo, 1948.

514. Thulstrup, Niels. "Kierkegaards Verhältnis zu Hegel," *Theologische Zeitschrift*, 1957 (13), 200-26.

515. ——. "Sören Kierkegaard, historien de la philosophie de Hegel," *Tijdschrift voor Filosofie* (Leuven), 1965 (27), 521-72.

516. ——. *Kierkegaards Verhältnis zu Hegel und zum spekulativen Idealismus : 1835-1846*. Stuttgart, Kohlhammer, 1972.

517. Hagen, Eduard von. *Abstraktion und Konkretion bei Heigel und Kierkegaard*. Bonn, Verlag H. Bouvier, 1969.

518. Wahl, Jean. "Hegel et Kierkegaard," *Revue philosophique*, 1931.

See also 148, 417, 429, 632 and 785.

Spaventa

519. Alderisio, F. *Esame della riforma attualistica dell' idealismo in rapporto a Spaventa e a Hegel*. Todi, tip. Tuderte, 1941.

520. Agrimi, M. "Bertrando Spaventa e l'eredità hegeliana," *Trimestre*, 1967, 141-53.

521. Cubeddu, Italo. "B. Spaventa riformatore di Hegel nella cultura italiana del 1900," in *Incidenza di Hegel*, a cura di Fulvio Tessitore, 759-90. Napoli, Morano Ed., 1970.

See also 739.

Marx and Marxism

522. Albrecht, Erhard. "Ueber das Verhältnis des Marxismus zur Philosophie Hegels," *Deutsche Zeitschrift für Philosophie*, 1955 (3), 225-35.

523. Almaleh, G. "De Hegel à Marx," *La Dialectique*, 1969 (1), 59-62.

524. Althusser, Louis. "Sur le rapport de Marx à Hegel," in *Hegel et la pensée moderne*, ed. Jacques d'Hondt, 85-111. Paris, Presses universitaires de France, 1970. Reprinted in *Contemporary Philosophy*, ed. Raymond Klibansky, IV, 358-77. Firenze, La Nuova Italia Editrice, 1971.

525. ——. "Lénine et la philosophie," in *Marx et Lénine devant Hegel*. Paris, F. Maspero, 1972.

526. Antoni, C. *Considerazioni su Hegel et su Marx*. Napoli, Ricciardi, 1946.

527. Apel, Karl Otto. "Reflexion und materielle Praxis. Zur erkenntnis-anthropologischen Begründung der Dialektik zwischen Hegel und Marx," *Hegel-Studien*, Beiheft 1 (1964), 151-66.

528. Apostol, Pavel. "Entäusserung, Vergegenständlichung-Objektivierung et Entfremdung chez Hegel et chez Marx. Remarques sur la dialectique de la spiritualité contemporaine," in *Hegel. L'esprit objectif. L'unité de l'histoire*. (Actes du IIIème congrès international de l'Association internationale pour l'étude de la philosophie de Hegel), 23-32. Lille, 1970.

529. Araud, R. "Critique de Hegel par Marx : abstraction et analyse," *La Dialectique*, 1969 (1), 112-16.

530. Avineri, Shlomo. "The Hegelian Origins of Marx's Political Thought," *Review of Metaphysics*, 1967 (21), 33-56.

531. ——. "Consciousness and History : List der Vernunft in Hegel and Marx," in *New Studies in Hegel's Philosophy*, ed. Warren E. Steinkraus, 108-18. New York, Holt, Rinehart and Winston, 1971.

532. Badaloni, Nicola. "L'idea hegeliana del conoscere ed il rapporto Hegel-Marx," in *Incidenza di Hegel*, a cura di Fulvio Tessitore, 567-92. Napoli, Morano Ed., 1970.

533. Ballestrom, Karl G. *Die Sowjetische Erkenntnismetaphysik und ihr Verhältnis zu Hegel*. Dordrecht, D. Reidel, 1968.

534. Barion, Jakob. *Hegel und die marxistische Staatslehre*. Bonn, Bouvier, 1963.

535. Barth, Paul. *Die Geschichtsphilosophie Hegels und der Hegelianer bis auf Marx und Hartmann : Ein Kritischer Versuch*. Leipzig, Reisland, 1890.

536. ———. "Zu Hegels und Marx' Geschichtsphilosophie," *Archiv für Geschichte der Philosophie*, 1895 (8).

537. Becker, W. *Idealistische und materialistische Dialektik*. Das Verhältnis von "Herrschaft und Knechtschaft" bei Hegel und Marx. Stuttgart, Berlin, Köln, Mainz, Kohlhammer, 1970.

538. Bedeschi, Giuseppe. "Il marxismo e Hegel," *Giornale critico della filosofia Italiana.*, 1970 (1), 100-14.

539. Bekker, Konrad. *Marx' philosophische Entwicklung. Sein Verhältnis zu Hegel*. Basel, Volksdruckerei, 1940.

540. Benner, Dietrich. *Theorie uod Praxis*. Systemtheoretische Betrachtungen zu Hegel und Marx. Wien und München, Oldenbourg, 1966.

541. Benz, Ernst. "Hegels Religionsphilosophie und die Linkshegelianer," *Zeitschrift für Religions- und Geistesgeschichte*, 1955 (7), 247-70.

542. Berki, Robert N. "Perspectives in the Marxian Critique of Hegel's Political Philosophy," in *Hegel's Political Philosophy*, ed. Z. A. Pelczynski, 199-219. Cambridge, 1971.

543. Bonnier, C. "Hegel und Marx," *Die Neue Zeit* (Berlin), 1891 (2), 653-62.

544. Bottigelli, Emile. "Comment Lénine lit Hegel," *Pensée*, 1954, n. 57, 110-14.

545. Breysig, K. *Die Macht des Gedankens in der Geschichte in Auseinandersetzung mit Marx und Hegel*. Stuttgart, 1926.

546. Bueckling, K. "Elemente der Hegelschen Geschichts- und Rechtsphilosophie im Marxismus," *Jahrbuch für Gesetzgebung*, Heft 3 (1919), 173-200.

547. Camporeale, Ignazio e Verde, Felice. "Resoconto di un recente dibattito su 'Dialettica hegeliana e dialettica marxista'," *Sapientia*, 1965 (18), 475-97.

548. Capograssi, G. "Le glosse di Marx a Hegel," in *Scritti filosofico-giuridici dedicati a G. Del Vecchio*. Modena, Soc. tip. Modenese, 1930/1931.

549. Carbonara, C. *Hegel e Marx nella polemica del diritto pubblico*. L.S.E., Napoli, 1967.

550. Caton, Hiram. "Marx's Sublation of Philosophy into Praxis," *Review of Metaphysics*, 1972, 233-58.

551. Cerroni, Umberto. "La critica di Marx alla filosofia hegeliana del diritto pubblico,' *Rivista internazionale di Filosofia del Diritto*, 1961 (38), 281-308.

552. Cerutti, Furio. "Hegel, Lukács, Korsch. Zum dialektischen Selbstverständnis des kritischen Marxismus," in *Actualität und Folgen der Philosophie Hegels*, hrsg. Oskar Negt, 195-210. Frankfurt am Main, Suhrkamp, 1970.

553. Colletti, Lucio. *Il marxismo e Hegel* (Biblioteca di cultura moderna, 665). Bari, Laterza, 1969.

554. ———. "Il marxismo e la *Filosofia della storia* di Hegel," in *Incidenza di Hegel*, a cura di Fulvia Tessitore, 595-623. Napoli, Morano Ed., 1970.

555. Composta, Dario. "Hegel e Marx e la filosofia del diritto," *Aquinas,* 1970 (13), 392-411.

556. Cooper, Rebecca. *The Logical Influence of Hegel on Marx* (University of Washington Publications in the Social Sciences, Vol. II, n. 2). Seattle, 1925.

557. Cornelissen, Christian. "Ueber den Einfluss der Hegelschen Dialektik auf die sozialistische Doktrin von Karl Marx," *Sozialistische Monatshefte* (Berlin), 1898, 547-57.

558. ——. "La dialectique hégélienne dans l'œuvre de Marx," *Revue socialiste,* 1901.

559. Cornu, Auguste. "L'idée d'aliénation chez Hegel, Feuerbach et K. Marx," *Pensée,* 1948 (17).

560. ——. Die Ueberwindung der hegelschen Philosophie durch Karl Marx," *Wissenschaftliche Annalen,* 1953 (2), n. 12, 754-68.

561. ——. "Ueber das Verhältnis des Marxismus zur Philosophie Hegels," *Deutsche Zeitschrift für Philosophie,* 1954 (2), 69-112; 344-83.

562. ——. *The Origins of Marxian Thought*. Springfield, Thomas, 1957.

563. Croce, B. "L'ortodossia hegeliana del Marx," *Quaderni della critica,* 1947, n. 8.

564. Damnjanović, Milan. "Arbeit und Sprache im System Hegels und bei Marx," *Praxis* (Zagreb), 1971 (8), 161-65.

565. Deborim, A. "Hegel und der dialektische Materialismus," in *Die Sowjetphilosophie,* hrsg. Wilhelm Goerdt. Basel, Stuttgart, Darmstadt, 1967.

566. Della Volpe, Galvano. "La critica marxiana della filosofia dello stato de Hegel e la problematica attuale," in *Atti del congresso internazionale de filosofia* (Roma), 1947, I, 235-49.

567. ——. "Marx e il segreto di Hegel," in *Per la teoria di un umanesimo positivo.* Bologna, Zuffi, 1949.

568. D'Hondt, Jacques. "L'histoire chez Marx et chez Hegel," *Hegel-Jahrbuch,* 1968/1969, 38-44.

569. ——. "La dialectique de Marx et de Hegel," *La Dialectique,* 1969 (1), 112-16.

570. ——. "La dialectique spécifique de l'histoire selon Hegel et Marx," *Hegel-Jahrbuch,* 1971, 184-88.

571. ——. "L'histoire et les utopistes selon Hegel et Marx," in *Hegel et Marx. La politique et le réel.* Poitiers, Publications de l'Université de Poitiers, 1971.

572. ——. *De Hegel à Marx*. Paris, Presses Universitaires de France, 1972.

573. Di Gona, Goriano. "Sgrammaticature della dialettica hegeliano-marxista," *Humanitas,* 1948 (3), 131-33.

574. Dupré, Louis. *The Philosophical Foundations of Marxism.* New York. Harcourt, Brace & Wourd, 1966.

575. ——. "Dialectical Philosophy Before and After Marx," *The New Scholasticism,* 1972 (46), 488-511.

576. ——. "Hegel's Concept of Alienation and Marx's Reinterpretation of It," *Hegel-Studien,* 1972 (7), 217-36.

577. Easton, Lloyd D. "Alienation and History in the Early Marx," *Philosophy and Phenomenological Research,* 1961-1962, (32), 193-205.

578. Engels, F. "Hegel und die Marx'sche Kritik der politischen Ökonomie," *Die Neue Zeit,* Jahrgang 39, Heft 1, 417-21.

579. Falk, Werner. "Hegels Freiheitsidee in der Marx'schen Dialektik," *Archiv für Sozialwissenschaft und Sozialpolitik*, 1932, 165-93.
580. Farias, Domenico. "Conformismo e rivoluzione : sulla filosofia della cultura di Hegel e di Marx," *Rivista di Filosofia Neo-Scolastica*, 1963 (55), 167-210.
581. Feller, W. *Von Hegel zu Marx*. Vortrag. Kaiserslautern, Verlag für Literatur und Politik, 1947.
582. Fetscher, Iring. "Das Verhältnis des Marxismus zu Hegel. Politische Hintergründe einer philosophischen Diskussion," in *Aus Politik und Zeitgeschichte* (Beilage zu "Das Parlament," Bonn, 1958), 241-75. Reprinted in *Marxismus-Studien*, Folge 3, Beiträge von L. Landgrebe, hrsg. I. Fetscher. Tübingen, Mohr, 1960.
583. ———. "Hegel et le marxisme," *Archives de Philosophie*, 1959 (22), 323-68.
584. Flam, Leopold. "La relation de Hegel et Marx, un problème d'actualité philosophique," in *Akten des XIV. Internationalen Kongresses für Philosophie*, Wien, 2.-9. September, 1968, VI, 243-49.
585. Friedrich, Paul Joachim. "Lenin und die Philosophie Hegels," *Zeitschrift für Religions- und Geistesgeschichte* (Köln), 1965 (17), 340-52.
586. Frozini, Vittorio. "Considerazioni sulla critica di Marx alla filosofia del diritto di Hegel," *Rivista internazionale di filosofia del diritto*, 1968 (45), 587-92.
587. Gancikoff, L. "L'hegelismo in Russia," *Rivista di filosofia neo-scolastica*, (23) Suppl.
588. Gentile, G. "Tra Hegel e Lenin," in *Guerra e fede*. Napoli, Ricciardi, 1919.
589. Grégoire, Franz. *Aux sources de la pensée de Marx*: Hegel, Feuerbach (Bibliothèque philosophique de Louvain, 7). Paris, J. Vrin, 1947.
590. Gropp, Rugard Otto. "Ueber den Gegensatz der marxistischen dialektischen Methode zur idealistischen Dialektik Hegels," *Wissenschaftliche Zeitschrift der Karl-Marx-Universität Leipzig*, 1952/1953, H. 9-10 (Gesellschafts- und Sprachwissenschaftliche Reihe, n. 4-5), 477-85.
591. ———. *Zu Fragen der Geschichte der Philosophie und des dialektischen Materialismus*. Berlin, Deutscher Verlag der Wissenschaften, 1958, 1959.
592. Grujić, Predrag M. *Hegel und die Sowjetphilosophie der Gegenwart. Zur materialistischen Dialektik*. (Dalp-Taschenbücher, Bd. 393) Bern, München, Francke Verlag, 1969.
593. Gulian, C.I. "Hegel, Marx, Lenin und die Fragen der Kulturphilosophie," *Revue Roumaine des Sciences Sociales* (Serie de Philosophie et Logique) (Bucarest), 1966 (10), 233-53.
594. Günther, Hillman. *Marx und Hegel. Von der Spekulation zur Dialektik*. Interpretation der ersten Schriften von Karl Marx im Hinblick auf sein Verhältnis zu Hegel (1835-1841). Frankfurt am Main, Europäische Verlagsanstalt, 1966.
595. Hartmann, Otto Julius. "Hegel und Marx. Ein Geisteskampf um das Schicksal des Abendlandes," *Die Kommenden*, 1970 (24), N. 20. 12-15.
596. Hartwig, Walter. "Marx und Hegel," *Aufbau* (hrsg. Kulturbund zur Demokratischen Erneuerung Deutschlands, Berlin), 1948 (4), Helft 10, 842-52.
597. *Hegel et Marx. La politique et le réel*. Travaux du Centre de Recherche et de Documentation sur Hegel et sur Marx (Publication de la faculté des Lettres et Sciences Humaines, année 1969/1970). Poitiers, Publications de l'Université de Poitiers, 1971.
598. Heiss, Robert. "Hegel und Marx," *Symposium*, 1949 (1), 169-206.

599. ——. *Die Dialektik bei Hegel und Marx*. Bremen, Angel-Sachsen Verlag, 1961.

600. Helander, Sven. *Marx und Hegel. Eine kritische Studie über sozialdemokratische Weltanschauung*. Jena, G. Fischer, 1922.

601. Henrich, Dieter. "Karl Marx als Schüler Hegels," in *Marxismus-Leninismus, Geschichte und Gestalt*, 5-13. Berlin, De Gruyter, 1961.

602. Henry, Michel. "De Hegel à Marx. Essai sur la *Critique de la philosophie de l'état de Hegel* de Marx," in *Hommage à J. Hyppolite*, par Suzanne Bachelard, et al., 81-143. Paris, Presses universitaires de France, 1971.

603. Hillman, Günther. *Marx und Hegel. Von der Spekulation zur Dialektik*. Interpretation der ersten Schriften von Karl Marx im Hinblick auf sein Verhältnis zu Hegel (1835-1841). Frankfurt am Main, Europäische Verlagsanstalt, 1966.

604. Himmer, J.G. "Marx und Hegel," *Nationalwirtschaft*, 1928 (1), Heft 2, 127-48.

605. Hogan, J. "Hegelianism and Marxism," *Irish Ecclesiastical Record*, 1948 (70), 1057-62.

606. ——. "Hegelian Dialectic and Dialectical Materialism," *Irish Ecclesiastical Record*, 1949 (71), 332-47.

607. Hommes, Jakob. "Von Hegel zu Marx. Die materialistische Fassung der dialektischen Methode," *Philosophisches Jahrbuch*, 1953 (62), 359-93. Reprinted in *Dialektik und Politik*, hrsg. J. Hommes. Köln, 1968.

608. Hook, Sidney. "Hegel and Marx," *Studies in the History of Ideas* (New York), 1935 (3), 331-404.

609. ——. *From Hegel to Marx*. Studies in the Intellectual Development of Karl Marx. London, Gollancz; New York, Reynal & Hitchcock, 1936.

610. Höppner, Joachim. "Zu einigen irrigen Auffassungen des Uebergangs von Hegel auf Marx," *Deutsche Zeitschrift für Philosophie*, 1957 (5), 327-44.

611. Hyppolite, Jean. "La conception hégélienne de l'état et sa critique par Karl Marx," *Cahiers internationaux de sociologie* (Paris), 1947 (2), 142-61.

612. ——. *Études sur Marx et Hegel*. Paris, M. Rivière, 1955.

613. ——. *Saggi su Marx e Hegel*. Milano, Casa Ed. V. Bompiani, 1963.

614. ——. "Alienation and Objectification," *Philosophy Today*, 1966 (10), 119-31.

615. ——. *Studies on Marx and Hegel*. New York, Basic Books, 1969.

616. Janko, Mitrju. "Hegel and Marx' Auffassung des Bewusstseins als Widerspiegelung der materiellen Welt," *Hegel-Jahrbuch*, 1971, 341-46.

617. Javurek, Zdenek. "Vernunft und Geschichte bei Hegel und Marx," *Hegel-Jahrbuch*, 1971, 170-74.

618. Jordan, Zbigniew A. "The Influence of Hegel's Philosophy," in *The Evolution of Dialectical Materialism. A Philosophical and Sociological Analysis*, 65-110. London, Melbourne, Toronto, The Macmillan Company; New York, St. Martin's Press, 1967.

619. Kangrge, Milan. "Révolution politique et révolution sociale. Rapport de la société et de l'état chez Hegel et chez Marx," *Praxis* (Zagreb), 1969 (5), 353-70.

620. ——. "Arbeit bei Hegel und Marx," in *Hegel und die Folgen*, hrsg. Gerd-Klaus Kaltenbrunner, 295-312. Freiburg-im-Breisgau, Rombach, 1970.

621. Kern, Walter. "Hegel, Marx und die Frankfurter Schule. Ein Streiflicht auf die Aktualität Hegels," *Stimmen der Zeit*, 1970 (186), 217-33.

622. Kline, George L. "Hegel and the Marxist-Leninist Critique of Religion," in *Hegel and the Philosophy of Religion*, ed. Darrel Christensen, 187-202. The Hague, Martinus Nijhoff, 1970.
623. Kojève, Alexandre. "Hegel, Marx et le Christianisme," in *Critique*, 1956 (1), 339-66.
624. ———. "Hegel, Marx and Christianity," *Interpretation*, 1970 (1), 21-42.
625. Krahl, Hans-Jürgen. "Bemerkungen zum Verhältnis von *Kapital* und Hegelschen Wesenslogik," in *Actualität und Folgen der Philosophie Hegels*, hrsg. Oskar Negt, 137-50. Frankfurt-am-Main, Suhrkamp, 1970.
626. Landgrebe, Ludwig. "Hegel und Marx," *Marxismus-Studien*, 1954, 39-53.
627. ———. "Das Problem der Dialektik," *Marxismus-Studien*, 1960 (Folge 3), 1-65.
628. Lange, Klaus. "Der Gegensatz Marx zu Hegel. Mit besonderer Berücksichtiging von Nationalökonomie und Philosophie," *Zeitschrift für Philosophische Forschung*, 1971 (25), 89-98.
629. Levy-Koref, H. *Karl Marx und Hegel*. Zur Widerlegung der Legende vom Jüdischen Marxismus. Berlin, 1925.
630. Lichtheim, George. *From Marx to Hegel*. New York, Herder & Herder, 1971.
631. Losurdo, Domenico. "Il periode jenese ed il rapporto Hegel-Marx," *Rivista di Filosofia Neo-Scolastica*, 1962 (54), 370-78.
632. Löwith, Karl. "La conclusione della filosofia classica con Hegel e la sua dissoluzione in Marx e Kierkegaard," *Giornale Critico della Filosofia Italiana*, 1935 (16), 343-71.
633. ———. "Man's Self-Alienation in the Early Writings of Marx," *Social Research*, 1954 (21), 204-30.
634. Lunatscharski, Anatol. "Hegel in Russland," *Osteuropa*, 1931 (7), 65-72.
635. MacIntyre, Alasdair. "Hegel and Marx," in *A Short History of Ethics*, 199-214. London, Routledge & Kegan Paul, 1966.
636. ———. "From Religion to Philosophy : Hegel," in *Marxism and Christianity*, 7-17. New York, Schocken Books, 1968.
637. Marck, S. "Hegelianismus und Marxismus," *Philosophische Vorträge der Kantgesellschaft* (Berlin), 1922, n. 27.
638. Marini, Giuliani. "Il rapporto Hegel-Marx in una recente indagine," *Rivista Internazionale di Filosofia del Diritto*, 1962 (39), 511-19.
639. Marx, S. *Hegelianismus und Marxismus*. Vortrag. Berlin, 1922.
640. Masaryk, T.G. *Die philosophischen und soziologischen Grundlagen des Marxismus*. Wien, 1899.
641. Maschner, Horst. *Dialectic, Money and Commodity*. Hegel's *Science of Logic* and the *Capital* of Marx. Published by the author, 1971.
642. Mazlish, Bruce. "The Tragic Farce of Marx, Hegel, and Engels : A Note," *History and Theory*, 1972 (11), 335-37.
643. McLellen, David. *The Young Hegelians and Karl Marx*. London. Macmillan, 1969.
644. Mercier-Josa, S. "Le thème du conflit dans la pensée occidentale. Genèse et destin de la dialectique hégélienne du maître et de l'esclave," in *Hegel et Marx. La politique et le réel*. Poitiers, Publications de l'Université de Poitiers, 1971.

645. Michaux, B. "Hegel et Marx. La politique et le réel," *Revue de Métaphysique et de Morale*, 1972 (77), 237-41.
646. Molnàr, Erik. *L'influence de la philosophie de l'histoire de Hegel sur l'historiographie marxiste* (Studia historica Academiae Scientiarum Hungaricae, 47). Budapest, Akad. Kiadó, 1960.
647. Mönke, Wolfgang. "Ueber das Verhältnis des Marxismus zur Philosophie Hegels," *Deutsche Zeitschrift für Philosophie*, 1955 (3), 235-41.
648. Moore, Stanley. "Marx and the Origin of Dialectical Materialism," *Inquiry* (Oslo), 1971 (14), 420-29.
649. Naniwada, Haruo. "Smith-Hegel-Marx. Ueber den inneren Zusammenhang der drei Sozialphilosophien," *Zeitschrift für die gesamte Staatswissenschaft*, 1955 (111), Heft 3, 397-417.
650. Niel, Henri. "De Hegel à Marx," *Vie Intellectuelle*, 1953, n. 3, 69-74.
651. ——. "Dialectique hégélienne et dialectique marxiste," in *Aspects de la dialectique*, 225-35. Paris, Desclée de Brouwer, 1956.
652. ——. "La suppression de la philosophie, à propos de Hegel et de Marx," *Critique*, 1961 (17), n. 174, 975-90.
653. Oiserman, T.I. "W.I. Lenin über die Dialektik Hegels," *Deutsche Zeitschrift für Philosophie*, 1958 (6), 273-86.
654. ——. "W.I.Lenin und die Hegelsche Dialektik," *Deutsche Zeitschrift für Philosophie*, 1970 (18), 791-808.
655. Olssen, E.A. "Christianity and Political Theory : a Study in St.John, Hegel, and Marx," *Landfall* (Christchurch, New Zealand), 1966 (20), 268-79.
656. O'Malley, Joseph. "Methodology in Karl Marx," *The Review of Politics* (Notre Dame), 1970 (32), 219-30.
657. O'Neill, John. "Hegel and Marx on History as Human History," in *Akten des XIV. Internationalen Kongresses für Philosophie*, II, 96-103. Wien, 1969.
658. Plenge, J. *Marx und Hegel*. Stuttgart, Engelmann, 1911.
659. Pöggeler, Otto. "Die Verwirklichung der Philosophie. Hegel und Marx," *Philosophische Perspektiven*, 1970 (2), 186-208.
660. Popoff, Peter Nikoloff. "Die hegelsche Konzeption der bürgerlichen Gesellschaft und ihre Ueberwinding durch Marx," *Hegel-Jahrbuch*, 1971, 37-44.
661. Porchner, B.F. "La périodisation du progrès historique universel chez Hegel et chez Marx," *Hegel-Jahrbuch*, 1968/1969, 173-86.
662. Régnier, M. "Hegelianism and Marxism," *Social Research*, 1967 (34), 31-46.
663. Reinig, Richard. *Zur Grundlegung der polytechnischen Bildung durch Hegel und Marx* (Beiträge zur vergleichenden Erziehungswissenschaft, 3). Braunschweig, Westermann, 1967.
664. Riedel, Manfred. "Grundzüge einer Theorie des Lebendigen bei Hegel und Marx," *Zeitschrift für Philosophische Forschung*, 1965 (19), 577-606.
665. ——. "Hegel und Marx. Die Neubestimmung des Verhältnisses von Theorie und Praxis," in *Hegel und die Folgen*, hrsg. Gerd-Klaus Kaltenbrunner, 273-94. Freiburg-im-Breisgau, Rombach, 1970.
666. Rohrmoser, G. "Die Religionskritik von Karl Marx im Blickpunkt der Hegelschen Religionsphilosophie," *Neue Zeitschrift für Systematische Theologie und Religionsphilosophie*, 1960 (2), 44-64.

667. Rossi, Mario. "La crisi del primo hegelismo tedesco e gli esordi filosofici di Marx e di Engels," *Rivista storica del socialismo* (Milano), 1959 (2), 425-62.
668. ———. *Marx e la dialettica hegeliana.* Roma, Editori riuniti, 1963.
669. Salvucci, Pasquale. "Hegel nella storiografia della filosofia italiana di ispirazione marxista," *Nuova Rivista pedagogica*, 1958, n. 3-4, 53-61.
670. Sartori, Giovanni. *Da Hegel a Marx.* La dissoluzione della filosofia hegeliana. Firenze, Copisteria a macchina, 1951.
671. Schleifstein, Josef. "Ueber das Verhältnis des Marxismus zur Philosophie Hegels," *Deutsche Zeitschrift für Philosophie*, 1955 (3), 711-27.
672. Seidel, Helmut und Gäbler, Klaus. "Ueber das Verhältnis des Marxismus zur Philosophie Hegels," *Deutsche Zeitschrift für Philosophie*, 1956 (4), 206-17.
673. Sitkowski, J.P. "Lenin und die Philosophie Hegels," *Sowjetwissenschaft.* Gesellschaftswissenschaftliche Beiträge (Berlin), 1970, n. 8, 793-806.
674. Steiner, R. "Das Ewige in der Hegelschen Logik und ihr Gegenbild im Marxismus," *Das Goetheanum* (Basel), 1937 (16), 237-38, 245-46, 253-54, 261-62.
675. Stiehler, G. "Die Methode des Aufsteigens vom Abstrakten zum Konkreten bei Hegel und Marx," *Hegel-Jahrbuch*, 1961, n. 2.
676. Stroie, I. "The Dialectic Relationship between Hegelian and Marxist Dialectics," *Analele Universitatii Bucureşti*, (Serie Estetica), 1970 (19), 83-91.
677. Tota, Enzo. "Das Verhältnis Hegel-Marx. Eine Diskussion marxistischer Philosophen in Italien (1962)," *Hegel-Studien*, 1965 (3), 294-96.
678. Touilleux, P. *Introduction aux systèmes de Marx et Hegel.* Paris, Desclée et Cie, 1960.
679. Tucker, Robert C. "The Symbolism of History in Hegel and Marx," *Journal of Philosophy*, 1957 (54), 144-45.
680. ———. "Cunning of Reason in Hegel and Marx," *Review of Politics* (Notre Dame), 1956 (18), 269-95.
681. Valentini, Francesco. "Diritti e torti della dialettcia," *Società*, 1959 (15), 810-23.
682. Verde, Felice e Camporeale, Ignazio. "Resoconto di un recente dibattito su dialettica hegeliana e dialettica marxista," *Sapientia*, 1965 (18), 475-97.
683. Vogel, P. *Hegels Gesellschaftsbegriff und seine geschichtliche Fortbildung durch Lorenz Stein, Marx, Engels und Lassalle* (Ergänzungshefte der Kantstudien, 59). Berlin, 1925.
684. Vorländer, Karl. *Kant, Fichte, Hegel und der Sozialismus.* (Vorwärts, Wege zum Sozialismus), Berlin, 1920.
685. Zanardo, Aldo. "Il primo Marx e Hegel," *Studi storici*, 1967 (8), 828-31.
686. Zelený, Jindrich. "Die Grundlegung der Wissenschaft bei Hegel und Marx" *Filosofický Časopis* (Praha), 1965 (13), 204-13.
687. ———. "Die Marxsche Hegelkritik in den Pariser Manuskripten," *Filosofický Časopis* (Praha), 1966 (14), 448-63.

See also 170, 173, 229, 235, 238, 260, 285, 286, 287, 288, 290, 325, 454, 470, 473, 474, 477, 478, 480, 495, 500, 501, 717, 744, 761, and 786.

Dilthey

688. Marini, Giuliano. "Dilthey e il giovane Hegel," in *Incidenza di Hegel*, a cura di Fulvia Tessitore, 793-841. Napoli, Morano Ed., 1970.

689. Schalk, Fritz. "Hegel und Diltheys Kritik der historischen Vernunft,"in *Festschrift für Leo Brandt zum 60. Geburtstag*, 431-39. Köln, 1968.

Green

690. Routh, D.A. "The Philosophy of International Relations, T. H. Green versus Hegel," *Politica* (London), 1938 (3), 223-35.

Mach

691. Miranda, L. "Mach o Hegel? Conversazioni intorno alle loro teorie filosofiche," *Rivista filosofica*, 1908, n. 3.

Peirce

692. Elton, William. "Peirce's Marginalia in W.T. Harris' *Hegel's Logic*," *Journal of the History of Philosophy*, 1964 (2), 82-84.
693. Fairbank, Matthew J. "A Note Concerning Peirce's Debt to Hegel," *The New Scholasticism*, 1962 (36), 129-24.
694. Santucci, Antonio. "Peirce, Hegel e la dottrina delle categorie," in *Incidenza di Hegel*, a cura di Fulvio Tessitore, 965-84. Napoli, Morano Ed., 1970.
695. Townsend, H.G. "The Pragmatism of Peirce and Hegel," *Philosophical Review*, July, 1928.

Hartmann (E)

696. Bolland, G.J.P.J. *Alte Vernunft und neuer Verstand, oder der Unterschied im Princip zwischen Hegel und E. v. Hartmann.* Leiden, 1902.
697. Grubich, Johannes. *Ueber das Verhältnis Hartmanns zu Hegel und Schopenhauer.* (Zeitschrift für Philosophie und Philosophische Kritik Ergänzungsheft 1). Leipzig, 1909.
698. Purpus, W. *Eduard von Hartmanns Kritik der dialektischen Methode Hegels.* Ansbach, Brügel, 1911.
See also 437 and 535.

James

699. Wilkins, Burleigh Taylor. "James, Dewey, and Hegelian Idealism," *Journal of the History of Ideas*, 1956 (17), 332-46.

Nietzsche

700. Brann, H.W. "Hegel, Nietzsche and the Nazi Lesson," *Humanist*, 1952 (12), n. 3, 111-15; n. 4, 179-82.
701. Castelli, Enrico. "A proposito di teologia della storia. Nietsche contro Hegel," *Rivelazione e Storia* (*Archivio di Filosofia*, 1971, n. 2). Padova, CEDAM, 1971, 11-14.
702. Greene, Murray. "Hegel's Unhappy Consciousness and Nietzsche's Slave Morality," in *Hegel and the Philosophy of Religion*, ed. Darrel Christensen, 125-41. The Hague, Martinus Nijhoff, 1970.

703. Hennemann, Gerhard. *Von der Kraft des deutschen Geistes*. Fichte, Hegel, Nietzsche. Köln, Staufen-Verlag, 1942.

704. Levy, H. "Nietzsche und Hegel," *Hamburger Fremdenblatt*, 10. und 17. Oktober, 1925.

705. Marion, Jean-Luc. "Généalogie de la 'mort de Dieu'. Contribution à la détermination théologique des présupposés conceptuels de la 'mort de Dieu' chez Hegel, Feuerbach, Stirner et Nietzsche. *Résurrection* (Paris), 1971, n. 36, 30-53.

706. Martin, Alfred von. *Geistige Wegbereiter des deutschen Zusammenbruchs*. Recklinghausen, Bitter und Co., 1948.

707. Rohrmoser, Günther. "Das Atheismusproblem bei Hegel und Nietzsche," *Der evangelische Erzieher* (Frankfurt), 1966 (18), 345-53.

708. Rosenstein, Leon. "Metaphysical Foundations of the Theories of Tragedy in Hegel and Nietzsche," *Journal of Aesthetics and Art Criticism*, 1970 (28), 521-33. See also 725.

Bosanquet

709. Trott, A. von "Bosanquet und der Einfluss Hegels auf die englische Staatsphilosophie," *Zeitschrift für deutsche Kulturphilosophie*, 1938 (4), 193-99.

Bergson

710. Prabhu Datta Sastri. *The Conception of Freedom in Hegel, Bergson, and Indian Philosophy*. Albion Press, Calcutta, 1914.

Dewey

711. Thayer, Horace S. "Dewey : Continuity — Hegel and Darwin," in *Meaning and Action. A Critical History of Pragmatism*, 460-87. Indianapolis, New York, The Bobbs-Merrill Co., 1968.

712. Ward, L.R. "John Dewey in Search of Himself," *Review of Politics*, 1957 (19), 205-13.
See also 699.

Husserl

713. De Wealhens, Alphonse. "Phénoménologie husserlienne et phénoménologie hégélienne," *Revue Philosophique de Louvain*, 1954 (52), 234-49. Reprinted in *Existence et Signification*. Paris, 1958.

714. ———. "Réflexions sur une problématique husserlienne de l'inconscient, Husserl et Hegel," in *Edmund Husserl 1859-1959* (Recueil commémoratif publié à l'occasion du centenaire de la naissance du philosophe), 221-37. La Haye, M. Nijhoff, 1959.

715. Kuspit, Donald. "Hegel and Husserl on the Problem of the Difficulty of Beginning Philosophy," *Journal of the British Society for Phenomenology*, 1971 (2), 52-57.

716. Ladrière, Jean. "Hegel, Husserl, and Reason Today," *The Modern Schoolman*, 1959/1960 (37), 171-95.

717. Pažanin, Ante. "Das Problem der Geschichte bei Husserl, Hegel und

Marx," *Phänomenologie Heute* (Festschrift für Ludwig Landgrebe, hrsg. Walter Biemel, Phaenomenologica, 51), 173-203. Den Haag, Martinus Nijhoff, 1972.

718. Werkmeister, W.H. "Husserl and Hegel," in *Akten des XIV. Internationalen Kongresses für Philosophie*, Wien, 2.-9. September, 1968, VI, 553-58.

719. Wilson, Arnold. "Husserl and the Idealists," *Telos*, 1969 (4), 83-94.

Blondel

720. Henrici, Peter. *Hegel und Blondel*. Eine Untersuchung über Form und Sinn der Dialektik in der *Phänomenologie des Geistes* und der ersten *Action*. Pullach bei München, Verlag Berchmanskolleg, 1958.

721. McNeill, John J. "The Influence of Schelling and Hegel," in *Studies in the History of Christian Thought*, Vol. I : *The Blondelian Synthesis*. A Study of the Influence of German Philosophical Sources on the Formation of Blondel's Method and Thought, 237-64. Leiden, E.J. Brill, 1966.

722. ——. "The Relation Between Philosophy and Religion in Blondel's Philosophy of Action," *Proceedings of the American Catholic Philosophical Association*, 1970 (44), 220-31.

Whitehead

723. Kambartel, Friedrich. "The Universe is More Various, More Hegelian. Zum Weltverständnis bei Hegel und Whitehead," *Collegium Philosophicum*. Studien. (Joachim Ritter zum 60. Geburtstag), 72-98. Basel, Stuttgart, 1965.

724. Whittemore, Robert C. "Hegel's 'Science' and Whitehead's 'Modern World'," *Philosophy*, 1956 (31), 36-54.

Weber

725. Meusel, Alfred. *Intelligenz und Volk*. Ueber Max Weber, Georg Friedrich Wilhelm Hegel, Ludwig Feuerbach, Friedrich Nietzsche. Berlin, Verlag Tägliche Rundschau, 1947.

Croce

726. Antoni, C. "Croce e Hegel," *Rassegna d'Italia*, 1946 (1).

727. Chaix-Ruy, Jules. "Benedetto Croce et la dialectique hégélienne," *Les études philosophiques*, 1957 (12), 21-25.

728. Ciardo, Manlio. *Le quattro epoche dello storicismo*. Vico, Kant, Hegel, Croce (Biblioteca di cultura moderna, 418). Bari, Laterza, 1947.

729. De Gennaro, Angelo A. "Croce and Hegel," *The Personalist*, 1963 (44), 302-08.

730. Franchini, R. "Morte e resurrezione della dialettica da Hegel a Croce," *Letterature moderne*, 1951.

731. ——. *Croce interprete di Hegel e altri saggi filosofichi*. Napoli, Giannini, 1964.

732. Lunati, Giancarlo. *La libertà : saggi su Kant, Hegel e Croce*. Napoli, Giannini, 1959.

733. Nyman, Alf. *Croce, Hegel, Avenarius*. Contribution à l'histoire du motif

de la fiction en philosophie (Essays dedicated to Gunner Aspelin on the occasion of his sixty-fifth birthday). Lund, Gleerup, 1963.

734. Rivetti Barbò, F. "Dialettica e storicismo : punto di divergenze tra Croce ed Hegel," *Rivista di filosofia neo-scolastica*, 1951 (43), 399-420.

735. Stella, V. "Un saggio su Croce interprete di Hegel," *Humanitas* (Brescia), 1965 (n.s. 9), 894-961.

736. Tessitore, Fulvio. "Storicismo hegeliano e storicismo crociano," in *Incidenza di Hegel*, a cura di Fulvio Tessitore, 845-910. Napoli, Morano Ed., 1970.

737. Tinivella, Giovanni. *Critica dell'idea di progresso*. Hegel, Croce, Gentile. Milano, Gastaldi, 1955.

Russell

738. Ushenko, A. "The Logics of Hegel and Russell," *Philosophy and Phenomenological Research*, 1949/1950 (10), 107-14.

Cassirer

See 353.

Gentile

739. Bellezza, Vito A. "La riforma spaventiano-gentiliana della dialettica hegeliana," in *Incidenza di Hegel*, a cura di Fulvio Tessitore, 685-755. Napoli, Morano Ed., 1970.
See also 737.

Hartmann (N)

740. Heiss, Robert. "Hartmann and Hegel," *Philosophy Today*, 1961 (5), 221-22.

Jaspers

741. Lichtigfeld, A. "Jaspers' Philosophical Basis," *Kant-Studien*, 1961/1962 (53), 29-38.

742. Pellegrino, Ubaldo. "Storia e metafisica in Kant, Hegel e Jaspers," *Rivista di filosofia neo-scolastica*, 1960 (52), 46-72.

Bloch

743. Fetscher, Iring. "Ernst Bloch auf Hegels Spuren," in *Ernst Bloch zu Ehren* (Beiträge zu seinem Werk), 83-98. Frankfurt am Main, 1965.

744. Schumacher, Joachim. "Anmerkungen zur Vorgeschichte des Begriffes Nichts bei Hegel und seine Aufhebung durch Marx und Ernst Bloch," *Praxis* (Zagreb), 1971 (8), 177-86.

745. Vattimo, Gianni. "Ernst Bloch interprete di Hegel," in *Incidenza di Hegel*, a cura di Fulvio Tessitore, 913-26. Napoli, Morano Ed., 1790.

Tillich

746. Westphal, Merold. "Hegel, Tillich and the Secular," *Journal of Religion*, 1972 (52), 223-39.

Heidegger

747. Angelino, Carlo. "Heidegger interprete di Hegel," in *Incidenza di Hegel*, a cura di Fulvio Tessitore, 987-1014. Napoli, Morano Ed., 1970.

748. Bröcker, Walter. "Hegel zwischen Kant und Heidegger," in *Auseinandersetzungen mit Hegel*, 7-32. Frankfurt am Main, 1965.

749. Coreth, Emerich. "Das fundamentalontologische Problem bei Heidegger und Hegel," *Scholastik*, 1954 (29), 1-23.

750. ——. "Zum Verhältnis Heideggers zu Hegel," in *Studi filosofici intorno all' "esistenza", al mondo, al trascendente*. (Relazioni lette nella Sezione di Filosofia del Congresso Internazionale per il IV Centenario della Pontifica Università Gregoriana, 14-16 ottobre 1953) Romae, Apud Aedes Universitatis Gregorianae, 1954.

751. De Waelhens, Alphonse. "Identité et différence : Heidegger et Hegel," *Revue Internationale de Philosophie*, 1960 (14), n. 52, 221-23.

752. Dubsky, I. "Bemerkungen zum Problem der Zeit bei Hegel und Heidegger," *Hegel-Jahrbuch*, 1961, n. 1.

753. Fabro, C. "Problem of Being and the Destiny of Man : Heidegger and Hegel," *International Philosophical Quarterly*, 1961 (1), 407-36.

754. Flam, Léopold. "Le devenir de la vérité de Hegel à Heidegger," in *Actes XIIe Congrès soc. Philos. langue française*, I. Louvain, Editions Nauwelaerts; Paris, Béatrice-Nauwelaerts, 1964.

755. ——. "Les symboles, de Hegel à Heidegger," *Revue de l'Université de Bruxelles*, 1966/1967 (19), 225-36.

756. Gadamer, Hans-Georg. "Anmerkungen zu dem Thema 'Hegel und Heidegger'," in *Natur und Geschichte* (Festschrift für Karl Löwith zum 70. Geburtstag), 123-31. Stuttgart, Verlag W. Kohlhammer, 1967.

757. ——. "Heidegger et le langage de la métaphysique," *Archiv für Philosophie*, 1973 (36), 3-13.

758. Garotti, Loris Ricci. *Heidegger contra Hegel e altri saggi di storiografia filosofica* con una presentazione di Arturo Massolo. Urbino, Argalia, 1965.

759. *Hegel, Hölderlin, Heidegger*. (Veröffentlichungen der katholischen Akademie der Erzdiözese Freiburg 27), von Hans-Georg Gadamer, Max Müller und Emil Staiger. Karlsruhe, Badenia-Verlag, 1977.

760. Hommes, Jakob. *Zweispältiges Dasein*. Die existentiale Ontologie von Hegel bis Heidegger. Freiburg-im-Breisgau, Verlag Herder, 1953.

761. ——. *Krise der Freiheit*, Hegel-Marx-Heidegger. Regensburg, Verlag Friedrich Pustet, 1958.

762. Hübscher, Arthur. *Von Hegel zu Heidegger*. Gestalten und Probleme (Reclams Universal-Bibliothek, 8651/8654). Stuttgart, Reclam, 1961.

763. Hyppolite, Jean. "Étude du commentaire de l'introduction à la *Phénoménologie* par Heidegger : *Hegels Begriff der Erfahrung*," in *Figures de la pensée philosophique*. Écrits (1931-1968), II, 625-42. Paris, Presses Universitaires de France, 1971.

764. Langan, Thomas D. "Heidegger Beyond Hegel. A Reflexion on 'the Onto-theo-logical Constitution of Metaphysics'," *Filosofia*, 1968 (19), 735-46.

765. Marx, Werner. *Heidegger und die Tradition*. Eine problemgeschichtliche Einführung in die Grundbestimmungen des Seins. Stuttgart, 1961.

766. Nadler, K. "Die systematische Entwicklung des 'Grundes' in Hegels und Heideggers Philosophie," *Die Idee*, 1933, Heft 1.
767. Ricci Garotti, Loris. "Heidegger contra Hegel?", *Il Pensiero*, 1963 (8), 303-26.
768. ———. "Leggendo Heidegger che legge Hegel," *Studi Urbinati di Storia, Filosofia e Letteratura*, 1962 (36), 258-87.
769. Rüfner, V. "Innere Zusammenhänge in den Denkmotiven bei Thomas von Aquin, Kant, Hegel und Heidegger," *Kant-Studien*, 1966 (57), 90-99.
770. Schneider, Herbert W. "Hegel, Heidegger, and 'Experience'. A Study in Translation," *Journal of the History of Philosophy*, 1972 (10), 347-50.
771. Siewerth, Gustav. "Martin Heidegger und die Frage nach Gott," *Hochland* (München), 1961 (53), 516-26.
772. Smith, P. Christopher. "Heidegger, Hegel, and the Problem of *Das Nichts*," *International Philosophical Quarterly*, 1968 (8), 379-405.
773. ———. "Heidegger's Critique of Absolute Knowledge," *The New Scholasticism*, 1971 (45), 56-86.
774. Stratton, Jon D. "Identity and Difference as *Austrag* : Hegel and Heidegger," *Kinesis*, 1971 (3), 81-92.
775. Taminiaux, Jacques. "Finitude et absolu. Remarques sur Hegel et Heidegger, interprètes de Kant," *Revue Philosophique de Louvain*, 1971 (69), 190-215.
776. Trivers, Howard. "Heidegger's Misinterpretation of Hegel's Views on Spirit and Time," *Philosophy and Phenomenological Research*, 1942/1943 (3), n. 2.
777. Van der Meulen, Jan. *Heidegger und Hegel oder Widerstreit und Widerspruch* (Monographien zur philosophischen Forschung, 13). Meisenheim/Glan, Westkulturverlag Anton Hain, 1963.
778. Werkmeister, W.H. "Hegel and Heidegger," in *New Studies in Hegel's Philosophy*, ed. Warren E. Steinkraus, 142-55. New York : Holt, Rinehart and Winston, 1971.

Sartre

779. Biemel, Walter. "Das Wesen der Dialektik bei Hegel und Sartre," *Tijdchrift voor Filosofie*, 1958, 269-300.
780. Gromczynski, Wieslaw. "Sartre et Hegel" *Studia Filozoficzne* (Warszawa). 1970. n. 4, 67-80.
781. Hartmann, Klaus. *Grundzüge der Ontologie Sartres in ihrem Verhältnis zu Hegels Logik*. Berlin, Walter de Gruyter, 1963.
782. ———. *Sartre's Ontology*. A Study of *Being and Nothingness* in the Light of Hegel's Logic. Northwestern University Press, 1966.
783. Kemp, Peter. "Le non de Sartre à la logique de Hegel," *Revue de Théologie et de Philosophie*, 1970 (5), 289-300.
784. Kopper, Joachim. "Sartres Verständnis der Lehre Hegels von der Gemeinschaft," *Kant-Studien*, 1960/1961 (52), 159-72.
785. Poole, Roger C. "Indirect Communication. Hegel, Kierkegaard and Sartre," *New Blackfriars* (Cambridge), 1966 (47), 532-41.

786. Wroblewsky, Vincent von. "Sartres existentialistische Hegeldeutung und Revision des Marxismus," *Deutsche Zeitschrift für Philosophie*, 1970 (18), 869-78.

Merleau-Ponty

787. De Waelhens, Alphonse. "The Philosophical Position of Merleau-Ponty," *Philosophy Today*, 1963 (7), 134-49. Reprinted from *Les Temps Modernes*, 1961.

INDEX

Aarsleff, H., 104n
Absolute, the, 33, 44, 74, 78, 84, 111
Absolute knowledge, 23, 28, 49, 53, 73; individual's growth toward, 56-61
Absolute spirit, 45, 71-72; and objective spirit, 154-155, 157
Alcibiades, 64
Alexandrian school, 41
Alienation, 16, 74-75, 138, 139
Anaxagoras, 33
Anselm, 44
Antinomy of freedom and necessity, 123-133, 135-136, 138, 140
Aristotle, 26, 31, 33, 34, 37, 41, 44, 63, 64, 66, 68, 69, 70, 73, 78, 79, 81, 118, 143, 144, 145, 165, 166, 167, 169, 174, 175, 176, 178n, 179; *Metaphysics*, 37, 69, 81; *De Anima*, 66
Atomism, 62, 115
Augustine, 41, 44
Avenarius, 62
Ayer, A.J., 85

Bacon, Francis, 162
Baille, James B., 176n
Being: and thought, 35-40, 88; and self-consciousness, 41; as pure beginning, 48; and value, 73-74; and nothing, 179, 190
Berkeley, George, 86, 87n
Bernstein, Richard, 77n
Blavatsky, Mme., 167
Böhme, Jakob, 41, 101
Bonitz, Hermann, 176
Boole, George, 178

Bosanquet, Bernard, 77
Boutroux, Émile, 163
Bradley, F.H., 77
Brahmanism, 167
Brockmeyer, Henry Conrad, 183, 191
Brumbaugh, R.S., 80
Buddhism, 167
Buzzelli, Donald E., 174n

Cabot, J.E., 191
Categorical imperative, 148
Categories: and Kant, 71, 110, 113-115, 119-123, 134; and Peirce, 172, 175-177, 182, 184
Certainty: and truth, 49-53, 85-86
Chaadayev, Peter, 160
Classical theism, 7
Conscience, 145-146, 148-150, 152-155, 157
Consciousness: natural vs. philosophic, 50-61
Cotton, J.H., 188n
Critias, 64
Critical philosophy, 112, 113
Criticism, Kantian, 31-32, 109, 112-115, 126
Cunning of reason, 136, 137, 138, 149, 150-151, 154, 156, 158

Descartes, 31, 38, 40, 41, 114; and doubt, 83-94; *Meditations*, 83, 86, 90, 93, 94
Dewey, John, 180
Dostoyevsky, Feodor, 163
Duty, 132, 133, 136, 142, 143, 150

Eleatics, 30, 33, 80
Elton, William, 183n

INDEX

Empirical concepts : and Kant's transcendental idea, 123-128
Empiricism, 34, 35, 38, 87, 115, 124, 161-162
Enlightenment philosophers, 126-127
Epicureanism, 26
Ethical community, 133
Ethical life : and morality, 143-156
Ethical order, 132
Euclid, 113

Fairbanks, Matthew J., 171n
Faith, 5, 28, 41, 127, 157
Faith, 5, 28, 41, 127, 157
Fichte, Johann Gottlieb, 32, 35, 39, 41, 42, 45, 64, 127, 190
Findlay, J.N. : on Hegel, 77-82, 118, 124, 125, 156n; "Hegel's Use of Teleology," 78; *Re-examination*, 78, 80; *Values and Intentions*, 78
Finite : and infinite, 37, 88, 90
Freedom, 24, 29, 31, 131-155 *passim*, 167; and necessity, 8, 129-140, 144; and philosophical thought, 29-32; and nature, 109; in Kant and Hegel, 129-133, 141-158
Frege, Gottlob, 121n
Fisch, Max H., 174n, 179n
Fitzgerald, John J., 186n

Gans, Edward, 142
Goethe, Johann Wolfgang von, 67
Good : objective vs. subjective, 146-151
Cray, J. Glenn, 44n
Green, T.H., 179

Hamilton, William, 190
Harris, H.S., 184n
Harris, W.T., 172, 183, 187, 188, 191, 192; *Hegel's Logic : A Book on the Genesis of the Categories of the Mind*, 183; "Introduction to Philosophy," 190; "Paul Janet and Hegel," 190
Hartmann, Eduard von, 162, 163
Hegel, Georg Wilhelm Friedrich : on the history of philosophy, 1-20, 21-46, 62-68, 109-110; on the unity of philosophy, 23-27; on Eleatics, 30, 33; on Plato, 30-31, 33-34, 36-37, 40, 41, 63-68; on Socrates, 30, 36, 40, 64; on sophists, 30, 40; on Aristotle, 31, 33, 34, 37, 41, 44; on Descartes, 31, 38, 41, 94; on Kant, 31-32, 35, 38-39, 42, 45, 72, 109-128; on Luther, 31, 41; on scepticism, 31; on stoicism, 31, 37; on Fichte, 32, 35, 39, 41, 42; on the Ionians, 32; on Schelling, 32, 35, 39, 42, 45; on Anaxagoras, 33; on Heraclitus, 33, 36, 63; on Leucippus, 33; on Parmenides, 33, 36; on Zeno, 33, 36; on Hume, 34, 38; on Leibniz, 34-35, 96, 105-108; on Locke, 34, 38; on Spinoza, 34, 38; on pre-Socratics, 36; on Philo, 37; on empiricists, 38; on Newton, 38; on Plotinus, 38, 68; on Proclus, 38, 68; on Protagoras, 40; and the question of subjectivity, 40-43; on Jakob Böhme, 41; on the neo-Platonists, 41; on Protestantism, 41; on sceptics, 41; on stoics, 41; and Plato, 62-76, 77-82; his realism, 64; on being and value, 73-74; his dialectic, 78, 113; his method, 78; his teleology, 79; and Descartes, 83-94; and Leibniz on language, 95-108; his critique of Leibniz's universal characteristic, 96, 105-108; on relation of German language to philosophy, 97-103; on language and thought, 97-99; on philosophical language, 105-108; on Kant's categories, 110, 119-123; on Kant's critique of knowledge, 111-118; on Kant's subjectivism, 118-123; on Kant's thing-in-itself, 118-123; on Kant's transcendental idea, 123-128; and Kant, 129-140, 141-148; his critique of Kant's antinomy of practical reason, 134-140; and Christianity, 136, 144; on transition from morality to ethical life, 145-149; his inclusion of Kantian autonomy in ethical life, 149-152; and Solovyov, 159-170; and Peirce, 171-193; and System, *see* Hegelian system; *Phenomenology of Mind*, 4, 21, 22n, 23, 24, 31, 37, 38, 40, 42, 44,

47-61, 67, 71, 80, 93, 94, 97n, 111, 141, 148, 152, 166, 168, 183, 191, 192; *Lectures on the History of Philosophy*, 21, 22, 23, 29, 40, 45, 55, 57, 62, 63, 68, 79, 83, 111, 112, 115, 120, 141, 157; *Science of Logic*, 21, 22, 23, 26, 27, 29, 33, 35, 39, 42, 44, 45, 47, 48, 49, 50, 53, 62, 79, 96, 183; *Introduction to the History of Philosophy*, 21n, 22, 27, 29, 44; *Lectures on the Philosophy of Religion*, 44; *Lectures on the Proofs for God's Existence*, 44; *Encyclopedia*, 56, 60, 96, 105, 111, 112, 113, 116, 122, 175, 176, 177, 183, 184, 190; *Jena-Realphilosophie I and II*, 97n; *Philosophische Propadeutik*, 105, 183; *Glauben und Wissen*, 111, 115, 125, 127; *Philosophy of Right*, 111, 141, 142, 145, 149, 151, 154, 157, 165, 168; *Lectures on the Philosophy of History*, 139, 149, 157

Hegelian system : as system of total mediation, 2-3; and historicism, 18-19; problem of its beginning, 47-61, 83; as circle, 60-61
Heintel, E., 149n
Heraclitus, 33, 36, 80, 160
Historicism, 17, 20; and system, 18-19
Historicity : and temporality, 15, 16, 17
Historiography of philosophy, 1, 2, 17, 18
History of philosophy, 1-20, 21-46; relation to philosophy, 1-2, 26, 60, 61; and world-spirit, 27-29, 57-58; stages of development, 27-29; and *Phenomenology of Spirit*, 47-61
Hofmeister, H., 146n
Hume, David, 34, 38, 87, 116, 118
Hyppolite, J., 105n

Idea, the, 6-7, 46, 71-73, 79, 110, 125, 136, 139; and truth, 6-7; self-generation of, 7-13, 18, 19, 162; logical and temporal development of, 11-20; and time, 14-16; as self-determining reality, 109
Individual : and universal, 43-46; and state, 151-157
Infinite : and finite, 37, 88, 90

Ionians, 32

James, Henry, the elder, 189
James, William, 172, 173, 179, 180
Journal of Speculative Philosophy, 172, 187, 188, 190, 191

Kant, Immanuel, 31-32, 35, 38-39, 42, 45, 54, 62, 64, 68, 71, 72, 79, 87, 96, 109-128, 129-140, 159, 160, 162, 168, 174, 175, 188, 189, 190; his categories, 71, 110, 113-115, 119-123, 134; his critique of knowledge, 111-118; transcendental idea, 123-128; his theory of moral will, 130-137; his individualism, 140; and ethics, 142; and Hegel, 141-158; on freedom, 142; *Critique of Judgment*, 109; *Critique of Pure Reason*, 110n, 112, 126, 129, 130n, 134, 147n; *Foundations of the Metaphysics of Morals*, 130, 147; *Critique of Practical Reason*, 142n, 147; *Über das Misslingen aller philosophischen Versuche in der Theodicee*, 146; "On a supposed Right to Lie from altruistic motives," 146n; *The Metaphysical Principles of Virtue*, 155
Kimmerle, Heinz, 47, 55, 56
Kireyevsky, Ivan, 163
Kline, G., 78n
Kojève, Alexandre, 163n
Kroner, R., 143n

Language : Hegel and Leibniz on, 95-108; and thought, 97-99; and mind and reality, 101; and philosophy, 103-105, 176; hieroglyphic, 106-107
Lasson, Georg, 79
Lauer, Quentin, 1n, 7n, 31n, 44n, 45n
Leibniz, Gottfried Wilhelm von, 34-35, 54, 62, 116, 123, 126, 162, 174, 178, 190; on language, 95-108; on language and thought, 97-99; on relation of German language to philosophy, 97-103; on language, mind, and reality, 101; on philosophical language, 103-108; theory of universal characteristic, 103-108 passim; *Ermahnung an die Deut-*

schen, ihren Verstand und ihre Sprache besser zu üben, 96n; Fragmente zu Logik, 96n; New Essays Concerning Human Understanding, 96n, 101; Philosophical Papers and Letters, 96n; Von deutscher Sprachpflege. Unvorgreifliche Gedanken betreffend die Ausübung und Verbesserung der deutschen Sprache, 96n
Leontiev, Konstantin, 163
Leucippus, 33
Liebrucks, B., 153n
Locke, John, 34, 38, 54, 68, 86, 87, 100, 115, 116, 118, 123, 162
Loemker, Leroy, 96n
Lucretius, 26
Luther, Martin, 31, 41

Maguire, T., 80
Malebranche, Nicolas de, 62
Marx, Karl, 96, 100; *Das Kapital*, 100
Mediation, 2, 6, 9, 11, 20, 37, 53, 86, 172, 176, 178
Medieval Christian theology, 64
Michelet, Karl Ludwig, 21n, 141
Mill, J.S., 162
Mochulski, Konstantin, 163n
Moore, G.E., 77
Moral law, 130, 132, 135, 138-139, 142-143, 147
Moral will : Kant's theory of, 130-137
Morality : and ethical life, 143-156; and legality, 142n, 143-144, 152-155
Mure, G.R.G., 79, 87n
Murphey, Murray, 174n, 189

Natural will, 134-139
Nature : and mind, 12, 14; and time, 14; and history, 64; and freedom, 109; and reason, 134
Negation, 83-94, 189; and affirmation, 37; as determination, 89, 92
Neoplatonism, 27, 41, 64, 68
Nethery, Wallace, 183n
Newton, Sir Isaac, 38, 178
Newtonian world-view, 131
Niel, Henri, 9
Nietzsche, Friedrich, 163
Nizolius, 100

Nominalism, 179; and realism, 191
Norton, Charles Eliot, 189
North American Review, 189, 191

Oriental philosophy, 26, 30

Parmenides, 33, 36, 190
Pascal, Blaise, 159
Paton, Herbert James, 116
Peirce, Charles, 163, 171-193; Cambridge Conferences, 172, 173, 177; and Hegelian dialectic, 176, 177, 178; proof of pragmaticism, 178-186; classifications of the sciences (table), 181; theory of signs, 184-188; "New List of Categories," 172, 173, 174, 183, 187, 189, 190; "On Reasoning and the Logic of Things," 172; "The Logic of Science," 175n, 189; "The Logic of Mathematics : an Attempt to develop my categories from within," 184; *Minute Logic*, 185; "The Place of Our Age in the History of Civilization," 188; *Three Papers on Logic*, 190; see also Pragmaticism
Perry, Ralph Barton, 172n, 179n
Petrick, Joseph A., 188n
Philo, 37
Philolaus, 66
Philoponus, 66
Philosophical thought : types of, 24; and freedom, 29-32; as speculative thinking, 36
Philosophy : and its history, 1-2, 16, 60, 61; as historical process, 1-20; and truth, 5-6; unity of, 23-27; and religion, 44; and the world-spirit, 57-58; and German language, 97-103; history of, see History of philosophy
Plato, 30-31, 33-34, 36-37, 40, 43, 44, 165, 166, 169; and Hegel, 62-76, 77-82; idea of the Good, 72, 73, 75; on soul's relation to the ideas, 72; on being and value, 73, 74; *Parmenides*, 30, 62, 66, 67, 73, 75, 80; *Phaedo*, 43, 62, 66, 72; Socratic dialogues, 59; *Theaetetus*, 54, 71; *Cratylus*, 63; *Philebus*, 66, 81; *Republic*, 62, 65, 67, 73, 74, 75, 81; *Sophist*, 62, 66, 73, 75, 81; *Timaeus*, 62, 66, 67,

70, 72, 73, 74, 75, 81, 82; *Phaedrus*, 72
Plotinus, 38, 68, 73, 79
Pöggeler, Otto, 47
Popper, K., 80; *The Open Society and its Enemies*, 77, 156n
Pragmatism, 179, 180
Pragmaticism, 172, 173; Peirce's proof of, 178-186
Pre-Socratics, 36, 63, 79
Price, Richard, 85
Proclus, 38, 68, 79, 80
Protagoras, 40
Protestantism, 38, 41
Psychological idealism, 115-118

Randall, John Herman, 79
Rational will, 130, 131, 134, 136
Rationalism, 87, 161-162
Realism : and nominalism, 191
Reason, 24, 39, 46, 93; instinct of, 5; finite, 39; and understanding, 111, 123-128, 190-191; practical, 130-140; rule of, 131; and nature, 134; and moral right, 135-140; in history, 138; and revelation, 161
Regulative ideas, 123-125
Renouvier, Charles Bernard, 163
Representation, 8, 30, 31, 33, 44; and thought, 40, 44, 89
Repression, 136, 138, 139
Right, 134-139, 142, 144, 151, 156, 168
Roberts, Don D., 186n
Roman Catholicism, 161
Romanticism, 50, 51
Rosenkranz, Karl, 55, 98n
Royce, Josiah, 172, 173, 180, 187, 188, 192; *The World and the Individual*, 178; *The Problem of Christianity*, 187
Russell, Bertrand, 62, 120
Russian messianism, 163
Russian orthodoxy, 163

Santucci, Antonio, 171n
Scepticism, 31, 41; toward philosophy, 3, 4
Schelling, Friedrich Wilhelm Joseph von, 32, 35, 39, 42, 45, 50, 64, 159, 161, 190
Schiller, Friedrich von, 180; *Ästhetische Briefe*, 184

Schlegel, Friedrich von, 63
Schleiermacher, Friedrich, 65
Scholasticism, 44, 45, 161, 176
Schopenhauer, Arthur, 163, 168, 190
Sextus Empiricus, 74
Smith, John E., 129
Socialism, 162
Socrates, 30, 36, 40, 43, 59, 63, 64
Solovyov, Sergei M., 161
Solovyov, Vladimir S., 159-170; his philosophical system, 164 (diagram), 165-170; *The Crisis of Western Philosophy*, 159, 161, 163; *Philosophical Principles of Integral Knowledge*, 159, 169; *A Critique of Abstract Principles*, 160; *Lectures on Godmanhood*, 160; *Three Conversations : on War, Progress, and the End of History*, 170
Sophists, 30, 40, 63, 66
Spencer, Herbert, 162
Speusippus, 70, 81
Spinoza, Baruch, 34, 38, 44, 45, 62, 79, 116, 159, 166; on determination as negation, 38; *Ethics*, 178
State, 138-140, 144, 168; and individual, 151-157
Stirling, James Hutchison, *The Secret of Hegel*, 189
Stoicism, 31, 37, 41
Strawson, P.F., 124n
Sylvester, James Joseph, 182
Synechism, 172, 174, 178, 179, 186

Temporality : and history, 15-16; and historicity, 15, 16, 17
Thales, 21, 26, 27
Thing-in-itself, 92, 111, 118, 135, 140
Thought, 23, 24, 25, 29, 32, 36, 88, 89; as self-creative movement, 8; forms of, 10; speculative, 22, 37, 45, 109, 110; as objectivity, 32-35; and being, 35-40, 88; and substance, 37; as self-concretizing, 38; as self-determining, 38; and representation, 40, 44, 89; and perception, 90; and negativity, 93; and language, 97-99
Thompson, Manley, 182n
Time, 9, 11, 12, 24, 26; and eternity, 3, 16;

ideal genesis of, 13-15; metaphysics of, 13; and nature, 14; and mind, 14, 15; and the Idea, 16; and historical process, 18, 19; and language, 106, 107

Totalitarianism, 156

Townsend, H.G., 171n

Transcendental apperception, 119

Trancendental consciousness, 15, 130

Transcendental deduction, 72

Transcendental ego, 71, 72

Transcendental ethics, 147

Transcendental idea : and empirical concepts, 123-128

Transcendental imagination, 111

Transcendental philosophy, 116-117, 126, 147

Truth, 84, 91-93; and history, 3; and thought, 5; unity of, 5-6, 17; as architectonic, 6; and the Idea, 6-7; and philosophy, 6; in terms of presence and absence, 6; as spirit, 44; and certainty, 49-53, 85-86; and immediacy, 52-53; and falsity, 87-88; philosophic, 88, 107; as self-developing whole, 89; and error, 94; and truthfulness, 146-148

Ulmer, K., 153n

Understanding : and reason, 123-128, 190-191

Universality : and particularity, 15, 42, 43-46, 74-76, 130, 136, 138

Universal characteristic, 96, 101-108

Universals, 64, 65, 70, 71, 75

Value and being : Hegel and Plato on, 73-74

Vico, Giovanni Battista, 161

Walsh, W.H., 156n

Whitehead, A.N., 62

Wiener, P., 102n

Wittgenstein, Ludwig, 62, 77

Wolff, Christian von, 162

World-spirit, 27, 149; and history of philosophy, 27-29, 57-58

Zeno, 33, 36